WASHINGTON D.C.
PLEASE, DON'T HURT ME

WASHINGTON D.C.
PLEASE, DON'T HURT ME

WE ARE THE PEOPLE
2024

By
ALILA BARRERAS

Copyright © 2024 by Alila Barreras

All rights reserved. No part of this publication may be reproduced, distributed, or transmitted in any form or by any means, including photocopying, recording, or other electronic or mechanical methods, without the prior written permission of the copyright owner and the publisher, except in the case of brief quotations embodied in critical reviews and certain other noncommercial uses permitted by copyright law. For permission requests, write to the publisher, addressed "Attention: Permissions Coordinator," at the address below.

ARPress
45 Dan Road Suite 5
Canton MA 02021
Hotline: 1(888) 821-0229
Fax: 1(508) 545-7580

Ordering Information:
Quantity sales. Special discounts are available on quantity purchases by corporations, associations, and others. For details, contact the publisher at the address above.

Printed in the United States of America.

ISBN-13: Paperback   979-8-89389-350-2
          eBook   979-8-89389-351-9

Library of Congress Control Number: 2024916605

COLOSSIANS 3:12-14

Therefore, as God's chosen ones, holy and beloved, clothe yourselves with tender compassion, kindness, humility, gentleness, and patience. Continue to bear with one another and generously forgive each other, even if someone has a reason to complain against another. Just as Jehovah generously forgave you, so you must also do. But above all these things, clothe yourselves with love, which is the perfect bond of unity.

INSPIRATIONAL THOUGHTS

Dr. Manuel Sans Segarra: A licensed physician and surgeon with a doctorate cum laude from the Faculty of Medicine at the University of Barcelona.
"Everything imaginable exists in the universe in the form of energy, waiting for someone to conceive of it and bring it to life."

Elon Musk: An entrepreneur and investor known for his key roles in the space company SpaceX and the automotive company Tesla, Inc.
"Life is too short for long-term grudges."
"Love is a battle, love is a war; love is growing. Love is a friendship that has caught fire. It is silent understanding, mutual trust, sharing, and forgiving. It is loyalty in good and bad times."
"When something is important enough, you do it even if the odds are not in your favor."

Robert Smalls, U.S. Congressman, 1895
"My race needs no special defense, for the past history of this country proves it to be equal to any people anywhere. All it needs is an equal chance in the battle of life."

José de la Luz y Caballero, Cuban educator and philosopher born on July 11, 1800.
"I would rather see, not the institutions of man, but the stars of the firmament collapse, than see the feeling of justice fall from the human heart, that sun of the moral world."

ABRAHAM LINCOLN, February 12, 1809. One of the most admirable presidents in American culture. He assumed the presidency at the age of 52 and was involved in the Whig Party before switching to become the first Republican president of the United States. He abolished slavery. His thoughts have been inspiring to this day. "Those who deny freedom to others deserve it not for themselves."

"**America will never be destroyed from the outside. If we falter and lose our freedoms, it will be because we destroyed ourselves.**""I am not bound to win, but I am bound to be true. I am not bound to succeed, but I am bound to live up to what light I have."

MARTIN LUTHER KING, January 15, 1929, Atlanta, GA. Nobel Peace Prize Winner
"I am not black, I am a man." "Your truth will increase as you learn to listen to the truth of others.""Nonviolence is a powerful and just weapon which cuts without wounding and ennobles the man who wields it. It is a sword that heals.""The ultimate tragedy is not the oppression and cruelty of the bad people, but the silence of the good people."

Oprah Gail Winfrey. She is a talk show host, television producer, actress, author, and American media owner.
"Turn your wounds into wisdom."
"Create the highest, grandest vision possible for your life because you become what you believe."
"Your legacy is every life you have touched. Feel everything with love because at every moment you are building your legacy."

JACK CANFIELD. He graduated from Harvard with a master's degree in Psychological Education.
"If you can dream it, you can do it."

"Everything you want is out there waiting for you to ask for it. Everything you want also wants you. But you have to take action to get it."

"If you love your work, if you enjoy it, you are already a success."

DEDICATION

I dedicate this book: "Washington D.C., Don't Hurt Me 2024. We the People," to all government agencies, especially to the Supreme Court of our country. From 2016 to 2024, we have witnessed abusive events of persecution against former President Donald J. Trump. It is your responsibility to restore Truth, Justice, and Peace to us. Remember: fulfilling the sacred duty of upholding Justice and serving the people "honestly," regardless of which political party we belong to or which president appointed you to your position. May God Bless our country and enlighten the members of our institutions, always remembering that "transparency in presidential elections" must be respected, and any discrepancies should be resolved according to the law, as was done in the past with Gore and Bush, and other challenges in our country. Not with the compromised words of members of different political parties today. Always remembering that "Only the truth will put on the virile robe." —José de la Luz y Caballero.

The four characteristics of a judge:

Listen courteously.

Respond wisely.

Consider prudently.

And decide impartially.

—Socrates

INTRODUCTION

This book is a gift of gratitude to the American people. They welcomed us when we arrived on this land in 1980 during the Mariel Exodus between Cuba and the United States. I have to thank the corrupt dictator Fidel A. Castro for allowing me to live in this wonderful country during the last years of my life, and for that, I am grateful. I never hold a grudge for the bad situations I've experienced. They are lessons learned to move forward. We don't fail; we learn, and we start again every day.

This book is not just about my subjective opinions; it's about realities that have been objectively lived in this era by all Americans, with global repercussions. It is not a legal defense of Donald J. Trump, the 45th former President, because he has his own good lawyers, and I emphasize that I am a "housewife" with a hobby of writing. Donald Trump is an example of stoicism in the face of cowardly attacks by the Washington D.C., Democrats, and some Republicans who have probably regretted their actions, never before seen in this Nation. What is happening to the 45th former President is what could happen to all of us in a corrupt Democratic government with communist infiltrations. Our duty is to denounce them.

This book is a defense of the Constitution, Democracy, Justice, Truth, and Order, so they do not die. NASA dreamed of going to the moon and succeeded. Elon Musk dreams of conquering Mars and traveling among the stars, and he will achieve it, just like everything he has set out to do, even if many of us might not see it. We saw people set foot on the moon; why not on Mars? Amazon was born and has left a legacy to those of us who dream of being writers but cannot afford publishing costs, and we find everything we need on that platform, completely free and with a way to do it ourselves. Bezos, with his success, made us all successful as well. Success is not just about money but about seeing your work accomplished. Seeing our books on his platform is a wonderful satisfaction, and that only happens in the USA. We have seen dreams become realities on Facebook and X, communicating worldwide, seeing news, all kinds of information, friendships, and even love has been found by many. Google brings everything to our fingertips without leaving the house, and YouTube offers us opportunities to learn, as do many institutes that we can enjoy thanks to the technology provided. How could we not be happy and proud in a country like this, being American citizens?

Having lived through part of this technological science that moves the world from the USA is more than feeling proud of the achievements made. Young millionaire figures have realized they must do something different to guide our country in the right direction; millions of thanks to them.

The country's progress will not fall into communist hands but rather into the privileged minds that lead us into the future. This is the capitalist country we will always defend, even if I am labeled ignorant, but my love for it will always be genuine and greater than my ignorance.

As an independent writer or with a hobby I love, I dream of making our country a UNITED AND RESPECTED people. Housewives also dream. Democrats in our neighborhoods, along with Republicans, will take a step forward like a giant wave of love and respect for the country that shelters and needs us.

As in the past, when we could state our political affiliations without being mistreated by citizens, mostly intransigent communist Democrats in the streets and Washington D.C.

Without losing family and friends, and that is what communism united with terrorism does to the people, it separates them and spreads hatred among everyone. Those who do not know those systems in practice will never see it as those who know it through literature.

The USA faced terrorism directly on 9/11. Communism, along with terrorism, is in Washington D.C., because they are the same thing, COMMUNISM. The Democrats wanting to destroy Donald Trump with the 14th Amendment, and precisely that same amendment, is the one President Joe Biden violated by helping terrorists through corrupt UN agencies to the Palestinians and indirectly to Hamas, has sparked controversy.

Words in this amendment, section 3: "No person shall be a Senator or Representative in Congress, or elector of President and Vice President, or hold any office, civil or military, under the United States, or any state, who, having previously taken an oath to support the Constitution of the United States as a member of Congress, or as an officer of the United States, or as a member of any State legislature, or as an executive or judicial officer of any State, shall have engaged in insurrection or rebellion against the same, or given aid or comfort to the enemies thereof. But Congress may, by a vote of two-thirds of each House, remove such disability."

We have verified Biden's actions when he helped our enemies, the Palestinians. The Constitution does not specify whether the aid was humanitarian or not. Nor does it specify that an insurrection was committed, and for the Democrats, an attack on the Capitol, because no one saw Donald Trump attacking, but we saw a government breaking our laws. This is the shame we are immersed in as a people, and it must end.

Nancy Pelosi wanted to award a Nobel Prize to that great help that was a betrayal by all of them and a violation of the Constitution with the approval of those who support causes without seeing the facts. The ones indicated to help those affected by the war in their territories are the Palestinians and Iranians to whom Biden has given billions of our dollars. They should use it to save their people, and they have categorically seen that they did not, having our dollars in their hands; because they don't even help each other. Wars have cause and effect, and terrorists attack people and then accuse those who defend themselves of genocide, as in the case of Israel and Hamas. We can no longer endure more social and political misery coming from Washington D.C., Democrats.

To live in harmony, bringing back loyalty, truth, justice, respect, empathy, solidarity, and sanity that we have left behind due to politicians and political parties, we need Truth and Justice and not to give votes to the Democrats until they rectify their serious attacks on democracy. Trump is not democracy, he is not the country, he is the means used by the "Woke" communists to eliminate those who oppose them.

Martin Luther King dreamed of racial equality, and our values, and left us many beautiful things, including the Civil Rights Act and his legacy of pacifism, even suffering the harshest episodes for his race. If we all cooperate individually, we will achieve this in the next presidential elections for a new beginning and awakening, using the laws that are there to decide who is lying and who is not. Denied to the 45th former President in 2020.

With this purpose, without being a politician, historian, or even intellectually literary, I offer my contribution and my pain to a people that became mine from the moment I received the American nationality certificate when I heard the judge say (in my broken English) that we must defend the country from internal and external enemies. I took it seriously because we did not come to undermine public assistance; we came to work and free ourselves from cruel communism. At that moment, I didn't fully understand the meaning of his words, mentally criticizing the judge for saying "from internal enemies," thinking that kind of enemy only existed in communist countries. Since 2016, I have seen our democracy deteriorate, along with our ethical, moral, political, social, and religious values, forming a great amalgamation of social destruction. I wanted to start defending it, as I swore that day at the naturalization ceremony, through my political ignorance but as an American citizen. For that reason, I present what I have lived through, not just for myself, but for all the millions of citizens in the country, regardless of which political party we belong to or what social status we have.

Addressing the topics I humbly present to you. And as Martin Luther King said in his beautiful thoughts:

"Injustice anywhere is a threat to justice everywhere."

THE SUPREME COURT

WORDS FROM THE SUPREME COURT'S WEBSITE IN WASHINGTON D.C.:

"Justice is one of the most recognized symbols in the architecture of the Supreme Court Building. Depicting Justice as a female figure dates back to ancient mythology. Do we wish for a robotic woman with artificial intelligence (subjective thinking) to govern our laws? We've already seen how Justice Sonia Sotomayor thinks and speaks, filled with hatred, and that's not how American laws should be legislated. They should be enacted with pragmatism at all times. What's sad is that when Obama appointed her to the Supreme Court, the same thing happened as with Kamala Harris and Biden. It seems she was chosen for being a Democrat and Hispanic. If she had studied the Constitution, she wouldn't have spoken the way she did. A pragmatic person is characterized by not theorizing but rather by pursuing concrete actions to find solutions to problems or answers. To achieve this, a pragmatic individual frees themselves from all emotions that might hinder their goals. The judge failed us and should resign out of decency, in accordance with the principles of pragmatism.

Over time, Justice became associated with a balance to represent impartiality and a sword to symbolize power. (They will need to reconsider these concepts with what they do to Donald Trump daily, and, to top it off, the attempted assassination on 7/13/24.) In the 16th century, Justice was often depicted with a blindfold. The origin of the blindfold is unclear, but today it is generally accepted as a symbol of impartiality. Let's add "Blind Justice" to what we are witnessing today. In the statue of the Contemplation of Justice, 9 she holds a smaller blindfolded figure in her right hand. Blindfolded Justice holds a balance in her arms.

What extraordinary work the justices of the SUPREME COURT of the Country have to do to end the evil and restore the political, judicial, and moral division and hatred of this decade. The words of Isaiah make it clear in divine justice. "Isaiah first says what practicing justice is not, before describing what it is. It is not shouting, it is not violence, nor the imposition of an order; these do not represent the justice of God. Isaiah tells us that God will bring justice through truth. Bearing witness to the truth requires patience, endurance, and sacrifice." A figure representing Justice, shown without a blindfold, is ready to wield her sword to fight against the powers of evil in the Supreme Court. That is how the statue stands. In the battle between good and evil, will the Supreme Court's Justice help to defeat it?

These words are inscribed in the Supreme Court of the United States. In this era of non-bipartisan persecution, with investigations into citizens and the 91 trials for Donald Trump without involving Hillary Clinton, does this mean that if we had seen Hillary Clinton alongside Donald Trump in all those trials, we could believe justice was being done, even if we didn't like it? Seeing that it has only been done to Donald Trump with premeditation, we do not believe in our Justice system until we see the results.

Will Justice help to defeat evil? Powers of Good and Powers of Evil. We wish that in these difficult times of political wickedness, the Power of Good will always shine in all the Courts, whether state or the Supreme Court of the Country, demonstrating that Justice is ready to cut through obstacles so that truth may triumph.

Justice Sonia Sotomayor: Member of the Supreme Court

Judge Sonia Sotomayor, when interviewed by CNN, responded in a manner that was unacceptable and filled with Democratic hatred. Her words, laden with malice toward former President Donald Trump, have shown us that within the Supreme Court, very fine lines are being walked when it comes to upholding Constitutional Justice by some members. Mrs. Sotomayor committed an extraordinary act of defamation publicly on CNN in Spanish. The difference between an ignorant populace, unaware of the law, and a magistrate who is supposed to enforce the laws enshrined in our Constitution, marks a stark contrast between the uneducated masses, who lack legal training, and a jurist ignorant of the laws and disrespectful to the people by harboring hatred in her heart.

Her words were extremely damaging when referring to the Supreme Court's ruling on former President Donald J. Trump's immunity. Mrs. Sotomayor's statement: "The President is now a king above the law" by Devan Cole on CNN en Español, is exactly what I read. If the article belongs to others, my credits belong to them as well. Sonia Sotomayor's antagonism towards Donald Trump made her forget that she is a member of the SUPREME COURT and that under these conditions of partiality, she should resign her position.

"We allow the President to break the law, let him exploit the perks of his office for personal gain (additional benefits), let him use his official power for perverse ends. Because if he knew that one day he could be held accountable for breaking the law, he would not be as bold and courageous as we would like him to be. That is the message of the majority today. Even if these nightmare scenarios never come to pass, and I pray they never do, the damage is already done. The relationship between the President and the people he serves has changed irrevocably. In every use of official power, the President is now a king above the law," she wrote.

"Does he order the Navy's Seal Team 6 to assassinate a political rival? Immune."

"Does he organize a military coup to cling to power? Immune. Does he accept a bribe in exchange for a pardon? Immune. Immune, immune, immune," she added.

The judge did not end her dissent with the traditional "respectfully." "With fear for our democracy, I dissent," Sotomayor wrote.

According to the article by Mr. Devan Cole on CNN en Español, Judge Sonia Sotomayor could not hold back and disagreed. "Let him use his official power for perverse ends."

Are the "perverse ends" the judge refers to those where Trump denounced the swamp where everyone is involved? Mrs. Sotomayor, could you explain to the American people why the Supreme Court or the district courts in conflict over the presidential elections did not count the votes? Whether the votes were stolen or not, the people demanded that they be counted. Can you explain to the American people why the Senate, the House of Representatives, which together form Congress, and the Electoral College involved did not fulfill their duty to count the votes as the people wanted, which the Democrats refused to do? Why, if the votes were counted in the six previous challenges to Donald Trump's, which have historically occurred in the country, were they not counted to know if Biden had stolen them or if Donald Trump was lying to us? The people are asking why none of these government agencies used the law?

We understand, Mrs. Sotomayor, that when there are legal differences, the law must intervene. Were they Democratic plots or laziness from the aforementioned agency members who did not want to work on counting the votes? When you said, "Let the President violate the law, let him exploit the perks of his office for personal gain," explain to the people what you mean by Donald Trump's personal gain. Why must we remind you, Mrs. Sotomayor, that Donald J. Trump does not need personal gain? He needs the law to be correct and upheld. The one who abused his perks was Obama, touring the world with Air Force One full of friends, closing hotels in Spain just for them, and we accepted it because, after all, it was his term, and he deserved to enjoy it. Obama, his agent, left with $68.5 million and entered the White House with one and a half million. Our government failed not only Donald Trump as President or former President, but it also failed his voters, which include all of us, regardless of the color of our vote. We are American citizens who need third-world country corruption not to alter our laws, through you.

I inform you that if anyone has broken the law, it is Joe Biden, not Donald Trump. That is the Democratic-Communist political strategy. Biden allowed 9 or 10 million illegal immigrants into the country, endangering sovereignty with the entry of illegal spies VIOLATING OUR IMMIGRATION LAWS. Joe Biden, under the 14th Amendment, violated the Constitution by sending aid to the Palestinians (our enemies), benefiting Hamas with that aid, and our Constitution does not specify what kind of aid can be given to an enemy; it simply states that aid cannot be given to "the enemies of the country." And don't tell me that this part that pertains to Biden is interpreted differently from what is written in the Supreme Law because we are not blind. Amendment 14, section 3. Do we need to repeat it?

Mrs. Sotomayor, you are the ones who feel above the law due to the hatred you have fostered and by violating our laws and professional ethics. This affects the morale of our country, affects the belief in judges, leading to a loss of trust in the law. The "perverse ends," as you say in the CNN article, do not belong to Trump; they belong to Biden and Kamala, allowing communism tied to TERRORISM to destroy us, but rest assured, they will not succeed. We want a country like the one we had before the Biden administration. DEMOCRATIC, NOT COMMUNIST, although Obama paved the way.

You, as a Supreme Court Judge, spoke with unacceptable Democratic hatred when accusing Donald Trump on CNN. It gives us the authority, as the people, to ask that you step down from your position in the Supreme Court. The statue is supposed to have its eyes covered in its chamber, but not you, nor "we the people." That is a conflict of political and party interests and presidents who appointed them. What is at stake is our Justice more than Democracy, and that is something I fear because I come from a communist country, and I know how they work. This is what justice means: "Moral principle that leads to determining that everyone should live honestly. Fulfill it!

In your hatred, the photograph shown in the commentary you made speaks more than a hundred thousand words combined about how your partially felt before the law manifests itself. The law does not know partiality, only impartiality, and our Constitution also knows this, except you, who are a member of our Supreme Court. Your personal hatred toward Donald Trump is not the people's business but yours alone, and we do not want you to involve us in those shady dealings. With your words, you have committed harakiri. For that reason, it is time for the American people to wake up and ask Congress for term limits for the Supreme Court, and for all politicians in Washington D.C., to avoid the hatred and corruption of human thought, as we have seen in your words and actions.

Mrs. Sotomayor, referring to Donald Trump, says, "Because if he knew that one day he could be held accountable for breaking the law, he would not be as bold and courageous as we would like him to be."

Although you are bothered by Donald Trump's conduct and we as a people are bothered by yours, we must act justly. We, the voters for Donald Trump, are patriots of the USA, not the MAGA gangsters as Nancy Pelosi calls us, nor the deplorable baskets as Hillary Clinton says. Stop poisoning the ignorant voters. Specifically, I have not written "stupid." These are the honorable Democratic politicians who hate their opponents. Can they act justly? Trump is more than bold because he has risked everything for us, and we sincerely thank him for it.

Mrs. Judge, you exude Democratic hatred; Republicans do not hate our Democrats because we are one people, regardless of the party. We denounce what happens, we open your eyes to the filth happening daily so that many do not do what happened in Germany, Spain, France, and Cuba, idolizing leaders and suffering their people. We Republicans want President Joe Biden to be tried for violations of the law and for his cognitive dementia, which is evident, although they want to hide it. (YouTube is full of videos proving it). You defend him and do not want to conduct the political trials that were held against Donald Trump without violating anything. Mrs. Sotomayor, where is American justice? It is the country, Mrs. Sotomayor, that you should defend, not the position that Obama accommodated you in, and sadly without legal knowledge, and I don't say that, you just demonstrated it.

That is the majority's message today. No, Mrs. Sotomayor, the people's message, who think like me, is missing, and if not, it is solely mine with a benefactor and responsible attitude, asking you to leave the Supreme Court. You have failed us with your hatred and words. That is not American Justice. As the entire judicial system fails its people, except for a few. We are not yet a third-world country. We are on the brink, and for that, we will defend it from internal enemies, and you are an enemy of your own country and have betrayed your career as a jurist.

Mrs. Sotomayor says: "Even if these nightmare scenarios never come to pass, and I pray they never do, the damage is already done." In that, you are right, the damage is already done, and not by the Republicans but by the Democrats. The political party you defend. But this time, it is not the parties that interest me, or us if they think like me, because we are all Americans. We are interested in the integrity of the laws and the country. Which you should serve with dignity and are not doing with these words out of order. The damage, Mrs. Sotomayor, was done by you as a government, and you do not want to talk about it because it is easier to talk about others than yourself.

And do not pray, because the word of God is not compatible with politics. Politics is dirty, and the divine justice of Jesus Christ does not relate to you until you repent. If you do not want to repent of your hatred, wait for the Final Judgment to be judged. Hatred and blindness in the Supreme Court is corruption equal to what we have in the Department of Justice, the FBI, CIA, and the Joe BidenKamala administration. Our Justice is dying, but we will revive it all on November 5, 2024.

You say: "The relationship between the President and the people he serves has changed irrevocably." We answer that it is true; Americans have seen that since the Democrats took power from the swamp we are living in. We must be just, and you are violating that justice with your hatred. That is why I ask Congress to set time limits for Supreme Court members who should not be above the law. Many years in power with conflicts of interest cause corruption. Your hatred leads you to accuse Donald Trump of murder publicly, and that is very serious, without yet having found him guilty. That is judicial incompetence on your part, and it has shown us your legal inefficiency based on gossip? Or on concrete evidence?

Mrs. S. Mayor wrote: "In every use of official power, the President is now a king above the law."

No, Donald Trump is not a king because we are neither living in a dynasty nor in kingdoms. We wish to live in democracy, and the envy of Donald Trump's fortune has caused many tensions, seeking to destroy him, while our people deteriorate morally, and you do nothing to stop it. Your hatred of Donald Trump breeds hatred among the people. Watch your words and be a little more just, and if you do not remember what it means to be fair, consult the dictionary because our Constitution is so crumpled that it cannot be read very well.

Your public accusation, Mrs. Sotomayor: "Does he order the Navy's Seal Team 6 to assassinate a political rival? Immune." You must prove it before accusing him; do not forget that you are a Supreme Court Judge of the country. Trump did not organize any political coup. No one can accuse him of that. You invented it, covering up inefficiency by not counting the votes with the law directed at a people who do not seek the information that is in their hands through cell phones. It was organized by American patriots who have every right to protest, but the white supremacists are accused, and none of you accused Black Lives Matter when they took to the streets, killed a police officer, and intimidated us with their bad behavior, breaking everything in their path. (It must be repeated constantly because you forget events). It is true that the Constitution says to protest "peacefully." You must be fair, Mrs. Sotomayor; you are in the Supreme Court of our country and are failing in justice. You say: "Does he organize a military coup to cling to power?" It is not a military coup; it is telling the truths we are tired of all of you saying otherwise, and you do not want to see or are not allowed to see reality. Do you know why? Because we cannot denounce because the Department of Justice is rotten. And its other agencies take orders and cannot do anything, but the truth will make you all fall together. There is no evil that does not come to an end.

Accuse him with evidence, and we accuse all of you for negligence, incompetence, failure to enforce the laws, including Nancy Pelosi, whose duty was to protect the Capitol, and she refused to use the help that Trump offered her.

What she wanted was for the disturbance to form to accuse him and remove him from future elections. It was all of you, in silence, without seeking the law, to stop the people out of hatred. You said:

"Does he accept a bribe in exchange for a pardon? Immune. Immune, immune, immune," she added.

I cannot tell you the truths there because I do not know the subject of the bribe you refer to. Prove it to us, and we will discuss it. But if we talk about bribes, I believe that the ones who should talk the least about that word are President Obama, who appointed you, who entered with one and a half million dollars and left with 68.5. In the end, it was 70 million. Can we think that the drug dealers he pardoned donated or gave him those amounts as bribes? We wonder where that money came from. The bribe is the one he accepted and that he is chasing Donald Trump with the FBI in Florida, and they are slowly falling. Only judges with morals are needed to not interpret laws that are already explicit in our Constitution, but since the people do not know these matters, we must accept everything good or bad that you unjust and inefficient judges tell us.

Accusing Donald Trump of ordering someone to be killed is a severe case, Mrs. Sonia Sotomayor, and you must prove it. The murder or attempted murder must be proven, not just with your wounded words because the Supreme Court did not consider your report but with evidence. (For obvious reasons, the members of the Court ignored your report). The Supreme Court of the country is not a neighborhood park in Washington D.C., Please place yourself! See if everything turns against you that you just accused him of wanting to assassinate, and the one they want to assassinate is Donald Trump on 7/13/24.

Referring to your fear for democracy, we see that we differ in opinions because the desire to preserve the moral values that you are destroying is a patriotic duty. (Your proof, saying everything you wanted without weighing your words to the press, showed that you are incompatible with your professional career, being more compatible as a neighborhood resident).

Although the journalist expressed his concern by referring to you not ending your dissent with the traditional "respectfully." I was very glad you did not use it because that would have been another disrespect on your part. See what he said in words and body language.

"With fear for our democracy, I dissent," wrote Sotomayor.

Do not fear for our democracy because we will defend it from judges, presidents, representatives, and senators who feel above the law by accusing former President 45 of what you all do, wanting to be above the law. That happens when corruption is great, and the ship starts sinking, and everyone swims to save themselves. You see one thing in the air bubble where you live, and the people see another in the immoral miseries that affect us, and it is time to start uniting and asking for Redress of Grievances, and we do not accept interpretations of the laws that come from the Democratic system and not from the justice system, the CONSTITUTION!"Is Justice at stake or not?"

POLITICAL CORRUPTION DEMORALIZES THE COUNTRY

"When you forgive, you don't change the past, but you change the future." (Bernard Meltzer), a U.S. radio host for several decades, reminds us of this. This is something we must remember as we continue to accept political situations we do not deserve. We will forgive the Bidens and their corrupt family, but we want them far away from the American government, along with all those who, for decades, have done nothing for the country. They have violated laws, acted as frauds, persecuted a citizen and political colleague who, whether they like it or not, must be respected as a human being because he was chosen by the American people just like the others. They have fabricated laws that are not in the Constitution, laws that never fell under their jurisdiction, while they made their fortunes in the corridors of Washington D.C. They have created a witch hunt. This is unhealthy for the citizens and for international opinion. It is immoral and has no other name.

Did Obama make his millions in Washington D.C.? We forgive him for that too. Does he want to continue leading the corrupt Democratic Party? Did he fail to pursue Iranian spies and all the other issues the public knows about? Shall we forgive him for that too? He has found a new profession in real estate, buying mansions with the money obtained from Washington D.C.,—shall we let him enjoy it? Did Nancy Pelosi, alongside Hillary Clinton, in their grief over losing the 2016 election, invent the persecution and destruction of Donald Trump? We forgive them. Did both of them enrich themselves with millions of dollars in Washington D.C.? We all know it—Democrats, Republicans, and other political parties active in the public arena. We forgive them for that too. Are they all supported by the communists? We forgive them since the party is officially recognized. Did Chuck

Schumer become a millionaire in Washington D.C., with luxury yachts and collections of cars? We forgive him, and after so many years in power, they now want to do for the country what Donald Trump wanted to do from the beginning. We forgive their lack of vision toward the American people, but we will fulfill it as Republicans and patriots, defending what the Democrats have thrown to the ground—their prestige! Did the inept jurist Adam Schiff lead the failed start of the Witch Hunt? We forgive him. Let's wipe the slate clean! But let their Democratic constituents hold them accountable in the 2024 presidential elections—it's time to clean our Big House together.

We are not the plucked chickens they think we are. We do not belong to any party when the country is in danger, nor did they buy us—we chose them, and that is different. The Democratic American people hold the keys to help us clean the Big House (our country) with their votes. Voting is crucial because if we have mentally unstable people in Washington D.C., governing us, it's because we put them there. Wisdom is found in correcting mistakes.

We, as a people, are not satisfied with these senseless situations occurring every day. Hatred consumes us; we have lost family and friends because of politics. The influx of hatred, supported by an irresponsible press, has resulted in us hating each other as if each group were the best, which is not the case. I reiterate that we will vote not only for Donald Trump, even though he performed excellently in his first term, nor because the Democrats wanted to destroy him and steal his votes. We will vote for our Democracy and what we have seen from our corrupt Departments of Justice.

The American people have always been distinguished by their mercy, altruism, patriotism, and law-abiding nature, having corrected the abuses against slaves (abolition of slavery) alongside unique and global capitalist progress. Today, Biden's hypocritical racism wants to pay monetary compensation to Black descendants of slaves, much of which will go into the pockets of some, forgetting the descendants of Whites who died defending the abolition of slavery. That is hypocritical racism. There is no payment for Whites. That is creating a dirty racism, and no one wants to return to that disastrous era. We want bipartisan Justice.

When American families of all ethnicities and races discipline their children from birth until they reach adulthood, we do so out of love and to make them better people in society. Why don't the Democrats discipline their politicians? They deserve the electoral vote punishment so that they become honest representatives of the people and stop lying to them. Why isn't it done? Simple—the Democrats work well with the communists, who have their philosophies for staying in and infiltrating power. Destroying American society is their dream. This is what has happened up to 2024. Hatred is at its peak, being confused with racism. This is reflected in the comments on social media, where people insult you and say horrible things, and we don't even know why. That is hatred, bad education, lack of respect, and that comes from communism, which the Democrats don't realize exists. I am completely sure that Republicans know we will vote for Donald J. Trump because he did not deserve what the dirty Democrats did to him, and those who didn't do it but supported the toxic politicians are just as responsible as they are. We are civilized people, not wild animals in the jungle. Enough is enough!

The international community used to see us as world leaders more or less under Obama until Donald Trump arrived and restored our lost prestige. Biden put it back on the ground; the situation is disastrous. Today, the vision is entirely different, seeing us tearing each other apart, involving the most sacred part of the country— Justice! Soon no one will want to trade with the USA, as happened with Cuba, Venezuela, and Nicaragua, and we will become a third-world country like all of them.

The entire people are responsible for what will happen on November 5. We do not want communism and certainly no hatred among all of us. In these Government Departments lies the hope of recovering our values, which are represented in our Constitution in almost all its amendments explicitly, not interpretively, as those who break the law—judges and prosecutors who are detractors of Democracy— want us to believe. And if they interpret it, they should be honest and do their job well.

By attacking one citizen, they attack us all—Democrats, Republicans, or members of other parties. Corruption makes no distinctions. Former Presidents deserve respect for their service, regardless of the political party they represented, and if the accusations are based on correct evidence, which in politics, there is none in either group, they can be analyzed. They were chosen by the people and deserve the immunity that this country has generously stipulated. We cannot trust these organizations that were our bulwarks in the past and are now sadly compromised by bad behavior and legal corruption (based on current events). No former President has spoken out, asking to stop what is happening to a peer, and that has shown us that they were also very corrupt and do not want to commit themselves.

The criminal, according to the Democrats, is Donald Trump. To the people, it's them. This is the political division, and it must end now. We have suffered enough from the gossip that Trump attacked the Capitol and all the schemes they have assigned to him, and we will see that our government failed out of hatred and plots. The United States Capitol in Washington, D.C., became the meeting place of the United States Congress when the building was first completed in 1800. Since then, many violent, dangerous incidents have occurred, including shootings, fistfights, bombings, poisonings, and major riots (historical facts).In the era of Donald J. Trump, under the Democratic Government, they accuse him of an attack, and we cannot accuse Black Lives Matter of the same. And I repeat it whenever it is relevant so that comparisons can be made. They destroyed the country's historical statues because they considered them racist, violating our constitutional rights for those who do not think like them. They killed a police officer, but the murderers are not them. They killed each other, took our streets hostage over George Floyd's death, and called it Riots. What happened at the Capitol on January 6 is called an ATTACK because they did not do their job, nor did Nancy Pelosi do hers (laziness or plots).

Created by Article I of the Constitution, the Legislative Branch is composed of the House of Representatives and the Senate, which together form the United States Congress.We are completely fed up with hearing so many inconsistencies when they do not use the law, justice, and Truth! Riots and popular demonstrations are events that usually result from the dissatisfaction or demands of a group of people who know they are being lied to. They do so uncontrollably, violently, and destructively, expressing their frustrations about the unsatisfied desires of what is happening in their government.

If the government fulfilled its duties, the people would not demonstrate. In these turbulent political times we are living in, as American citizens, it is healthy to demonstrate and publicly denounce our dissatisfaction regarding the events in the best possible way, telling the truth, and expecting fair responses from the members of our Government Departments.

They accuse and condemn Donald Trump without anyone having seen him start a revolution, commit an act of violence, or wander the halls trying to stop the election results with weapons in his hands. That was done by the people tired of so many political abuses by those who should have counted the votes. The Democrats condone the present and the past of the racist Black community, which is unfair to the racist White community. It doesn't matter if both groups are criminals. What Black Lives Matter did on our streets, what the Black Panthers did in the past, what the Power groups, Antifa, and violent White Supremacists have done is unacceptable in any era, along with the many Hispanic gang members or criminals deforming American society. White supremacists are condemned, but Blacks are not. That is called political injustice and racism in the Biden-Harris administration.

Trump supporters (accused of being White Supremacists by the letter sent to the Pentagon by the Democrats, led by Bob Menendez, advising that the supremacists seen at the Capitol were bad influences, but they didn't say that the violent Black groups are as Supremacist as the Whites and that both act violently).This causes an imbalance in justice when you condemn one group and leave the other out to cover up the wrong or out of fear of them. The people lose confidence in their Democratic politicians and raise the truth to denounce them all.

They stormed the Capitol on January 6, 2021, protesting when sessions were being held to certify Joe Biden's election. If the Democrats had acted correctly, justly, and ethically, counting the votes according to the law, as was done when Bush and Al Gore contested the results and in other past challenges, none of this would have happened. We would have known who was lying to us. Whether it was the Democrats or Donald J. Trump. As a people, we have the constitutional right (we don't know if this is also interpretive or clearly stated) to protest what happened. We must continue to denounce it. We believe the Democratic Party acted quickly to seize power illegally because they did not use the laws that would have clarified whether the 2020 election was stolen. This brought about the consequences of violent protests, as our law enforcement institutions have always allowed, failing to uphold the laws that protect citizens. Therefore, we hold all those involved accountable for not upholding existing laws. As President, Trump had the unshakable duty to demand a vote count, but that did not suit the Democrats because their false information about the votes would have been exposed, and some unfortunate scapegoats paid the price to clean up the image of what happened. There are many cases in our history where presidential elections have been contested.

Contested Presidential Elections Before Donald J. Trump and Joe Biden. Showing the people how inefficient our politicians, both Democrats and Republicans who joined the disaster without analyzing the negative aspects of all of them, are. At that time, the laws were upheld in favor of democracy and the people. Ask yourselves, if this has happened since 1800 and the laws were used to clarify the facts, why weren't they counted in 2020? The persecution of Donald J. Trump by our own government had already been set in motion! What insolence!

In 1800, Thomas Jefferson and Aaron Burr received the same number of Electoral College votes. The House of Representatives, adhering to the Constitution, convened the special session required to resolve the tie. In 1824, Andrew Jackson won the popular vote against John Quincy Adams without obtaining the necessary majority from the Electoral College. Adams was selected by the House, following a procedure in the Constitution, naming him the winner over Jackson. The 1876 election between Rutherford B. Hayes and Samuel Tilden was also contested. Some Southern states did not clearly certify a winner. Here, Congress and its negotiations intervened. This was resolved through negotiations conducted by an electoral commission created by Congress. Hayes became President, and concessions were made to the Southern states that effectively ended the Reconstruction period.In 1960, the contest between Democrat John F. Kennedy and Republican Richard Nixon spread fraud allegations like wildfire, and Nixon's supporters aggressively pressed for recounts in many states. In the end, Nixon reluctantly accepted the decision rather than drag the country into civil unrest during the intense tensions of the Cold War between the U.S., and the Soviet Union. In 2000, Republican candidate George W. Bush and Democrat Al Gore were embroiled in a dispute in Florida. The Supreme Court determined that Bush was the winner, and Gore conceded defeat publicly, recognizing the legitimacy of Bush's victory, saying, "While I firmly disagree with the Court's decision, I accept it."

Does everything need to be repeated to the people for them to analyze it themselves? Not through the erroneous information of a totalitarian press bent on favoring communism and not democracy. Donald J. Trump was not responsible for what happened in the election fraud or the Capitol incident. Neither the White supremacists, nor the Black supremacists, nor the people demanding democracy were responsible. The lie dies when the truth arrives. It was our government, mired in a political plot and lack of work ethics, along with the international communists who run Woke. No detective skills are needed to recognize this.

The legal pack against Donald J. Trump is more than proven, with all the previous examples where justice was used, applied, and correctly sentenced. Why didn't they present themselves to civilly discuss the situation of Joe Biden and Donald Trump?Why didn't our governmental institutions defend democracy (which concerns the inept Judge Sonia Sotomayor because there is only one Constitution) by clarifying who was lying and who was not, as in the past with those six contests? None of these organizations took action to establish order with the justice that was their duty, demonstrating the truth. Not even the Supreme Court, seeing the danger and avoiding civil insurrection due to the mismanagement of laws, took action. They didn't even accept Trump's supporters who wanted recounts in the states involved in the fraud or alleged fraud, not clarified by the laws as was done before. Did Donald J. Trump fail? Or did our institutions fail by not working or plotting? For those unfamiliar with the word, the dictionary clarifies it. Conspiracy, from the derivative conspirer(se), means 'to plot or scheme, usually with political purposes.

We have the right to defend the country from within, and I denounce, or we denounce to those who want to understand the truth, that there was a mismanagement of justice. A Department of Justice sold to corruption. Is the head of the Department of Justice in contempt? Nothing happens.Precisely all those in Washington D.C., failed to defend the country's justice and democracy, and they didn't do it. They all failed—the Legislative Branch, composed of the House of Representatives and the Senate, which together form the United States Congress— maintained opportune silence with the "intention" of taking the presidential elections away from the winner along with the Electoral College. Cowardice!

Everything they have done to Donald Trump must be reversed for the good of the country. There is no other explanation because everything has been done based on extreme filth. And if Nixon's supporters, who aggressively pressured many states to recount votes at that time, succeeded, why did Donald Trump's supporters do the same and weren't heard?"Fraud allegations," silence from those who should defend justice. Unbelievable and dirty accusations like the Witch Hunt by the Democrats in Washington D.C., Donald Trump, in those presidential elections, the dirtiest and most unjust in history, being mistreated by non-existent laws of conspiracy, not as we sometimes think badly of the Constitution. A great shame staining the prestige of the USA, not Donald Trump, who has been persecuted without cause. Our government failed us by not acting quickly to solve the problems and grievances perpetrated by our justice agencies against the people by not clarifying the situation.

You are the guilty ones, and I publicly denounce you, loudly demanding Reparations for Grievances caused to the American people. We demand in our Reparations for Grievances that all this ends abruptly because you planned it very well, but the result has been exposing your political and human immorality. The boomerang has returned to you for fraud and illicit enrichment. There has never been a persecution like the one perpetrated against a citizen using the Constitution interpretively, denying him immunity to destroy him civilly. Where are these intentions written? Are they in the Constitution? Of course, they're not. You invented them without considering the historical document that prohibits it unless Congress and two-thirds of the chambers are involved—everything else has been a dirty theater, and its protagonist is TAINTED JUSTICE.

Violating the rights of a citizen, a former President, and a noble man, demonstrating that your sick hatreds are not ours as a people. Problems are not solved by persecuting but by working decently. None of those governmental agencies have the ability to solve problems? None of you have the right to drag us as a people into your hatreds and bad legal practices.

If I am wrong, tell the people with evidence and press conferences with detractors of Donald Trump and your accomplices in an open debate, as American democracy dictates. We are fed up with your bad behavior. You Democrats, with foolish yet silly words, categorically demonstrate the bad intentions of a political party called Democrats, soon to disappear if they do not make urgent favorable changes. We can all make mistakes and have the decency to admit it publicly. Nobody is perfect, and we know that. The Democrats, acting with the intention of destroying the country, apply the laws to Donald Trump. Time passes. While the Court deliberates to decide what to do and present its ruling again when the document is returned to them, the people will be impatient to know the facts. Still, with the bad reputation of not having used the laws, they left us mired in serious political conflicts and doubts. Fortunately for Donald Trump, the Supreme Court ruled in his favor. It gave him the necessary advantages to continue his political campaign, something the Democrats used as a lethal weapon, and they were the ones who were harmed. Sonia Sotomayor will probably have another neighborhood tantrum like she did in the CNN interview, which is unbecoming of a Supreme Court Judge.

By not adhering to laws as in the past, there is now a vulnerability in our trust in them—whether to believe in them again or not. The Democrats' damage has torn apart the Constitution, much like when Nancy Pelosi tore up Donald Trump's speech, displaying her lack of political and ethical control. The revenge is felt by the people as collateral damage, and it's not fair. We are defending the DEMOCRACY of the country, not just Donald Trump's or the corrupt Biden's.

We need Socrates' four points to reclaim the peace that has been stolen from us, demanding transparency and respect in the next presidential elections: Listen courteously. Respond wisely. Consider prudently. Decide impartially. All of these are crucial for restoring order in our country and reuniting everyone without bipartisan resentment. Considering the Supreme Court's decisions to restrict firearms for those involved in domestic violence, tomorrow they might restrict the First Amendment, so we can't denounce them. That's how Woke operates.

If students are sent to ETHICS classes when they violate them, all of our legal institutions should attend those same classes for not counting the votes according to existing laws, for being mentally out of control, fabricating evidence against a former president, and for everything we've seen in these fateful years, shamelessly violating our laws and the peace of the people.

Subversion, as defined on Wikipedia (for Democratic voters): The term subversion (from Latin *subvertor:* to overturn, to turn upside down) refers to something that aims to subvert an established order or is capable of doing so, whether political, social, or moral. Similarly, something that simply seeks to disrupt public order or political stability can also be called subversive.

According to the RAE dictionary, the term subversion is defined as "the action and effect of subverting." Its synonyms include alteration, disorder, rebellion, uprising, insurrection, revolt, sedition, revolution. Has anyone in this Nation seen Donald J. Trump with weapons, causing disorder, leading an uprising, or starting a revolution? If you have photos, publish them so we can know the truth and not doubt the "dishonest Democrats" who refused to count the votes, destabilizing political order by not fulfilling their duties as public servants, just as they did in the past by applying the law when there were disputes over electoral votes. They serve us, not Joe Biden.

Are they accusing Donald Trump of speaking out or shouting? Is that in the unread Constitution? What the most misinterpreted Constitution of all time says is, "Read me, please!" Many people went to law school without learning what reading comprehension means. Incredible!

How do we refer to the Democrats who refused to count the electoral votes? Corrupt. Adjective. It applies to people who commit irregularities or break the law to gain personal benefit. Example: A politician, an official, or a police officer can be corrupt when they benefit from their position of power. The DICTIONARY does not lie. (The Democrats broke the law by not counting the electoral votes).

They accuse Donald Trump of subversion, and we, the people, accuse the Democrats of corruption, because by not counting the electoral votes, they "benefited from their position of power" and broke the law, which exists for dealing with shady matters like vote theft in our country and for obtaining personal gain. What was that personal gain? Biden's presidency. They didn't use the laws applied during the Bush-Gore dispute, which contributed to the Capitol disturbances.

We really cannot punish or criticize any disorderly, violent group, or Donald Trump for shouting or not, nor the black or white supremacists who are imprisoned, because those who failed to act decently were all those in power who should have resolved the situation but did not do so on January 6, 2021. Our government acted more criminally than the population. They get paid and represent us, the people do not.

They are the ones who should be behind bars. The plot was set up and succeeded until everyone, analyzing history, could see that the culprits were the Democrats of Washington D.C., for not working or because the top brass (The Woke) ordered them to be silenced. That is their problem now for being fraudulent, and their voters should be grateful that we are alerting them. We are not attacking them. The people's judgment is: think carefully, exonerate all those who are not guilty, and return to the political arena with ethics and respect, so that we can repair the grievances caused.

Bob Menendez's letter to the Pentagon, blaming white supremacists while ignoring black supremacists, being complicit in violating our laws, is utterly immoral. They needed a scapegoat to cover up the plot: Donald Trump, the black and white supremacists, and the rest of the American population who demanded that corrupt politicians do their job. Don't look for scapegoats. Blame yourselves for not doing your jobs properly and apologize to "We the People."

Why weren't the laws used to count the votes? Were laws violated because Trump blasphemed? Can he be accused of insurrection without having violated the Constitution, as the Congress, the House of Representatives, and the Senate did by not working? They ignored the ethics of the process, the trust of the people, the peace, which is indeed established in the Constitution and is not open to interpretation.

If Trump is not above the law, as he is accused of being, neither are any members of our institutions. "We the People" formally demand that the government follow what the First Amendment of our Constitution says: the redress of grievances for the damages caused to the citizens. If I could, I would sue them, or we would sue them, seeking redress of grievances, for the damage done to the citizens, including myself, due to the failure to uphold the laws. I would sue them financially, not morally, because we already know that morality in Washington D.C., does not exist at the moment, but money does, and it flows in billions to our enemies while our elders receive paltry monthly Social Security checks and the Department of Justice gags its subordinates so they don't speak out and denounce.

LOSING FAITH IN OUR LAWS

Racism and division, fueled by Washington D.C., and supported by all its Democratic members and some Republicans, wreak havoc on society. Today, racism and division are intertwined, which is why they must be addressed in this discussion. Topics include: "Racism between Black and White Americans in our homes," "The violence of Black Lives Matter," "The legacy of the Black Panthers and their past violence," "The Democrats' Witch Hunt against former President Donald J. Trump," "Violent Black Supremacists," "Violent White Supremacists," "The Federalist Flag as a Nazi symbol for intolerants who should respect the history of the country, whether 'good or bad,' and which many still don't know," "Slavery and its psychological impact on future generations," "The beautiful memories of Martin Luther King," "Nancy Pelosi's emails calling Donald Trump a thug, a label she imposed, forgetting that Hillary Clinton has the same reputation, and with valid reasons, because her close friends have 'committed suicide'—and the list is long," "Chuck Schumer and his contradictory philosophy on his government website, criticizing the elite while he belongs to it, getting rich from his position," "Adam Schiff and his failed trials against Donald Trump out of hate and conspiracy, not justice, despite being a Harvard graduate with millions in his bank account," and "How many Americans view the death of Democracy in the U.S."

The philosophy of homosexuals, who are accepted as such, but whose acceptance is taken to elementary schools by politicians and the radical left, with their hidden agendas that the public does not accept. The famous word *tolerance* has been twisted by incorrect politicians and governors, who don't know the Constitution, yet they all sin in their intolerance toward other groups of citizens, including street "prostitutes." The Take Care Clause and whether President Joe Biden has violated it. The violations of immigration laws by President Biden and his betrayal of Israel by supporting Hamas terrorism. The ungratefulness of laws, mandates, or decrees, or simple governmental corruption by President Joe Biden, giving preference to millions of illegal immigrants while neglecting millions of Mexicans who have been settled in our territory for decades—two decades under Clinton (Democrat), one under Bush (Republican), two under Obama (Democrat), one under Trump (Republican), and one under Biden (Democrat).

Trying to legalize them all in emergencies to secure votes in 2024, we suppose the Supreme Court will have to intervene. Our Constitution and its laws can serve either to protect us or destroy us when they are misinterpreted by lawyers, prosecutors, and judges, and aggressors go unpunished. Street prostitutes should have a place in society, just like homosexuals and the accepted Porn Industry, for those who are not religious. How does Jehovah view all these groups that were once considered immoral and are now "rescued" by dictionaries and psychiatric medical books? The Bible condemns them as immoral if they do not repent. The public should not judge any group because we are not Jesus Christ. That concerns them alone, as long as they do not harm society.

The social rejection of adult prostitution and its persecution despite existing laws. Pornography with prostitutes now called "sex workers" or "porn stars" when, in reality, they are just as much prostitutes as those on the streets. Double standards in the country, protecting the mafias of the Porn Industry and the introduction of marijuana into society in competition with the Drug Cartels. Immigration brings all kinds of problems and marginalization to the country's citizens, who end up losing their rights in favor of others. These are the issues that Americans must address and resolve by draining the swamp of Washington D.C., united on November 5 if they want a healthy and productive country.

Unfortunately, the Democratic Party has failed its voters. They deserve to be punished with their electoral votes by joining the most conservative Republicans who uphold our moral values. Remember that if the Democrats consider the Republican Party as corrupt as theirs, it is always logical to choose the less corrupt option. Our veterans have sacrificed their lives or returned mutilated, whether they liked the wars or not, but they made great sacrifices for their country. Civilians must also sacrifice something and send a message to the usual politicians: we want new faces solving problems in the Democratic Party within four years. The person for the job now is Donald J. Trump, to take charge of the borders again, stop the uncontrolled flow of immigration, strengthen the economy, and erase the negative international opinion of us, among many other tasks.

When immigration is controlled, budgets are made. When it is uncontrolled, as with nearly ten million people entering the country illegally, it is madness and governmental irresponsibility. This is evident when Americans in need apply for public assistance like housing and other benefits, and immigrants who just arrived receive them before they do. Injustices. Does Biden want the votes of the illegals, or does he want a civil war? The Democrats have ignored Mexicans for decades, and still, Univision has the slogan "vote with me," lacking the courage to say what they truly think and want, "vote for the Democrats," and never has that TV channel run a campaign for Mexicans to be given parole. Their petitions were based on baseless scandals, marches with the Mexican flag until someone took action, promoting them with the American flag, as many of us sent letters calling for common sense. We must publicly denounce what is wrong if we want solutions.

Councilman Anthony Beale from the Ninth District expressed his dismay at a city council meeting, revealing that illegal immigrants in Chicago receive more than several thousand dollars per month in various forms of assistance. All of this makes this book a COMPENDIUM of situations that kill Democracy, hurting the emotions of citizens from any political party, and that is what I defend in it. We are all fed up with the incorrect attitudes of the Democratic politicians who drown and destroy us like a devastating tsunami. "The homeland is better served by those who tell it the truth." - José Martí. "Never judge the honest man by the harshness of his truths. Better beware of the hypocrite for the sweetness of his lies." - Paulo Coelho.

COMMON SENSE

If we don't create a red, white, and blue wave by voting on November 5, 2024, even if many don't like Donald Trump for his bluntness (defending oneself is not rudeness, it's speaking the truth), he is the right person to begin the cleanup of our Big House. We have two homes: our small house and the Big House, which is our country, and unfortunately, it's very dirty.

We are not defending one side or the other; we are defending our freedoms, which are now threatened even by the 8 members of the Supreme Court for restricting firearms for those involved in domestic violence. Clarence Thomas is the only one on that court whose brain still functions. The U.S. Supreme Court has upheld the federal ban on firearms for people under restraining orders due to domestic violence. The Second Amendment states: "A well-regulated Militia, being necessary to the security of a free State, the right of the people to keep and bear Arms, shall not be infringed." Are laws being invented by the Supreme Court, or should they follow the canons of our Constitution?

A violent person can kill with a pen, a baseball bat, a stone, a kitchen knife, any object at hand, and even with their own hands, and we can't restrict those weapons. We need to open more institutions that fight against insanity, violence, and drugs—drugs that our Democratic politicians and some infiltrators have unleashed without prior scientific studies, taking over the money that the Drug Cartels used to receive, and now, our government is collecting by selling marijuana and creating Sanctuary Cities. Please, Democrats, open your eyes. Don't let yourselves be poisoned by the hatred of the communists; that's their goal to govern us.

All political parties must unite and respect each other. We are one country, one society, and one God. If we are divided into groups, it was the politicians who did it, not us, not the Constitution, nor the citizenship certificate that clearly states we are Americans.

We are exhausted; let's join forces for the country and be honest. Recognizing the virtues or faults of others makes us greater. Let's be giants for mutual benefit. We don't know what Constitution we have anymore—the one that's dusty, crumpled, or mistreated, or the one they don't read. We must rescue it too. Does the Constitution specify whether violent people can bear arms or not? Wake up! Let's sacrifice for the country.

Judges are human beings and they make mistakes, and our Supreme Court is contaminated with the worst thing that could happen— interpreting what is explicit, making us believe that because we don't know the law, we don't read, or we aren't properly informed, we are considered idiots, and they are above the law. Where are the journalists spreading hate against Donald Trump and who don't see clearly who is really above the law? Sonia Sotomayor has shown that she doesn't know the law; she legislates under the influence of hatred toward Donald Trump. We think that the presidents who nominate these people for those positions don't know who they're nominating either. Before I leave this world, I would like to see a beautiful and intelligent female robot on the Supreme Court, using her AI, and leaving it to the only one whose neurons still function, Justice Clarence Thomas, to help her analyze the rulings.

The others should open their law firms in our neighborhoods for minor issues and see the misfortunes they've left us with due to poor legal interpretations when they served on the Supreme Court— unless they've corrected themselves and bring to the table what they did wrong by restricting firearms for those involved in domestic violence. "To err is human" comes from the poet Alexander Pope in a famous quote, "To err is human; to forgive, divine; to correct, wise." Forgiving others' mistakes is like forgiving our own.

Restricting arms is not in the Constitution; it's in laws outside the Constitution, made by individuals with subjective, not objective, opinions. In communism, one of the first atrocities committed in countries is modifying the Constitution, restricting the people's constitutional rights, and our jurists supporting Woke and not their own Democracy. Those who let themselves be influenced by others don't deserve to legislate our laws either.

The Second Amendment speaks clearly and explicitly; it is not up for interpretation. The United States Constitution, the supreme law of the nation, defines the structure of the federal government and divides it into three branches: legislative, executive, and judicial. The objective thing would have been not to restrict arms, obeying our historic document. What is the Constitution for if there are other laws that they don't show us?

We conclude that the CONSTITUTION should remain stored away, and each district and court should decide what is justice and injustice because none of them adhere to what the Founding Fathers left (and in my humble opinion, which is now subjective, they should create a new one, since many judges neither understand nor respect it as it was written, and this one should be left in the History Museum). How could we not have a swamp in Washington D.C.? Especially if the lawyers who destroy democracy graduated from Harvard, and it's like a curse. The saving grace for that university is that many good people have graduated with honors, like Ted Cruz. This slightly redeems the university's disgrace due to many of its alumni. My childhood dream was to graduate in Legal Sociology from Harvard University. "Life is a dream." This is a play written by Pedro Calderón de la Barca and premiered in 1635. The most famous poem from it is the one recited by Segismundo, which ends with the famous line, "life is a dream, and dreams are dreams."

THE FIRST TRIALS OF DONALD TRUMP

Nets have been woven around Donald Trump to destroy him, and this began in 2016, when the people started receiving messages devoid of common sense. This is part of the Democrat-Communist plan, which intensified from Biden's first day in office until 2024. It's a clear case of "Persecution Hysteria." This situation is unprecedented in U.S. history, with powerful forces, including the Woke movement, at play. As Nancy Pelosi stated, "We will remove him from power at any cost." The cost is a society deeply divided between the political good and evil established by the Democrats. People are paying for the hatred and inefficiencies of politicians from both sides, intensified by liberal, communist Democrats and silent conservatives in a society advancing in technology but deficient in moral values and mutual love.

The trials began to unfold one after another, leading to years of government litigation. They accuse Donald J. Trump of wanting to be above the law as a former president. (This was, and still is, the worst repeated line—like a scratched vinyl record—heard nowadays by journalists who don't investigate because they no longer know what to say.) If you ask, "Who is above the law?" the answer is clear. Those who are above the law, which is our Constitution, are the ones who invented "PARTIAL" trials instead of "IMPARTIAL" ones as the law requires. Added to everything that has happened and the violations without reading the dusty documents in the archives, we are all affected in some way by hearing such big lies disguised as truths or vice versa on a daily basis.

This is the peace that Washington, D.C., politicians steal from us every day. A press that violates all the principles on which information is based is a press sold out to the enemy. What enemies? The ones from within—ourselves. When politicians become corrupt and the government fails the people, we all eventually become corrupt.

The consecutive trials have led to extensive government litigation, raising significant questions about law enforcement for former President Donald J. Trump. It is crucial to ensure that trials remain impartial, in accordance with our law. It is clear that we are all affected by the prevalence of falsehoods and distortions.

We must work towards a transparent and accountable political system in Washington, D.C., where the interests of the people are truly represented. A responsible and ethical press plays a fundamental role in upholding the principles of information dissemination. Continuing to report based on lies and hatred destroys us all, and we lose faith in all of them.

It is important for us to work collectively to promote integrity and accountability in our government and media. All united. The press, which has rightly earned the label of incompetent among its readers, rejoices at the thought of Donald Trump going to jail. Where is the compassion for others? They have become involved in the same conspiracies as the Democrats, and it's all a fusion of monetary interests and corruption. These are the people who govern and inform us.

As the Bible says: "Jesus warned us that false prophets can disguise themselves as sheep when they are really ferocious wolves (Matthew 7:15)." This is yet another example of how the Bible encourages believers to have sensible, informed, and mature faith (Acts 17:11; 1 John 4:1). While these verses refer to religious leaders, it is appropriate to apply them to false politicians and journalists. "By their fruits, you shall know them."

Of course, none of them are punished for fake news and ethical violations that harm their readers or listeners because our country's Journalism School is also corrupt. If we don't see the corruption, then we are blind—not to mention deaf or mute. A nation without compassion for its fellow citizens is an empty nation, even if it's full of luxuries and material wealth. There are many things money can't buy, and among them are mental health, love, and dignity.

Many trials were held against President Trump while he was in office. Those who led the trials, mainly Democrats, will be remembered in history for their attempt to undermine the democracy of the United States of America. However, history will also remember the efforts to counter this attempt by American patriots.

We, the people, will not allow those in power to neglect their duties by misusing the law. The protests were not stopped, as was done in the past with similar challenges to electoral votes.

We need to review history and hold our legal experts accountable, as they dismiss charges against criminals and unjustly imprison decent people, including our heroic police officers. In the past, presidential candidates and their teams respected the law and prioritized the people's needs. Today, in Washington D.C., the focus is on lobbying, corruption, and law violations, along with that Woke movement that doesn't show its face legally but exists within our government alongside the puppet master Soros. In the 2020 election, the votes were not properly counted in the name of democracy, as it was believed they had been stolen—and indeed, although they won't admit it, they were. Those who claim otherwise either ignore the similar situation with Bush and Al Gore or don't want to remember the previous challenges where the laws were correctly applied.

It is important to remember that the Democratic Party is no longer what it once was, especially the current group of Democrats hungry for power. We, the people, will not allow the Congress, the House of Representatives, the Electoral College, the Senate, and others who participated in the last presidential election to neglect their duties. They could have stopped all those protests by applying the law, as was done in the past with the six challenges to the electoral vote mentioned in the first pages of this book.

"History is there. You just have to read it, dust it off, and keep it accessible to legal experts, not to the inept who dismiss charges against criminals and give access to prisons to decent people, including our incarcerated police officers. Others dismiss civil cases sold to the highest bidder. In the past, presidential candidates and their collaborators were deeply attached to the law and thought of the people. Please don't cling to the fact that the party you all joined as Democrats is the same! It's not!

Let's not dismiss the concerns of Cubans, Venezuelans, and Nicaraguans who fear reliving in their new homeland what they left behind. We have learned the lesson too late, but as the saying goes, 'Better late than never.' This time, if there are discrepancies or attempts to alter our votes in November, American citizens from all political parties will unite to hold the government accountable.

They will ensure that votes are counted accurately and that any suspicion of electoral fraud is investigated." Democratic voters are key to draining the Washington D.C., swamp by denying them votes until they reform. The toxic ones are Nancy Pelosi, Schumer, the Clintons, the Obamas, Adam Schiff, Ocasio-Cortez, the Bidens, and Sonia Sotomayor, among many others from both parties. It's time for them to retire from power, which they have never used to benefit the people but to fill their personal coffers. So much toxicity has sickened the country. Because she is the youngest representative, we ask the people of New York to vote differently than they have been doing so far for Alexandria Ocasio-Cortez. We don't want communists in Washington D.C. That's what the cleanup is about. Democracy ratified them as a political party. Those of us who know how communism works must denounce them and deny them votes, thinking of our freedoms and rights, but also our civic responsibilities.

Voting is a fundamental right of citizens, and it is important to ensure transparency and review the functioning of voting machines to prevent electoral fraud. This is necessary given cases like Venezuela and Capriles in 2013, and concerns about vote theft in the past U.S. elections.

Ensuring that the voting process is transparent to maintain the integrity of presidential or state elections is everyone's duty. There is also debate about granting citizenship to a large number of people (more than ten million illegals), and this will be debated if the Democrats attempt it. It is essential to consider these issues within the framework of existing laws and regulations to ensure fairness in the electoral process. Everything has a limit. It's not about bringing in illegals to perpetuate themselves in power; that is ultimately human trafficking. Do Americans want to restrict their rights because a group of ambitious and inefficient people want to destroy their political party? Stay away from what is useless, even if it harms you politically. I'm using what should not be done— mixing politics with religion, as they are incompatible, but now it is necessary to mention it. Proverbs 4:14-27 is for the religious, but I love how it portrays the Democrats.

We hope to return to political bipartisanship in Washington D.C., when the Supreme Court responds to the people, based on the laws, but not the laws the Democrats have for persecution, but the Constitution's laws. Always remember that what happens to one citizen can happen to all of us, and the sad thing is that it's already happening. Trump has left behind the bitter history we have lived through, led by the Democrats. We can make mistakes; it's human to do so, but on November 5, all united—Democrats, Republicans, and citizens of other parties—we will vote for Donald Trump to reclaim Political Moderation from the clutches of the communists and other destructive philosophies, including the Democrats of Washington D.C., for their bad behavior in evading the law to cause harm. Are they mentally ill?

Are they allowing marijuana to be sold freely to raise money like the Drug Cartel and turning their cities into Sanctuaries? They don't deserve the support of reasonable voters. The country should be a sanctuary for all of us, not just for those who are destroying it.

Several judges presided over the trials involving Donald Trump, claiming to defend the impartiality stipulated in our Constitution, and it was not upheld. However, it is evident that all were partial and had Democratic affiliations, which undermined the impartiality of the trials.

Legal proceedings should have involved consulting independent experts and legal professionals to ensure those impartial trials. While I am not well-versed in politics, I recognize the harmful actions of certain factions within the Democratic Party in Washington D.C., aligned with communists. Cubans have experienced it on a large scale.

The Witch Hunt against Donald Trump began when he announced his presidential candidacy in 2016. The Democrats panicked at the thought of someone who was not a politician coming in to expose the dirty dealings in Washington D.C. Those of us who supported him are grateful for his positive impact on the economy, the reduction in unemployment rates, and his effective negotiation skills, which are recognized by the majority of the population, while he served the country for free. In the new administration, he should be paid as the others have been.

However, his critics, who form a considerable opposition, do not recognize his achievements. The nation needed a non-political figure like Trump, as we were tired of the existing hypocrisy, and now we need him more than ever because we can compare who served the country better—Donald J. Trump or Joe Biden (though Biden governed with the most deficient cabinet in history, advising him poorly). I present to you those who unjustly accused Donald Trump, violating what the Constitution says about impartial trials. Beyond the Witch Hunt against the 45th President of the USA, due to collateral damage, they began to publicly destroy American Democracy, removing all their masks.

Adam Schiff, DEMOCRAT, 59 years old (California). A lawyer educated at Harvard University and Chairman of the House Intelligence Committee. He led much of the impeachment investigation and was in charge of the group of seven prosecutors, only for them to ultimately fail as jurists. Donald Trump was acquitted.

My recommendation to families affected by any case led by the OVERWHELMING AND FAILED LEADER of the House Intelligence Committee, Adam Schiff, in the trial where they failed to prove their lies and slander, is to reopen the cases of their imprisoned relatives. It's no wonder they failed; if the House Intelligence Committee chose him as chairman, it means the name should be changed and from now on called the Committee of Inept Jurists of the House of Representatives.

Jerry Nadler, DEMOCRAT, 72 years old (New York). Chairman of the House Judiciary Committee who has been a Trump adversary since the 1980s.

Zoe Lofgren, DEMOCRAT, 72 years old. Congresswoman who participated in the impeachment investigation against Richard Nixon (who resigned to avoid impeachment) and voted against the impeachment of Bill Clinton. (California). It had to be, the Californian Swamp in action.

Hakeem Jeffries, DEMOCRAT, 49 years old (New York). Trained as a corporate lawyer and Chairman of the Democratic Caucus. If the accused is a Republican, there should be a bipartisan effort to ensure both Republican and Democratic perspectives, avoiding injustices. It's clear that the Democrats were not fair, as we've already demonstrated. The trials of Donald Trump seemed like a plot to remove him from power, which was harming all of us. If you disagree, ask anyone who has lived in communist countries.

Val Demings, DEMOCRAT, 62 years old (Florida). She was the first female Chief of Police in Orlando. She serves on the House Judiciary and Intelligence Committees. If constitutional procedures are not followed (even though interpretations of our laws vary), trust in the administration of justice diminishes, whether by prosecutors, judges, and Democratic lawyers or by former police chiefs.

Jason Crow, DEMOCRAT, 40 years old (Colorado). He served as a U.S. Army Ranger and is a veteran of the Iraq and Afghanistan wars. Coming from Colorado, we cannot ensure impartiality. We have seen it as a people. But for serving the USA in those wars, we respect him. But one thing doesn't cancel out the other—he helped with the Witch Hunt, erasing his good deeds in Iraq and Afghanistan.

Sylvia Garcia, DEMOCRAT, 69 years old (Texas). Congresswoman in her first term as a legislator, who previously worked as a judge in Houston's municipal court system.

The unjust scrutiny directed at the 45th president of our nation may have originated from the public's reluctance to thoroughly evaluate situations that impact us as a society. Is it fair to appoint a Chairman of the House Judiciary Committee who openly opposes the accused? This presents a conflict of interest and an injustice, as an impartial figure should be sought instead. Our Constitution must defend justice for all, not just for some. Amendment VI. In all criminal prosecutions, the accused shall enjoy the right to a speedy and public trial, by an impartial jury of the state and district wherein the crime was committed...

The trial of Donald Trump under our Constitution was an absolute political disaster and clearly unconstitutional. The selection of a person who is openly hostile to him as prosecutor raises serious concerns about the fairness of the trial and therefore our Justice system.

This violates the fundamental principles of justice and undermines the existing laws designed to protect us. By failing to meet these standards, they also fail Democratic voters who have placed their trust in a system that should be fair and equitable. Are we allowing ourselves to be governed by individuals who ignore the very laws that shape our society, or by vindictive individuals with prestigious credentials but lacking good judgment and integrity?

The Woke movement is fiercely active and unwavering in its efforts in Washington, D.C., to infiltrate the branches of government. Critics in numerous Western countries have used the term "Woke" to describe leftist movements as fanatical or insincere, accusing them of dogmatically censoring any deviation from their ideological perspective. As an independent writer, unaffiliated with any literary institution, I replace the terms "insincere and fraudulent" with their appropriate equivalents: "inefficient, hypocritical communists who deceive the people."

These words have tarnished our country's reputation, both internally and, most importantly, on the international stage. The Woke philosophy is born from political misery (we might say Political Corruption) and seeks to erase the past to build a new future. This "starting from scratch" is simply a way to continue corrupt practices. How do we survive an increasingly dominant ideology? If Americans don't wake up, we may need to meet in heaven to discern that on this earth, in this country, communism—and now even infiltrated terrorism—is present.

Bad philosophies are leading us from the highest levels of government. Remember Ronald Reagan, who did not allow the communists to advance even an inch; today, with the Democrats, they are everywhere, starting in our elementary schools, where it is easier to brainwash children than adults. No one can cast the first stone in Washington, D.C.

Let's assume there are fair and just judges, prosecutors, and lawyers within the Democratic Party (hard to find). Still, in the trials held against Donald Trump, I don't believe any of them raised their voice to ask, "Are we violating the Constitution? Have we been impartial? Are we being fair?"

If judges and prosecutors don't consult the Constitution, they are no different from corrupt press journalists who don't consult the dictionary or religious individuals who attend churches, harbor animosities toward Donald Trump, and read the Bible without any remorse. They simply absorb what others tell them. It is essential that we all adopt critical thinking before acting and actively participate in meaningful dialogue, but never silence the truths that will lead us to reform the future that is filled with lies. Lies and hypocrisy are exhausting!

Very little is said about the Woke ideology. From my perspective, it is not just an ideology but an organization that persecutes whites, patriotic values, and religious, political, and social values. It is an organization aimed at the destruction of the American people and any country where it is applied.

We have already seen this from Washington, D.C., in the persecution of a white man, Mr. Donald J. Trump, whom this ideology could not reach because it collided with the strength of truth and the repudiation of decent people, whether Hispanic, Black, White, mixed, or of different ethnicities. In Washington, D.C., the Woke movement or philosophy remains alive. The FBI, CIA, Department of Justice, Senate, Congress, House of Representatives, Supreme Court, and Pentagon have much work to do for ALL American citizens. Is the word "investigation" lost? Or was it erased from the dictionary?

Not long ago, the word "Woke" seemed to belong to American campuses or the most radical circles. It strongly marked a particularly active sector of North American students. These students were convinced they were the defenders of social justice, mobilized particularly by issues of "race" and "gender." They were willing, by any means necessary, to embark on a definitive judgment against the

Western world and, more specifically, against the white man, who they saw as embodying all vileness, humiliation, persecution, and ignominy. Are Nancy Pelosi, Hillary Clinton, Chuck Schumer, Adam Schiff, and many others part of the Woke organization pursuing Donald Trump? It seems so because now they are targeting whites—a new version of the Democratic Ku Klux Klan.

Reading books written by communists is to witness the destruction of capitalism without putting it into action, but they decorate it so beautifully that in the end, the reader almost feels like a communist. They are experts, and no one can take that credit from them. In all the countries where communism operates or has operated, it's the same story. The traces of destruction are visible simply by walking through the streets. It's an oppressive sensation of decay. A depressing sadness.

THE BOOMERANG

How do we perceive the actions of the Democrats? How should we respond to them? In short, injustices lead to mockery, criticism, hatred, the desire for revenge, and division, among other miseries. This is the imperfection of humanity, both in the aggressor and the one who refutes it.

Observing the failures of Democratic judges, ignoring the law, stripping Trump of his immunity to subject him to various civil trials, and attempting to condemn him for his wealth, it's understandable that degraded souls feel envy for the possessions of others. The hatred toward Donald Trump has been overwhelmingly unhealthy among the Democratic population. If you ask them, they don't know why.

This is called envy, and it's part of the inner darkness many carry within, like Pandora's Box when it's opened. Finally, some light was shed on the Supreme Court's ruling, and the immense anger of the inept Judge Sonia Sotomayor during her interview with CNN en Español was unacceptable.

Why should the American people care about Donald Trump's wealth, whether he has lied or not? We're more interested in the wealth of Nancy Pelosi, Schumer, the Clintons, the Bidens, the Obamas, and Adam Schiff, who have enriched themselves without working, solely by manipulating their positions among Wall Street, the pharmaceutical industry, donations, and everything related to Washington, D.C., claiming they serve the people.

While Donald Trump worked, sweated, and negotiated without holding any political office, whether he lies or not is not our concern. We need him as our president. If those mentioned above were asked about their wealth, they would lie to us, and they haven't been accused, much less tried or persecuted.

Today, everyone in Washington, D.C., should be facing the charges brought against Donald Trump. They are the ones who will go down in history negatively, while the persecuted will be crowned with laurels. In fact, he's already been awarded them by the American people. That is the best accolade: being recognized as a great governmental worker without being a politician, serving the people without stealing. Can previous politicians and presidents cast the first stone? No, because they've all done the impossible to destroy their own country, becoming traitors to their homeland, and this is how they were congratulated.

CONGRATULATIONS

Congratulations to all the Democrats in Washington D.C.! You have taken a significant step toward losing the 2024 presidential election, and we are very grateful to you. Let's hope everyone returns to normal and goes back to working as they always did in the past. Thank you for supporting our next President, Donald J. Trump, with more media coverage and more of our donations. We are very thankful for all the mistakes you have made. November 5th is the day to take back Democracy, and we are convinced that many Democrats will cross the line as Abraham Lincoln and Ronald Reagan did in the past. Our country needs the sacrifice of its citizens, and this is the best time to do it. Thank you very much for these several years full of persecutions. Thank you for helping us make America great again, while also strengthening our Republican Party. We love you all, and our country will never forget this extraordinary success, which will give us the opportunity to elect our president from jail if it comes to that. Something new in our Democracy, implemented by you, the corrupt Democrats. God bless you all for the beautiful generosity shown to the American people. God Bless America.

Clarification. I do not speak on behalf of the American people in general. I speak on my behalf and on behalf of all those who think like me, or who have lived through these Political Odysseys both abroad and in the USA.

The Plucked Chicken: Attributed to Stalin

In one of his meetings, Stalin (Soviet dictator) asked for a chicken to be brought to him. He grabbed it tightly with one hand and began plucking it with the other.

The chicken, desperate from the pain, tried to escape but couldn't. He managed to remove all its feathers. And he said to his aides: "Now watch what will happen." He placed the chicken on the floor, moved a bit away from it, and grabbed a handful of grain in his hand while his aides watched in astonishment as the chicken, scared, in pain, and bleeding, ran after Stalin as he tossed handfuls of grain, circling the room.

The chicken followed him everywhere.

Then Stalin looked at his aides, who were totally shocked, and said:

This is how easily the stupid are governed."

"Did you see how the chicken followed me despite the pain I caused it?This is how most people are; they follow their rulers and politicians, despite the pain they cause them, just for the simple fact of receiving a cheap gift, a stupid promise, or a bit of food for a day or two."Although the last words of the metaphor may displease us, we must nobly accept that this is how most voters behave, always doing the same thing and with the same results. Our decision is to do something different, and we will have different results. Without fear of social changes.

SOME OF WHAT DONALD TRUMP DID DURING FOUR YEARS IN OFFICE

For those who have forgotten what Donald Trump did for the country, here are some unforgettable examples that came to my phone from a woman who wrote them, but we don't know who she was. All credit goes to her because we immediately identified with her clarifications and memories. **Donald J. Trump and his work while serving "for free" to the American people. 2016-2020**

The article begins like this.

"The one whom the Democrats call the clown of the White House just negotiated four Peace agreements in the Middle East, something that in 71 years of political intervention and endless wars previous presidents before Donald Trump did not achieve.

The one whom the Democrats call the White House clown was the first president who did not involve the US in a foreign war since Eisenhower. That White House clown has had the greatest impact on the economy, bringing jobs and reducing unemployment among the black and Latino population more than any other president.

That White House clown has always exposed the deep, widespread, and long-standing corruption in the FBI, CIA, NASA, and both Republican and Democratic political parties. That White House clown turned NATO around and made them start paying their dues. That White House clown neutralized the North Koreans, prevented them from developing additional nuclear capabilities, and warned that the United States had a more powerful nuclear button than Kim Jong-un when he threatened that his weapons were a threat to this country.

That White House clown, whom they discredit out of hatred, changed the relationship with the Chinese, brought hundreds of businesses back to the US, and revived the economy. That White House clown secured the appointment of three Supreme Court justices and nearly 300 federal judges. That same clown reduced taxes, increased the standard deduction in the IRS Declaration from $12,500 for married Filing Joint to $24,400, and caused the stock market to move to record levels more than 100 times, positively impacting citizens' retirements. That White House clown accelerated the development of a COVID cure, and did so in record time. We still don't have a vaccine for SARS, Avian Flu, Ebola, or a series of diseases that emerged in previous administrations. That White House clown rebuilt the military that the Obama administration had paralyzed and fired 214 key Generals and Admirals in his first year in office (wanting to destroy our country).

This Donald Trump, whom the corrupt press wants to destroy because he tells truths never before heard by the people from a president, uncovered widespread pedophilia in the government and Hollywood, exposed child sex trafficking worldwide, and brought children home with their families. Where were the presidents before Trump?

That White House clown worked for free and lost more than 2,000 million dollars of his own money while serving and did all this and much more in the face of relentless undermining and opposition from people who feel threatened because they know they will be exposed as criminals if he is re-elected.

Choose between a clown or a corrupt hypocritical liar with a forked tongue who speaks softly. Please make it known, I'm sure you won't want to have a beer with him (if he drank, which he doesn't) or even be his friend. The author of this piece says: "I don't even like him," referring to Trump. The USA needs a strong leader who is not afraid to kick asses when necessary and helps humanity.

We do not need a father figure in the presidency; we already have one. We do not need a liar, that's what Hollywood, CNN, MSNBC, ABNC, NBC, and The New York Times are for.

And please re-educate us on what Biden **did or accomplished in his 47 years in office * (making himself and his family rich)* I included what's in asterisks.**

Blessings to this woman wherever she is and to the one who achieved it, Donald J. Trump.

DEAR READERS

In this book, I express my deep gratitude to the American people for their compassionate help during the Mariel Exodus between Cuba and the United States in 1980. As "Marielitos," we will be forever grateful for the generosity and warmth with which we were embraced in this beautiful country.

From 2016 to 2024, we have experienced a concerning series of events leading to political and moral decline. Despite these challenges, I am filled with gratitude for the unwavering support of the American people from all walks of life, including the U.S. Navy, whose heroic rescue efforts saved us from death. My daughters and I cannot thank you enough for saving us, along with the rest of the crew of the Boca Chica ship, whom we never met again. Millions of blessings and thank you for the rescue.

Upon our arrival in Key West, we received invaluable support from compatriots, American organizations, and other ethnic groups. I was personally moved by the kindness and solidarity we encountered. When we were transferred to Fort McCoy in Wisconsin, we underwent an exhaustive legal process and medical exams, and soldiers, officers, and doctors provided us with the much-needed assistance during our 48-day stay in the shelter.

The empathy and care shown to us by everyone involved were extraordinary. This experience reminded me of the power of love and compassion, feelings I hope to convey in this book, even when pointing out what is wrong may upset those criticized. But the purpose is to unite us.

Being compassionate and loving is one thing, but accepting what is wrong as right is another. We hadn't set foot on the military base, and already there were strikes and attempts to transform the immigration system by my fellow countrymen. The Cubans overstepped there, just as the Democrats have overstepped now, and everything becomes history.

The FBI or CIA process began with individual interviews, asking us about the communist system and whether we had been involved in it. That's how it should be, not like now, with Biden violating all these laws protecting the country's security, allowing millions to enter without being investigated or medically examined, foreseeing the infectious diseases that occur in Third World countries. Many interviewees left with handcuffs on, which was also the right thing to do.

Alongside the political process, medical appointments began. The girls were not examined like the adults, as they were young, and my mother, so foresighted, had given us an envelope before we separated in Cuba, containing the medical records of the two girls with all their vaccinations.

This country was so orderly at that time under Democratic governance, and now with the current disorder, it causes dismay to those who love order and justice. The medical process was physical and mental, and the reports were sent to the Centers for Disease Control and Prevention in Atlanta, Georgia 30333. Under this information: "Cuban Refugee Processing Center Fort McCoy, Wisconsin." This letter was given to me along with those of my two daughters. It says: "Dear Doctor: Attached are copies of the medical documents we have issued to Cuban refugees. These refugees have been authorized to enter the United States by the Immigration and Naturalization Service pending the resolution of this 'political asylum' application. They are destined to reside in your state at the addresses indicated in their documents. These refugees have been medically examined in Wisconsin under excludable medical conditions (leprosy infection, active tuberculosis, the five venereal diseases, and certain mental conditions). This information is provided to you for what you consider necessary." Signed by the leader of the Cuban refugee team, John F. Hybarger.

A Democratic president worked responsibly in allowing about 125,000 Cubans to enter during that exodus. For the first time, we could vote emotionally, not physically, as the Democrats want, or as citizens suspect about the illegals due to the Democrats' past misconduct.

We did it for the Republican Ronald Reagan, after receiving visits from friends and family who had the right to vote as Americans. Even though we were Democrats and were allowed to enter as political exiles, we couldn't vote. The laws were upheld. Let's hope that is repeated now, and those who enter illegally or legally but without the proper documents do not vote. Emotionally, we did it, due to the hostage crisis in Iran and a deteriorating economy marked by inflation; we considered Ronald Reagan the right man.

As Donald Trump wanted, immigrants should enter authorized and processed politically and mentally, avoiding the spread of diseases and mental illnesses (which we already have enough of here). The people have a voice. Thanking all those who received us would be an endless list, and the best payment is to live in harmony and respect their laws, which are now ours, thanks to naturalization. The exodus officially ended on October 31, 1980.

Cuban soldiers ordered the last 150 boats in the Port of Mariel to leave without passengers. It is estimated that about one hundred twentyfive thousand Cubans arrived in the United States through the MarielKey West (Florida) sea bridge. If an exodus of that magnitude affects American citizens, about ten million is an astronomical figure with disastrous consequences. We all like to be praised and told positive and beautiful things, but if it's not true, we fall into hypocrisy. In the case of the "Marielitos," doubts were logical because Fidel Castro had allowed common criminals to leave, who never cared about politics, just as any country has its criminals.

He let the sick out of mental hospitals to discredit the Cuban dissidents who did not accept communism. That was the price to pay, and filmmakers live off these themes, exposing and preserving them in history. Scarface was released in 1983.

This happened in the spring of 1980. The Mariel Exodus saw 125,000 Cubans set sail from the Port of Mariel, Cuba, to Key West, Florida. As everyone says, in search of the American dream, the reality was not that. The poor Cuban did not emigrate; the rich did for pleasure, not out of necessity or to seek the American dream. The American dream was in Cuba before the Castro Revolution.

The film depicted not only the Cuban ambition for wealth and power but also aspects of the drug world in the USA through the Colombian drug cartel. The Cuban in beautiful Miami found the negative opportunity offered by that world of wealth, power, and sex, where many found love, even if distorted. He was Tony Montana. The world still remembers him by the name Scarface. Al Pacino, in my opinion, shone in that movie. Many Cubans felt offended by it, considering it a defamation of their ethnic group. It depends on who sees it that way, but the reality is that social problems have always been brought to the big screen. And I think it should be that way for history because the public remembers a movie better than several pages of history in the library.

In my view, they captured several aspects worthy of social analysis. I still consider it today a great film representing drug trafficking; the emotional touch is still remembered. "Say hello to my little friend!" The actors, all formidable, each in their character.

In all groups of exiles, there are criminals and infiltrated spies, and we should not be offended, but we have learned that over time and in a different culture. With the passionate Cuban character, for all Marielitos, it was a high price to pay. The reputation lost in that historical moment, but as integration progressed, the concept changed, and even so, we are extremely grateful to the American people for being patient and generous, knowing that we were fleeing communism. We say thank you a thousand times from the bottom of our hearts.

Thank you, and profound gratitude to all the officers and crew, of the aircraft carrier (for us, it was) who saved our lives. Our respect and eternal gratitude. We still keep the black sweater with the name "Caroline" in red, which one of the officers gave me for my small daughter, who was completely soaked during the rescue. The exodus was orchestrated on April 15th of the same year in Cuba. We left in the last half of May 1980. To all, our sincere thanks and deep gratitude on behalf of the rescued.

I believe the same sentiment is shared by millions of immigrants in this land, who identify with that feeling of gratitude for all the help received. Although many may not like the topics discussed in these pages, it is necessary to comment on them for the benefit of this wonderful country, especially for the young people and children who will be the bright future of tomorrow. Talking about the 2020 elections is taboo. It causes discussions and accusations among voters of different political parties, especially between Republicans and Democrats today.

Democratic voters are defenders (understandably) of their party and political attachments, not the country, often thinking that communism does not threaten them. Republicans accused by politicians as gangsters for being demanding because they know the Democrats' modus operandi, are united in the divisions and allegations. The humane, just, and wonderful thing would be for all of us to go back several decades when belonging to any political party was honorable, respectful, democratic, and no one remembered the matter until the next elections. And friendships and families were not lost. (The first thing that happens in a communist country). Focus on the reality we currently have and draw your conclusions.

Intellectuals who talk about the past, analyzing the Anti-Communist Hysteria developed in the USA during the era of Joseph McCarthy, considered it an exaggeration of the facts. The Anti-Communist Hysteria had its reasons, but those who were wrong were those who thought it was all a plot for many to rise to power and harm American democracy. Communists never sleep, and forgive me for those intellectuals who think differently.

Those of us who have lived under communism 90 miles from the United States have a duty to refute that communism is not a benign philosophy, that it should not be feared, and that the people should not turn it into Anti-Communist Hysteria.

We must denounce that this is not the case. Those who think otherwise are wrong. If they don't want to believe it, they have the free will to renounce capitalism and move to communist countries to see the differences.

In historical accounts, it is reported that many teachers were fired from their positions and nearly 600 were investigated for their associations with the communist system. Unlike Cubans, professors from various fields, many of whom had doctorates, voluntarily chose to resign rather than have to teach communist ideologies to their students.

They immediately identified as "anti-communists," which led to a shortage of professionals in the educational sector, known as the "Teacher Crisis," while others said the same, but more academically. As a result, pre-university students were hired as substitute teachers for lower grades. This is a remarkable situation worth mentioning.

Communism's tentacles have not separated from the USA; they extended to Latin America and the Caribbean, achieving their goals. Today, in third-world countries, almost all presidents are social democrats, progressives, socialists, liberals, etc., and the people in extreme poverty vote for them, and this sustains governmental corruption. To extend their tentacles where they desire, they use any situation. Communists are patient, and they know which groups to ally with to achieve their Machiavellian goals. Unfortunately, the Democrats in Washington D.C., have mostly allied with these philosophies, becoming their puppets. Many intellectuals defended the Anti-Communist Hysteria of the United States as exaggerated and unjust.

The sad thing is that those who harshly criticized it never lived under communism and consider it unimportant or do not believe it. They cannot imagine it, even though they advocate for it.

Many intellectuals considered that far from being a justifiable response to threats to national security, the Anti-Communist Hysteria of the post-war period represented the most sustained era of political repression in American history. I strongly disagree with that concept because if, in that era, the Anti-Communist Hysteria intimidated American society, the Democratic era has done the same since 2016, but more intelligently than in that era, using the Constitution, recruiting immoral judges, and social networks, which serve both ways, one to spread lies and the other for truths.

It is important to remember our rights and freedoms. A persecution of a former President never happened in that era. Where is the Department of Justice? Former President 45 has been threatened with putting national security at risk, his immunity has been stripped until the Supreme Court ruling in July 2024, bringing some light, but not the necessary one that should be applied to the fraudulent trials perpetrated out of hatred that did not exist in the post-war era. His followers are persecuted, called all sorts of names by the government (and by mobs of negative social elements) such as a basket of deplorables (Hillary Clinton), a mafia, a gang, etc. (Nancy Pelosi and her followers) for not having the same ideologies as the Democrats, inviting the people to do the same. Sowing hatred and division among American citizens. Politicians should carefully choose their words so that the mentally ill outside do not echo those hatreds by attacking the population. Now they want to take away the right to bear arms? Are they preparing another circus?

We have no post-war era, and persecutions and trials violating the Constitution are carried out continuously, and nothing happens. The most sustained era of political repression has returned to the forefront in the United States of America, brought by the Communist Democrats since Donald Trump announced his candidacy. Are we facing Democratic Hysteria similar to Anti-Communist Hysteria? Or are we facing reality? Are we hysterical about using the word tolerance in elementary schools? Or is it justified hysteria? Do we have more than just the radical left, terrorists in schools? Why are Palestinians and all those who support terrorism coming here? What kind of students confuse freedom of expression with urban terrorism? Will they be the professionals of the future? I think it's time to stop living in ignorance or demand that the government uphold the law. That they repair all the grievances caused, ending this corrosive persecution, as they are all responsible.

When teachers or politicians express their own ideas instead of following school curricula, conflicts arise between students' parents and their teachers, impacting students and violating their constitutional rights. The case of DeSantis in Florida, defending the constitutional rights of parents and children regarding homosexual influence in schools, was a significant event. Other governors, like

Gavin Newsom in California, don't want to follow suit, and his Attorney General is complicit.

This reflects the current state of hysteria. When hysteria arises, we must refer to its foundation: the Constitution, which is often overlooked. Many people believe that freedom of expression allows them to influence others with different philosophies, forgetting that each individual has a unique mind and should express themselves freely based on truth and lived experiences, rather than defaming or offending others, as is happening now. But never give in because others do not tolerate them. Truth and love are unique, and we all have them within us.

In 1947, 67% of the American population opposed the legalization of the Communist Party, but unfortunately, today we are living the same thing with actions carried out by the Democrats. In the era of anti-communism in the USA, the arrival of the FBI was associated with the destruction of life or a career destroyed by suspicions or real events, as intellectuals have said. Today, it happened to a former President, something never before seen in our history. What happens to a president or former president can happen to any citizen. Moreover, it is already happening, and you will read more about it later.

According to intellectuals, they say that the Anti-Communist Hysteria of post-war America became a horrible nightmare: lost jobs, divided families, blacklists compiled, and hearings held. With all due respect to those intellectuals and American history, we can say that everything repeats itself. Now it is not Anti-Communist Hysteria. Now it is true communism that never left the USA and that the Democrats have helped with their unconstitutional actions. It existed, exists, and will exist even if many don't believe it, and if they are not communists, they are deeply involved with them, working together, and possibly the high-ranking individuals pulling the strings of communism are at the international level.

We have divided families and friends because of political differences, lost jobs, hearings held supporting racism and delinquency (police officers imprisoned for defending us), not social integration and respect, and social networks like Yahoo News often threatening us (they will have it in their records) for defending Donald Trump from his detractors' attacks or erroneous concepts in their news. Injustices are not good.

Isn't that happening, or are we lying? That case was mine. I lived it by speaking the truth, not by offending anyone with vulgar words. Of course, after debating it, they didn't threaten me again, and I continued participating in the forums. Silencing me? I went through that situation several times. That was persecution and violations of my constitutional rights because if others expressed negative opinions, why weren't my positive comments accepted? How can I not denounce what is wrong? In the end, they left me alone. That's how communism works, which historians now don't see.

Words of Fidel Castro, a liar, thief, and murderer, like any good communist in power: "We will demoralize the American people." The communists' hatred of the United States is powerful and sickly (the same hatred the Democrats have against Donald Trump, who doesn't even know why they hate him, among them Adam Schiff, who hasn't reached the Senate yet and already wants to impeach Donald Trump again).

Those of us who suffered under communism know how they operate. This great power refuses to become communist, but they insist on subduing it. First, the Cuban people were demoralized (historically a proven reality that no intellectual historian can object to).

In these times, the Cuban communists, led by the shameless Díaz Canel, have minors imprisoned after beating them in the streets for thinking differently.

In May 2024, they are eager to return to the capitalism they always hated, asking to negotiate to stay in power. But they hide from the American government under Joe Biden what they are planning. What did the ships that visited the island in June 2024 bring, whether Russian, Canadian, or Chinese? And above all, why do they guard the cargo like a militarized zone? Could the Cubans have Chinese weapons for a future attack 90 miles from the USA?

In November 1961, Kennedy approved Operation Mongoose, a secret plan aimed at stimulating a rebellion in Cuba that the United

States could support. By the time everything was in place, and Brigade 2506 was formed, Kennedy betrayed them. The rest is history.

While the Kennedy administration planned Operation Mongoose, Soviet Premier Nikita Khrushchev secretly introduced mediumrange nuclear missiles into Cuba. The next day, on October 28th, Khrushchev issued a public statement saying that the Soviet missiles would be dismantled and withdrawn from Cuba. The crisis was over, but the naval quarantine continued until the Soviets agreed to withdraw their IL-28 bombers from the island, and on November 20, 1962, the United States ended its quarantine. The Democratic government at that time worked correctly, adhering to the law.

Russian or Chinese ships could have brought the atomic bomb from the Russians or the Chinese, who, by the way, are selling Cuban men as mercenaries to fight in Ukraine. Communism doesn't work; it destroys everything. Delegations enter through Miami airport, including extortionists who abused the Cuban people, spies, and all with paroles. Who is endangering national sovereignty? Donald Trump or Joe Biden? There's no need to ask; we all know that Joe Biden is violating our laws, and everyone is silent. The entrants are not investigated as they were years ago when we were quarantined.

In the 1950s, many artists, including Walt Disney, Ronald Reagan, and others, allied with Anti-Communist Hysteria, and not without reason, because it was true what was happening in the country. There's no worse blind person than the one who doesn't want to see (a street saying). Under Ronald Reagan's government, communism was contained and did not gain ground while this great man governed. Thanks to his memory on behalf of the American people for stopping the monster that others see as a simple fairy tale.

Joseph McCarthy reported that over two hundred communist allies were infiltrated in government ranks. They branded him a liar and homosexual for saying that without being able to prove it and claimed he only wanted to gain profit. As if communists would publicly offer to say "what they do and what they plan." Ridiculous to think so, even if you are an intellectual.

Richard Nixon began his American political career with this attitude, even identifying anti-Americanism. Nixon's words: "So a very characteristic attitude of the Democratic Party could be likened to a dangerous drift towards communism." We didn't say it; Richard Nixon did, and he was right. The infiltration of communism into our Universities, Colleges, and High Schools and the government is a reality, whether people like to hear it or not.

Algernon Hiss, denounced by a former communist Whitaker Chambers, and Nixon's intervention made the opinion of the muchtalked-about Anti-Communist Hysteria even more intense. It was considered that these cases were fueled by the population because they had the feeling that there was a conspiracy of spies at the highest levels of the American government. Communists spread their tentacles everywhere, and in 1959 the Great Revolutionary Scam occurred. The Cuban Revolution, also known as "Liberation Day."

From 1950 to 1959, it wasn't Anti-Communist Hysteria that was experienced in the USA; it was a disguised reality, much like the one we have now under the name of Democrats. And that force that the population felt, that there was a conspiracy of spies at the highest levels of government, today we don't just have that feeling; we have the certainty that terrorism and communists are closely linked to our government, along with the Democrats. Joe Biden is the promoter by helping terrorists and not standing firmly with Israel alone in this era. He gives millions of dollars to Palestine, and today foreign and national students unite to destroy everything in their path in over 25 universities in the country, and the government hasn't issued clear orders for imprisonments for the damages caused. Complicity? Governmental negligence? Of course, yes.

How many spies from different countries are taking advantage of the situation and are now walking our streets? In California, hundreds of them, from China, were detected, entering freely into the country with the new invasion. Joe Biden has placed our country's sovereignty in the hands of spies from any part of the world. And they accuse Donald Trump of the same for asking that the electoral votes be recounted, without giving him the opportunity to count them as happened with Bush and Al Gore. We must repeat it continuously, so we don't forget the facts. And the six historical challenges that happened before, which in this Biden era didn't use the laws for vote counting. Is there a conspiracy or not? Democratic communism in action. What will the intellectuals write in the future? That the defenders of freedoms were crazy? In Florida, there are many communists wandering the streets and constantly entering with the famous parole, just like in California, and many are even on vacations.

The most shameful thing, many of them are Cuban spies. Those words that: gave the feeling that there was a conspiracy or infiltration of spies at the highest levels of the North American administration... today, we have seen it with the unconstitutional trials perpetrated against former President Donald Trump, and tomorrow it will happen to us too, if we continue to protest.

With the intervention not only of Soros and many more millionaires, friends of the Democrats, because they are all interested in being in the Swamp, where they will continue to increase their fortunes in lobbying and government perks, the serious events that affect us all continue to happen. A big round of applause for the "Democratic millionaires" who supported Donald Trump by giving millions of dollars to the campaign. It was about time to see the light at the end of the tunnel.

Democratic politicians who don't think about their country are traitors to the nation, even from within the government. And although the people don't have the proof in their hands, we know these opportunistic donors exist, although we have more than we thought involved in communism and cooperating with them in wanting to destroy the country. The government in Washington D.C., knows it, and the Department of Justice will never tell us. The trials at the highest levels of the North American Democratic administration from Washington D.C., were broadcast to devour former President 45.

Those who had the vision that communism penetrates and envelops the masses were not wrong. It is so. Example: Cuba, Venezuela, Nicaragua in our Latin America and the Caribbean. Even in Europe, these harmful philosophies fluctuate as if they were holy water when in reality, they are the destroyers of societies.

Seen and proven. Communism's mission in this era is not to rush but to infiltrate highranking military, government, and intellectual positions, as Joseph McCarthy said, although terrorism is already at the door. The trial of a judge candidate questioned by Ted Cruz and other Senators demonstrates that all have been involved with the communists, and then they are the judges who attack citizens with their obsolete criteria, but they have the power in their hands to destroy the people. If Democratic voters don't want to understand, they will suffer the consequences. Those of us who have experienced communism will be the survivors.

In the Senate, McCarthy attracted national attention in February 1950 after a speech in which he allegedly possessed a list of "Communist Party members and members of a spy network" employed in the State Department. McCarthyism was also known as the Second Red Scare, a period characterized by political repression and persecution of leftist individuals. This movement generated widespread fear of supposed communist and Soviet influence within American institutions, as well as apprehension about Soviet espionage in the United States from the late 1940s to the 1950s.

Some intellectuals have been guilty of confusing their readers by perpetuating the notion of a "supposed communist influence." A closer examination reveals that after the 1950s, communism emerged as a tangible concern, as demonstrated by its expansion to Cuba – barely ninety miles from the United States – within just eight years. Therefore, McCarthy's claims, despite their controversial nature, had a semblance of truth.

His detractors can criticize him infinitely; they have that right under freedom of expression, but communists are indeed sly, spies, insolent, and immoral; they do infiltrate the highest government positions. From there, the persecution of Donald Trump from Washington D.C., has arisen, which sadly neither the CIA, the famous FBI, nor the Pentagon, or the Department of Justice investigates the aggressors, much less. All are implicated in terrible corruption.Top of Form.

The Witch Hunt is a method of operation used by the communists, and in this case, they are using Donald Trump. But the most serious thing is that they are harming the American people and their democracy both nationally and internationally, and that is the goal: to demoralize us, pitting us against each other under the stigma of hatred instead of the benevolence of love. Communists are already persecuting people through groups affiliated with them—our children, spouses, brothers, friends, and anyone who doesn't think like they do. Television has the events recorded of how they beat those who supported Donald Trump, spreading fear and terror among the people in front of the Department of Justice, without any response. Did they take action? No, they allowed them to act without punishment or legal consequences. Why? Because they are all corrupt; there's no other word for it.

The Democrats are cooperating with them and are secretly part of their ranks because, wherever communism operates, they bribe, pay large sums to the press, politicians, judges, and prosecutors, so they can control them like puppets in a circus. But once they take power, all of those mentioned are the first to fall. In many European countries where communism operated and destroyed nations, they relied on such bribes. Cuba in the Caribbean, Venezuela in South America, Nicaragua in Central America, and many others, with their communist philosophies, are ready to control the world with their sick delusions. Those of us who have lived under communism for years have our own story, because it's easy to be a communist or discuss it under capitalism. The hard part is being one or discussing it in a communist country.

We Cubans, who experienced it firsthand, know the Witch Hunt in our own flesh, unlike intellectuals, artists, historians, journalists, or political theorists writing and making big conjectures without risking jail or persecution of their families for what they say or do. Under the law, we are all equal according to the amendments of our Constitution, but the university protests across the country in favor of terrorism show us that this is not the case. Terrorism is already within, intimidating law enforcement officials who either cannot or do not want to act. We are witnessing this thanks to technology—cell phones, tablets, TV, etc.

This will go down in history, and in 40 years, journalists and experts in various fields will return to say that this never happened, and that it wasn't perfectly planned from Washington D.C. Years will pass, and they will claim that the Anti-Communist-Democrat Hysteria was not a reality, but rather "a hysteria against corrupt Democrats by Republicans," or "an anti-Democrat terrorist hysteria by citizens against them because they were part of Donald Trump's gang," or by Cubans obsessed with the topic. "We are the people," patriots, not political gangsters. If the Democrats weren't relentlessly pursuing Donald Trump with disrespect to voters, viciousness, disrespect to integrity, violating our laws with unjust and mafia-like trials, we would give them the benefit of the doubt. They would have to return the immunity that they have impudently stolen from him, and no one is being investigated by the Department of Justice. I won't erase what I've written in the previous paragraphs because that's what happened, and we waited months to learn part of the truth upon his official immunity being returned. Do you know why? Because they are all involved. We've impatiently awaited the Supreme Court's ruling obtained in July 2024, giving us the chance not only to see the verdict but also the face of some of its members, such as Justice Sonia Sotomayor, full of Democrat-communist hatred. Can this lady be impartial as the Constitution demands?

The judges are creating problems instead of solving them. They are pursuing Donald Trump with the joy of destroying him, not applying the dirty justice of this Biden-Kamala administration, because if they were just, they would judge themselves for being inept. Did they close the Department of Justice, and we haven't noticed? Is the Department of Justice now working for just one group? The Democrats? Are they obeying the Woke? Are they incompetent in their profession? Many questions that they will never answer because they don't have the right arguments, nor the courage to do so.

That is totalitarianism, not justice. Have any Democrats been sanctioned or tried? Think about it. The IRS has helped Biden's son cover his payments (penalty relief for tax filings), but Donald Trump must be destroyed. But they fixed it quickly, extending penalty relief to the population.

I'll give you an example from our Democratic politicians—words from Schumer on his government page: "Too many families in the United States feel that the rules of the economy are against them. Special interests and lobbyists have too much power in Washington, from the wealthy spending unlimited amounts of money in secret to influence our elections, to our tax code that helps corporations and the wealthy avoid paying taxes."

If he's referring to Donald Trump not paying taxes, and thanks to disinformation, the American people said Trump didn't pay them, but they didn't add that neither did they. And for Trump's detractors, it was very easy to shout it from the rooftops, making Trump look like a criminal while portraying his detractors as saints. Those are the injustices we must not tolerate. Just like all of you shouldn't either. So look at what the IRS did, fixing the tax messes and evasions of President Biden's son, Hunter Biden. What this politician says about the tax code for the rich was mentioned by Donald Trump to Hillary Clinton in one of their debates, arguing that they were the ones responsible for those regulations, good or bad, that they should have fixed, but they didn't because they all belong to the elite and also don't pay taxes. They would be affected if they fixed it. Now they accuse Donald Trump of the same thing that all millionaires have done to avoid paying large sums because of the tax code that benefits the wealthy. Schumer himself admitted it, showing us the Democrats' corruption in the swamp, blaming others for what they do as well.

The people deserve to know the truth about this tax code for the wealthy, to avoid speculations and arguments on social media accusing only Trump. That's called injustice. Having the correct information, provided by an elite Democrat like Mr. Schumer, who has become rich in Washington D.C., leaves no doubt that all millionaires use that code. If the tax code exists for that, what are they complaining about?

They're millionaires, not fools. The IRS is now helping those who owe due to pandemic-related problems. Will they erase Trump's debts if he has any? Are they doing it to secure votes for Biden in the presidential elections? Or are they erasing everyone's debts so they won't be criticized for erasing President Biden's son's debts? The Democrats are not pure as snow.

The goal is to eliminate the Republican political party and keep the Democrats in power. That's how communism works, first in complicity with the Democrats, and if they were to take power, they would eliminate them too. But that's just a hypothesis becaus they will never take control of the USA. We won't allow it. The Communist Party of the United States, officially the Communist Party of the United States of America (CPUSA), also known as the American Communist Party, was established in 1919 after a split in the Socialist Party of America, following the Russian Revolution. Finally, communism became official in the United States under the name Communist Party of the United States of America (CPUSA). They may be there, but we won't let them achieve their goals.

CONCLUSION

Karl Marx, the German philosopher and main developer of communist theory, along with significant philosophical doctrines such as historical materialism, and Friedrich Engels, his German philosopher companion, co-author of many of Marx's works and theorist of scientific socialism—these founders of such destructive ideologies criticized the bourgeoisie, yet they opened businesses, loved holding prominent positions, and sought fame. They brainwashed those who allowed it. They lived intensely all that their philosophies supposedly opposed.

The support of the Communist Party for Democratic presidents confirms what Nixon once said: "So, a very characteristic attitude of the Democratic Party could be seen as a dangerous drift toward communism." The Communist Party's support for the Democrats is undeniable in the U.S., and the people know it. The Communist Party endorsed these candidates to power. What do Democratic voters expect?

- Bill Clinton (1992-1996) was elected president.
- Al Gore was not elected in 2000. • John Kerry, not elected in 2004.
- Barack Obama (2008-2012), elected.
- In 2016, Hillary Clinton, thanks to Donald Trump voters, was not elected.
- Joe Biden, elected through electoral fraud that they didn't want to investigate (2020).

Why doesn't the Communist Party support and donate to the Republicans? Because the Republican Party knows them, rejects their practices and philosophies, and denounces them to the people. Communism is a Democratic extension, and we are seeing it without needing to be branded as crazy or extremist, much less as suffering from "Democratic Anti-Communist Hysteria."

Something beautiful from the Bible, Matthew 7:16-21: "By their fruits you will know them." Who has caused all that we are currently experiencing? The Democrats, without question. Wherever communism operates, there are electoral frauds, bribery, crime in the streets, imposing their rights while trampling on others'. We've seen it in past actions of the Black Panthers, Black Lives Matter, Antifa, the so-called Power groups, White Supremacists, the Government Elite, all sharing the same mistaken ideologies and supremacies, which today are obsolete in a time of informative dynamism in our homes via the internet and with many more technological advances at our doorstep.

There are communist influences trying to make the general public close their eyes. There are crimes, dirty sexual slanders, family, religious, social, and political disintegration. Dysfunctional families, regardless of financial status. When we speak of crimes, many are related to communists or to the madness of many. Joe Biden's is one, but it could also be in our homes. There is a deformation of moral values, there is divisiveness—and that's what they thrive on. Racism is created and promoted by them, creating divisions of races. There's everything, to the extreme of constantly accusing law enforcement of being killers, while they themselves act as benevolent angels.

I bring you this information, which you can corroborate on the internet, so that you reject communism, socialism, Marxism, and all the remaining ideologies that wish to end capitalism and turn us all into the destitute, as has happened throughout history. Open your eyes to what's being done by the Biden-Kamala government, though I don't even mention Kamala because she was chosen poorly by Joe Biden. Power is power, and she craved it, being selected not for her intelligence but simply for being a Black woman.

I disagree with former President Donald Trump when he calls her brilliant. She may be, but if she were, she wouldn't have lost the presidential race with a low approval rating of around 13%. It means that the people she served did not accept her.

I remember when Angela Davis, former member of the Black Panthers with her communist philosophy (hopefully, she has distanced herself from that social filth), traveled to Cuba to ingratiate herself with Fidel A. Castro Ruz. That was the first time I heard that a country could be destroyed if a germ bacillus was released, and it terrified me at the time. It was a threat to human destruction, and I always suspected that COVID-19 had some connection to the communists.

If Angela Davis wanted her own country to succumb to communism, we can tell her she was wrong, along with the past Black Panthers and their communist ideals, and other violent groups. They haven't advanced an inch. If they had followed their leader Martin Luther King, today they would be decent people.

Those who labeled it Anti-Communist Hysteria many years ago were mistaken. Angela Davis visited the island for the first time in 1969, with a delegation from the Communist Party of the United States. She returned in 1972 as part of an international conference tour following her acquittal on charges of murder and conspiracy, and her release from prison. She returned in 1974 to attend the Second Congress of the Federation of Cuban Women. Have you ever wondered why, if McCarthy was wrong about communist infiltration in high places, the party was still made official? Because they were already inside.

Wherever communism is born, it destroys everything. The Federation of Cuban Women was always full of shamelessness and lies. They took advantage of certain social favors, insulted and accused those who didn't think like them, and displayed an abysmal ignorance of the country's history, burning books to keep the people ignorant. Today they're in Florida cooling off. What a great failure for the communists and for their inspired members from the former Black Panthers and Angela Davis as promoters of all this social misery! What do they say now? Do you see the results?

Everyone has their own story to tell, but not all stories are honest. What can we ask of a president aligned with communism like Joe Biden? General social misery, and we all know it. People as intelligent as Winston Churchill said: "Socialism is the philosophy of failure, the creed of ignorance, and the gospel of envy; its inherent virtue is the equal sharing of misery." Can we compare W. Churchill with Democratic politicians, Angela Davis, or any member of the former Black Panthers trying to live communism under capitalism?

That happened in Cuba, word for word, and today we're wandering the world, begging for mercy to be saved from hell. No people emigrates if its leaders are good. When people emigrate, it's because their leaders are thieves—synonymous with governmental misery affecting humanity. Those who emigrate by choice are those who hope to give and receive the best in the country they choose. There are no bad countries; it's the leaders who are useless.

We did not suffer Anti-Communist Hysteria in Cuba; we suffered Immoral and Cruel Communist Hysteria, and millions of immigrants who had to flee to democratic capitalist countries can attest to that, as can the oppressed and mistreated people on the island. This is not an invented story, as many intellectuals try to make it seem, or felt that hysteria had no basis in the U.S. These are truths lived day by day, in the worst possible way. What we all need is courage to expose them with the truth.

The American people refuse to enter the henhouse, and I'm among them. We will not be Stalin's plucked chickens—Stalin, the corrupt communist political leader like all others. We will be what we've always been, through good times and bad: democratic citizens of the most beautiful and envied country in the world—the United States of America.

Another of the communist groups (they call themselves socialist, but remember, they are the same)—Anti-Communist Hysteria will not end as long as these communist, neoliberal, radical leftist organizations exist, led by members who want to change the course of others, and if allowed, they will succeed. There are more ignorant people influenced on the streets than those seeking true information. That's what they all thrive on. That's how brainwashing works. Among the groups are those who follow the masses without analyzing opposing situations.

Greta is an example of idealized environmental activism. She was created for that, and they succeeded in our society. It's not her fault. The fault lies with those who brainwashed her, and she lacked the strength to seek information in National Geographic, scientific writings, etc., on the subject she defends. At that time, she was a child, and they brainwashed her because that's where the communists operate.

PETA is another invented example, claiming that animals should not be touched. And many of its members go to church, yet they don't know that Jehovah clothed Eve and Adam in skins, and that in Genesis 1, God told humans to have "dominion over the animals and to fill the earth and subdue it."

They criticize women who wear leather shoes or accessories, they criticize hunters, and their concepts are not shared by others. We are full of "wise people" in these groups that form without any research and feel more powerful than God's word in defending animals. Imagine if no one hunted snakes—we would be without antidotes and left at the mercy of their bites and deaths. When these animals and other wild creatures are hunted, it is allowed by countries that accept such practices according to their needs. Killing animals for hunting is ultimately not satisfying.

It's beautiful to wear a mink coat and not be envious of those who can. We should not allow animal abuse, and we should help create shelters for them instead of leaving them on the streets. Hunting, God approves of; PETA does not. What they defend are the donations to their institutions, which are good for helping sick animals or their care, not letting them die without assistance. That's commendable, but criticizing those who wear leather accessories is envy. Every human being has different points of view, but letting ourselves be influenced by PETA would be the last thing in our lives.

I'm tired of hearing, "They discriminate against us, the police are killers, they don't tolerate us, they persecute us, they hate us, they don't help us, we are marginalized, the government is fascist, the government belongs to the Republican elite, Donald Trump is to blame for the wall on the southern border, he's to blame for the wave of millions of illegals that Biden has already given health insurance and money to while ignoring the Mexicans." Please, reconsider.

We're tired of hearing so many complaints disguised as lies, covering up bad Democratic behavior. Biden lies when he says Donald Trump is anti-immigrant; he said so recently when the Mexicans danced for him, and the journalist didn't ask him what was going on with his people.

Biden repeated that Trump is anti-immigrant to promote his party, and they've been using the same obsolete tactic for years. We see the news filled with hatred, sickening society, and it's time for a rebirth. I wanted to bring all these topics covered in this book into collision so that you can compare what we've been living through passively. Communism, radical leftism, socialism, or liberalism, along with terrorism—misguided in these times—are wreaking havoc on our society, all because of ignorance or listening to ignorant professors in the country's universities and colleges about what they proclaim. They may know much in books, but they lack practical experience in these matters.

By listening to ignorant groups on the topics they defend, the confusion is extreme. Listening to upset relatives, friends, and neighbors because they don't share the same political or religious ideas, but without a history book in hand to verify it—not the Bible, nor the Constitution—and so we go, each saying whatever comes to mind without consulting the facts. Proverbs 18:13: "To answer before listening—that is folly and shame."

Both Black supremacists and White supremacists have a common denominator in their actions, and that is Communism or their socialist philosophies, which are the same. The same goes for violent Hispanic groups. They should think twice before getting involved in these ideologies, which only sow hatred and division.

THE DSA ORGANIZATION

Who are the DSA? According to their own deceptions, they maintain the most significant socialist presence in U.S. politics since the early 1900s and 1920s. For them, it's a responsibility to keep talented organizers infiltrating American society. They assume they can succeed (but we won't let them easily).

In the late 1990s, the DSA focused much of its attention on closely collaborating with the Congressional Progressive Caucus and local global justice groups to oppose the Multilateral Agreement on Investment (MAI). This proposed international treaty, which would have stripped national governments of the right to legislate democratic controls over foreign investment capital, was a precursor to the Trans-Pacific Partnership Agreement proposed by President Obama. By 1999, it seemed that a new global left was emerging, with progressive and socialist unions joining younger, anarchist-oriented protesters to confront the International Monetary Fund and the World Trade Organization.

Remember when they said, "Obama wants to destroy the country"? And the people defended him? He was doing it, but he couldn't fully succeed.

"The Progressive Promise: Justice for All"—these are the lies we can no longer stand. This Caucus is more communist than progressive. So many affiliates earning salaries without working—that's what happens in these organizations, or whatever they call themselves. The Congressional Progressive Caucus (CPC) is made up of over 100 members of Congress who defend progressive ideals in Washington and across the country.

The key question is: Does Congress spend its time sitting in their chairs or actually working? One of their defenses is this: "Eliminating corruptive policies." Yet they were all corrupt for not intervening in Congress to count the electoral votes that Donald Trump's supporters demanded for justice and democracy. Who do they think they're fooling? Since 1991, the CPC has advocated for progressive policies that prioritize American workers over corporate interests, fight economic and social inequality, and promote civil liberties. Sorry, but it's time to dissolve that group that's been saying the same thing for years, with little progress, because the U.S. does not want communism. All those ideas are the same ones used in communist countries. The same literature.

Have you read their manuals? Most of the time, anything that's free doesn't work. Visit them, read their grand communist ideas, because progress comes from working, not from giving away free programs, and then they'll say they're not part of our government.

The four fundamental principles of the Progressive Promise:

1. **Fight for economic justice and security for all;** Donald Trump has lost his security by having his immunity stripped away. (It was like that for a long time.) For him, there is no justice in the U.S. Why do they lie?

2. **Protect and preserve our rights and civil liberties;** have they violated the civil rights of your former president while you sat by?

3. **Promote global peace and security;** what peace? It was stolen from us the day Congress, the House of Representatives, the Senate, and the Electoral College failed to fulfill their duty to their country by counting the votes and electoral fraud. Do they want to do that globally? Work! And stop lying because we no longer believe you.

4. **Advance environmental protection and energy independence;** (living as parasites, fundraising while doing nothing useful for society). This is the famous Caucus referred to in this writing. We're in a terrible state, no matter how you look at it.

DSA grew and gained popularity (just like those who get paid for ads, possibly influenced by Soros), with the press helping them with comments promoting "socialism" (which is communism). And of course, without hesitation, they joined that propaganda, stirring up the public (for some, a vague desire for a more egalitarian society, similar to Sanders' examples about Denmark). Communists daydream but incite young people in universities, parks, etc., trying to recruit them into their frustrated dreams and laziness, living off donations from their organizations.

Curious followers of Sanders who searched the internet for "democratic socialism" found that DSA appeared first (democratic socialism is communism under that name). DSA hoped that a Hillary Clinton victory would allow them to help lead an anti-neoliberal Democratic opposition that would push for Medicare for all, progressive taxes, stricter financial sector regulations, etc. (When you hear these words, "stricter financial sector regulation," say a prayer, *Our Father,* so that it doesn't happen. Communism, among many measures, first takes control of the country's currency, investments, purchases, businesses of all kinds, etc. They destroy the financial power of the countries they operate in. Cuba is the typical example.)

Cuba, Venezuela, and Nicaragua are examples, but Cuba is currently the most extreme case. They don't impose strict regulations on capital—they seize it, buying luxury yachts, staying in 5-star hotels, eating the finest seafood, drinking quality wines, wearing expensive clothes and perfumes, traveling to different countries, while the people are starving and can't even travel from one province to another, as happened before they had to reverse it. Is that what students in our universities and colleges want?

Thank goodness that despite the country's ups and downs, the financial power of the U.S. remains strong. But with Biden in power, or any Democrat, it's severely at risk because Democrats from within are allied with communist tendencies, printing money like postcards. This is not hysteria or personal opinions. This is what we are all living through, and they do it to steal more easily, leaving the people like Stalin's plucked chicken.

"Ironically, Trump's victory led thousands to join the DSA." That's what members of this organization said. Those who joined the DSA were the ignorant, who ardently wanted Hillary to win, but didn't even know what Hillary was offering in her political platform.

They only saw that a woman (the feminists) would be president. These are the ones who don't know communism, and for those reasons, they vote without knowing who or what for, and the saddest part is that they don't read the political platforms of the people they want to elect. They vote based on emotions, not logic.

Communist idealists feed off lies to gain followers, who then become addicts. DSA says that through a strong chapter mentoring program, their national leadership, volunteers, and staff helped people in 48 states and D.C. form countless DSA chapters and many new YDS chapters as well. What does YDS have to do with these promoters of socialism, which is communism? We don't see the logic of communists joining theologians or religious people. They are completely opposite doctrines, so what are these YDS youths doing with the communist scum when they have religious backgrounds? What do their professors say? Are they religious, or are they disguised communists?

The YDS Mission

What their website says:

The mission of Yale Divinity School (YDS) is to foster the knowledge and love of God, to prepare students for lives of transformative service, to promote broad inclusion and diversity in our community life, to encounter the sacred through music and the arts, and to advance the sustainability of the earth. People of different religions and even those who are not religious can belong. Yale Divinity School is a professional school within Yale University, preparing leaders to address the major issues facing the global community.

YDS prepares students with a variety of practical ministries through rigorous academic research, including spiritual formation. The school seeks to help students understand the theological dimensions of their vocations. If the DSA claims that YDS joined them, it should be investigated to see if it's true or not.

If it's true that YDS is joining the communists, the Yale professors will have to recruit them all again and show them the differences between one philosophy and another. We've never seen young people with religious, theological, or spiritual training support communism or its destructive ideologies, which are opposed to everything mentioned above. "Yale is uniquely positioned to prepare leaders to address the major problems facing the global community."

They should start practicing what they've learned because the major problems facing communities globally are precisely those communist, radical socialist, democratic socialist theories, which are all the same in reality, disguised according to the circumstances and with different names, and they all converge in Communism.

Theology means: theology that deals with God, His attributes, and perfections in the light of revealed principles. The Bible is similar to the dictionary. The **RAE** (Real Academia Española) has two meanings for the word "communism." The first: "Doctrine that establishes a social organization in which goods are collectively owned." The second: "Political movement and systems, developed since the 19th century, based on class struggle and the suppression of private ownership of the means of production."

This is what happened in Cuba when they began to seize (suppress) all companies, whether national or international, without compensating the owners (property thefts).And it's what happened in Venezuela and Nicaragua. Nothing should surprise us anymore—everything is upside down, with Democrats affiliating themselves with those communist philosophies, receiving money from all of them, trying to spread harm to the citizens from Washington D.C. What we must do is work hard and systematically to restore social order, benefiting all citizens everywhere, especially in the U.S.

The institutions tasked with investigating need to start deciphering why the Democrats want to destroy Donald Trump and, at the same time, democracy. It's something pathological. Trump is not above the law, but neither are they, and they've shown with their bad behavior that it's they who violate the law, and they don't work for the people but for hidden interests that we still can't decipher.

The task is great, but not impossible. In all these communist philosophies, totalitarianism is the backbone of the doctrine. DSA says: In many red states, new DSA chapters have led the opposition to the Trump administration's attempts to gut Medicaid. (You can see how they join together to want to destroy Trump.) All with communist philosophies and the Democrats undercover. That is a blatant lie. Until now, that is the policy that Nancy Pelosi and the others have long launched and they emphasize it in their emails that you will read later, winning voters to their coop, and the intelligent people of DSA follow them.

It is a conspiracy against Donald Trump, of the communist-democratic agenda that we all see, except the government departments that are there to investigate correctly and under the Constitution that says that we are equal regarding the law, but we do not see results or sanctions for the aggressors. DSA organized an openly socialist presence in March 2017 at the House and local town hall meetings, as well as sitting in local Senate offices during the July 4 recess. In blue states like New York, New Jersey, New Mexico, and California, DSA members are at the forefront of the fight for state Medicare for All legislation. What this organization should be investigating is why is there so much Medicare fraud from all sides of the country? For three days in the hospital $36,000 charged to Medicare. (As an example). They charge what is, and what is not, to Medicare in all states and that creates the national swamp, not just in Washington D.C.

Only idealists like them will believe them, all of this supported by communist Democrats or closely allied with them. Are there communist infiltrations in the high command? Of course there are. Don't believe their theories, they seduce with their lies, like enchanted snakes in children's stories. Look at what happens in Cuba and you will know the truth of the destruction caused by a communist government.

Americans under different organizations take student delegations to Cuba, flouting the laws of the opposition, but neither here nor there do they tell them the truth.

Nobody has work, you have to steal to live, you have to beg from countries to obtain medicines, they steal the capital of the workers, the people on foot or on bicycles and they in the best cars, and luxury yachts, they fish and Cubans cannot do it living on an Island. If they are not fishermen, they cannot fish to bring food to their homes. They light themselves and the people do not have electricity for up to 24 hours, if they have had a fine for some reason, they do not sell them the pittance of what they stipulate through the ration book (basic basket that the UN praised for how balanced it was) leaving them without food. What the famous members of the UN (who do not investigate) did not know is that no one could eat from that basic basket for a whole month, and they praised them for being intelligent.

The water service was disconnected and they had to go long distances to fill their buckets with water. All of them were accomplices of the shameless.

They are murderers and morbid, because they enjoy the damage caused to the people. What the Stalin metaphor says is not a lie. They destroy the country's capital, they destroy buildings, they go hungry, they prostitute themselves for a bath soap. The Cuban communists say that capitalism suffocates them, and that they have a blockade from the USA and what they have is a life annuity of millions given to Cuba from the USA annually for whatever reason.

Lies are their favorite bases and repeating them constantly is their objective, so that the people are indoctrinated and the most unusual thing is that it happens. This is what happens with the crumbs of the Democrats. Trump is bad, Trump is bad and for the Democratic voters, he is bad and they don't know why. That's how communism works.

The Castros, Putins and all those who proclaim that wealth should belong to the people are the new millionaires. It is the unattainable dream of the communists in the United States, that we all lose our freedoms, and they take control. Investigate before joining these organizations. The American veterans, and those who have given their lives, their families, will defend them, along with the rest of the population, and they will not leave even an inch of territory to the communists along with all of us.

Let all those organizations that infest the university classrooms know about it even though the country has recognized them as the communist party and we will achieve it like Lech Walesa in Poland, without firing a shot. Let them continue living off their great dreams of turning us all into miserable people, which they will not achieve.

This situation is not a problem of Republicans or Democrats or other political parties, this problem is of every American who does not act accordingly with what is happening to us.

Communists don't work, that's why the economy of the countries where they operate is destroyed, everything is wasted in propaganda and embezzlement, theft and suppression of civil liberties of the population. Money given for emergency budgets, or to feed the people, disappears. Winston Churchill was not illiterate, he was one of the most efficient and prominent men in England, and he knew what he said about communism. "The vice inherent in capitalism is the unequal distribution of goods. The virtue inherent in socialism is the equitable distribution of misery. That making profits is reprehensible is a socialist concept. I consider that what is truly reprehensible is making losses." With communism, which the literati call Anti-Communist Hysteria, we all lose, Republicans, Democrats and of course, the community in general.

There is no wealth in the group, they individualize it for their leaders and you will not even have jobs. They do not create any kind of wealth, they steal the wealth of others. Youth should be wary of communists and their frustrated philosophies in universities and colleges, more than any other biological virus.

Alexandria Ocasio-Cortez, Cori Bush, and Rashida Harbi Tlaib belong to this communist organization and belong to our government as Representatives. Can you imagine the ideological damage from within the government? Are they in our government or not? OcasioCortez wants to eliminate the Supreme Court and what she should advocate is to denounce her own wrongdoings. Both Ocasio-Cortez and Ms. Sonia Soto Mayor should leave their positions out of dignity. Both are totally inefficient.

The Supreme Court must take action regarding a member who expresses himself in the way that Ms. Soto Mayor did. Hatred towards former President Donald Trump, for legal misinterpretation and for not having read the Constitution is unacceptable. We have them within the American government, and historians when years go by will say that it was our "Political Hysteria against Democrats or Anti-Communists."

And that everything was invented. Remember, there is no socialism, that name is a camouflage, its real name is Communism. Everything is Communism with its destructive and hypocritical ideologies, because everyone ends up being bourgeois. They devalue the currency, turning those who have capital into those who do not.

The misery of which Churchill spoke. Just like the Democrats in this era, manipulating information, as they manipulated and edited the report of the Prosecutor who sanctioned Biden with velvet, calling him "forgetful old man."

Our universities are mined with ignorance spread by Students and Professors who practice these philosophies. Those who do not practice these philosophies graduate from their subjects and use them for the benefit of all. These are not my subjective opinions, they are objective denunciations. Throughout the fields of schools from High School to Universities of different subjects, students have emerged who discredit the universities where they graduated. Harvard has produced good professionals, but I think they come out more contaminated with dishonesty, bad practices and the communist virus than clean in some academic branches.

Joseph M. Schwartz has always been active in DSA since he served as the first DSOC campus organizer between 1979 and 1981. He teaches radical political theory at Temple University, has been an active member of its teachers' union (AFT) and is part of the DSA National Political Committee. Can you imagine, a unionist active in the theories they call Political Science but affiliated with communist groups wanting to recruit followers to the cause among teachers and students? (Who possibly graduated from Harvard too).

Most likely, many were contaminated and are in charge of brainwashing students who do not think (they follow multitudes without analyzing them). They follow their teachers thinking that they know everything, and they are not wrong, if they know everything that is in the books of the social democrats, radicals, progressives, communists, etc., from a placid and capitalist world.

Not living the hell of all those theories in political science that they know in their own field full of goodness as is this land. That an intelligent person like this gentleman leads or led a group that thinks this way is incredible in the USA because in Cuba it was with Fidel A. Castro Ruz and the country was destroyed. DSA understands that an equitable and sustainable future for people and the planet is possible only if workers obtain control of the wealth that we create together. Who told DSA that communists work? That is not true, they do not work together, they do not create, they live on dreams and they destroy everything. There is no prosperous communist country. Capitalism is what generates capital for the people. In the countries where capitalism is the one that generates capital for the people, it is not possible to achieve the same goals.

However, Congress, by a two-thirds vote in each House, will be able to remedy this incapacity. Why do I repeat this? Because the vast majority knows that the Constitution exists but they have not seen it.

Aid to Hamas under the UN organization in Gaza is aid to terrorists, which is quite clear in the fourteenth amendment, which Joe Biden has violated, but since Biden's intentions were humanitarian aid, this amendment cannot be applied to him, but Donald Trump does want to apply it to him for an insurrection that he never took part in, even though he has shouted as much as he wanted. Has Congress met by a two-thirds vote in each House to remedy this violation by Joe Biden or to remove him from power for being a traitor to the country, or to dismantle the Witch Hunt? We are fed up with so many poorly planned lies by the Democrats, or Social Democrats, who are ultimately as communist as the rest, the only thing that is hidden and that is what is socially bad for the USA. The deception of the citizens!

On their Facebook page they say that Biden is revitalizing the country. Is he revitalizing it or destroying it? Allowing more than 9 million immigrants to violate our immigration laws does not revitalize. He is destroying our country and putting us in danger as well with many spies entering our land. No more lies, please!

The debate on 6/27/2024 was prepared by the communists and democrats as a calculation of how things would be before the day of the votes arrives in November. Their ends are known only to them but their actions show that they are the power. There are many speculations, but where communism is allied with the democrats, anything can happen, but if the democratic voting people, pay them back for having deceived them for so many decades, the situations will change drastically, and the swamp could be cleaned sooner than we imagine. That would be taking a step forward in defending the country. Behind the removal of Joe Biden from the presidency, engineered by the Democrats, there is no similarity to the way they wanted to remove Trump with all the failed trials and all the Amendments mentioned. When the Democrats together with the communists want to keep power, it will not belong to them either, it is for the Woke wanting to get rid of the Democrats and the Republicans, even if you do not want to understand it. The same corruptions of all their accomplices continue. The Democratic Party should completely separate itself until it regains common sense, and along with them, its voters, do not let themselves be fooled. Do not love the political party that corrupted you, love the Country as your former president John Kennedy wanted.

JOE BIDEN AND THE COMMUNIST PLANS.

Talking about the President of the United States, Joe Biden, is having to endure constant mockery from others in videos on YouTube, which, by the way, there are some very instructive ones and others that are terrible and lying. An illness is not something to be mocked, but neither is it something to lead the World Power, which is our country. If he does not voluntarily retire, he should be impeached for being a traitor to the country by providing aid to Hamas through the Palestinians, either directly or indirectly. For having had the Classified Documents scattered everywhere and for not remembering where he had put them. For endangering the Nation with the number of spies that have entered. For violating immigration laws. A patient with cognitive problems should not be at the head of the presidency. Do the Democrats not have a brain? It seems that they all suffer from the same illness of hiding their shamelessness from the people. In short, the puppet was Biden and the puppeteer is Soros Together with the Woke. Democratic voters wake up!

The plans of Biden and his accomplices to win the 2024 presidential elections could be identical to those of Nicolás Maduro in Venezuela, who by means of a presidential decree nationalized a total of 8,331 illegal immigrants. (There were more but they lie when it is not convenient for them to give numbers).

Ronald Reagan, a Republican, gave the planned amnesty in 1986. Two million undocumented or illegal immigrants (because they violated the borders), unauthorized in that Reagan era became a major problem. Currently, there are about 11.1 million undocumented or so-called illegal immigrants living in the country. Many of them who met the requirements took advantage of that law.

Possibly there are more, without counting the millions of illegal entries that Biden allowed for a quota of about 21 million possible votes. If he does what Maduro instructed him.

This always causes discussions in the Senate. The Senate has an extraordinarily high authority, sometimes higher than that of the President or the House of Representatives. The Senate can judge impeachment cases, which can remove a president for misconduct. (We have already experienced those false impeachments of Trump and we say false, because they could not prove anything and he was found innocent although other presidents suffered the consequences). But that is the point, to work and negotiate what is best for the country, not to create persecutions among themselves. That is undemocratic, but it has been happening since 2016 until now 2024. Why did Republican senators, congressmen and representatives not demand that the votes be counted in 2020? Did they believe the Democrats? What is missing is Biden's violations in the desperate attempt to steal the electoral votes again with his long-awaited amnesty as requested by the President of Venezuela. There is very little left to see before the 2024 presidential election

All legislative power of the government resides in Congress, which means that it is the only part of the government that can write new laws or change existing ones. (It seems that they have taken a fouryear vacation, or are sleeping off the intoxication of inefficiencies), so as not to have to deal with the Witch Hunt of Donald Trump and much less tell the truth to the people.

That is not new, nor is it that they use groups for their political purposes with false promises, such as Hispanics, blacks, and now homosexuals too. The people know the truth.

Nicolás Maduro, President of Venezuela, to win electoral votes, made his political maneuver. (Remember the vote thefts in 2013 when Capriles). Maduro said: "I am approving the naturalization of 8,331 migrants from various countries of the world, "and I challenge the United States government to do the same and SIGN A DECREE to legalize all Latin American and Caribbean migrants, who reside in their country." What Maduro does not know is that the political system of the USA is not the same as their declared communist systems, but we already have doubts that this can happen, and since they are all corrupt we do not have a justice department to protest.

Living in the shadows is not easy for any group. These leaders like Nicolás Maduro do not nationalize illegal citizens for being good presidents, because they destroy the countries where they govern. They legalize them, to obtain presidential votes and stay in power.

Here in the US they want to perpetuate the Democratic Party and abolish the Republican Party, which is what we are all experiencing, but what the brainless Democratic politicians do not imagine is that they are in the crosshairs to be eliminated as well. So that there are no strong political parties that interrupt their plans, because the rest will be handled perfectly by them. When any party that interferes in Democratic corruption, or any institution of the government order, does not neutralize them by applying the laws, we are facing government corruption. We are already seeing it, no matter the bipartisanship.

These words below were said by Biden from the White House. Analyze them. "Biden also plans new legal avenues to regularize millions of undocumented people in his country and improve the process for those who request asylum," according to a report of the call with his Mexican counterpart, López Obrador, published by the White House.

The ace up his sleeve to win the presidential elections without being accused of electoral theft??? Legalize illegals so they can vote? Will it legalize Mexicans who already deserve it for having been forgotten for so many decades?

A few months before the presidential elections, the conference scheduled for 7/11/24. The conference scheduled so that Biden could be seen in perfect mental condition was ridiculous. It is the Democrats' way of hiding the facts. Those who edited a prosecutor's report because what was written did not suit them, editing any document in their government hiding facts is corruption.

In the next presidential elections, if you want to follow them and give them the votes, that is consciously. Everyone will contribute their part whether you like it or not. But the invitation for us not to hate each other as is happening, remains standing. The invitation to save our laws remains standing, The invitation to vote for Donald Trump, remains standing. You decide what part of history you want to be in!

Talking about the economy is not as easy as it is said: If his economists inform Biden that everything is fine, who can argue with him? It is as if they told us that everything is fine in the Justice system, when we know that it is not true, because of the rottenness in the Department of Justice. Everyone knows that, including the Democrats.

Talking about the Supreme Court as Biden said, there would be a lot to say, because restricting weapons to people who use domestic violence is a violation of the Constitution in the Second Amendment. Because two-thirds of the chambers have not met to make a change to the law. When violent people can even use their own hands to kill.

The children who die from gun assaults, it is not a question of restricting the weapons that citizens must carry, but rather opening hospitals for the mentally ill. Making changes to the Constitution so that the mentally ill should not buy weapons or use them. However, under the Biden-Kamala administration, the 8 justices of the Court, Congress and compliance with the laws based on the Constitution were forgotten.

Close to the presidential elections, the issue of illegal immigration of 9 million potential voters was not touched upon, as Biden gave them all the documents and aid. The Democrats do not work for the people. Only two questions that any journalist would have given us about the elections with the millions of illegals that he has benefited and could be potential voters for the Democrats, since that is the suspicion. That appearance was programmed terribly badly. Nor was it considered what the Russian ships and submarines were doing in Cuba. We were not born with political parties on our backs, we chose them as adults that we are, and it is an adult to analyze the current situations. What an inefficient Democratic government we have!

Do they need them now? Like the nine or ten million who entered illegally? In gratitude, will the voting relatives give the votes to the Democrats, or will they themselves?

They will have to hurry, because the days pass quickly and we assume that they do not continue to lose their minds. We already have the presidential elections of 2024 at the door. For the persecution of one man, they destroy a people. This is how communism and hatred towards capitalism work, and it seems that the Democrats do not analyze it. Do they have advisors? Well, they are asleep! When you vote for the Democrats, analyze whether you do it for them or for the communists, who will replace all of you and the entire nation. Communism in power!

The Democrats have worked to enrich themselves and for their personal interests, as have many Republicans until now, not for the people even if many do not accept it. Of two bad problems, we must follow the one that has the least, and that is the Republicans. More conservative and moral so as not to violate the laws.

Giving the Democrats the benefit of the doubt for the future is not advisable. They should analyze the moral damage that Nancy Pelosi and the entire clique have done to the people. (Many voters have Stockholm syndrome) and they will continue to cling to their ideas without analyzing reality because many think they should agree with the Republicans. This is not a competition or a power war between us, this is defending democracy together. We have already experienced a whole plot of Judges, Prosecutors, President, Department of Justice involved in the fecal mess along with the attempted assassination of our future president Donald J. Trump.

Mr. Merrick Garland graduated from Harvard. (Another studied at Harvard), we must clean up that university. If my grandmother were alive, who was a spiritualist, she would go with a basin full of water and basil, blessing the entire University so that the graduates there begin to work properly and be decent people in society. Or something like a Catholic exorcism.

The Attorney General, accused of contempt for not wanting to hand over information about Biden. Ana Paulina Luna, a Republican congresswoman, is doing to Merrick Garlad what a stone in the shoe bothers. All my respect for a congresswoman who wants justice to be done and for political corruption not to drown us, but many Republicans are not getting up from their chairs. That hurts us.

The laws are there to be enforced, but the Department of Justice feels above the law, and has the audacity to accuse Donald Trump without being covered in the manure of all of them, for what they are doing. "Being above the law." What does the press say? What does the Democratic people say about it? Is Donald Trump the one who is above the law, or is it the Democrats in weight?

CNN is either vindicating itself or it has received large sums from the Democrats who feed them the information they want, in order to justify getting Biden out of the way and making it easier for their plans not to be thwarted before November 5, 2024.

Many have become sick with the virus of power. Perhaps one day we will see that hammer in the History Museum with a sign that says: "The hammer in the hands of the Democrats when they wanted to destroy the Democracy of the USA" or something similar. We are in time to stop them if we use logic and not emotions. They say that they give public assistance in Venezuela to naturalized people, but Venezuelans are already living the ordeal of Cuba, emigrating to the USA and other countries. If Democratic voters analyze the situations, they will see that it is not that they have to change political parties, but rather wait for them to recover and for new Democratic faces to come who want to work for the people. We invite them to recover the lost values because this country belongs to everyone. As long as they keep doing the same, they will have the same. If Abraham Lincoln changed parties, Ronald Reagan, etc., why not the people? Although they can wait until 2028.

Remember that who they are defending is the country and not Donald Trump. He demonstrated that he worked excellently for all of us, for free, clearing the disrepute of how the international community was analyzing us. The pride of being American, of returning to moderate, peaceful patriotism, but firm in values, must be in the veins of those born and naturalized, who do not ask to be so, to obtain benefits, neither we nor our relatives, but to give the best of each of its citizens as a rescue team.

They do not defend the presidential candidates who will be passing through the White House, and even if they do not like them, they must make the electoral sacrifice. Citizen necessity, to leave a better future for current and future generations and that they are never persecuted as our former president Donald J. Trump has been. This is inhumane and immoral and it can happen to any of us.

It is absolutely clear that the Biden administration has divided the country, divided future electoral votes, violated all existing laws, and fostered racism for its political ends. Who is protecting it? All of our Departments that are trying to put the country in order through the laws? If they fail, they will be the masterminds of what is coming, due to the failure to comply with the laws that are there to create military and civil order. The injustices are obvious. You don't have to be a lawyer, prosecutor, or judge to know that there is a dirty, degrading, and unconstitutional persecution that is bringing the country's morale to the ground.

THE SITUATION IS TOTALLY SERIOUS. Biden has violated all current laws and his executive laws must be read to evaluate his mental health and that of the Secretary of the Interior, who seems to suffer from the same illness as Biden.

Never in my life have I written penises and vaginas so many times to be able to elucidate a writing. Dementia is in Biden's entire cabinet or ignorance along with Woke helping to pull the strings.

Executive Order 14121. Especially the one he dedicated to women and girls entitled: RECOGNIZING AND HONORING THE HISTORY OF WOMEN. All to carry out his political maneuvers behind the backs of his people. Most importantly, Biden does the same thing as the communists when they want to achieve their goals. Modify, change, or violate the laws that subject him, and as a good irresponsible Democrat, he takes refuge in that governmental rot. He updated the law to be able to bring in the millions of undocumented immigrants and if this was not planned, may God come and see it. On December 23, 2022: The Biden Administration's regulation is already in effect. The regulation confirms that public benefits for food, health and housing are not included in the rule that said they could be receiving public aid. (The plot to steal votes was hatched just as communists work). Hopefully these are just bad thoughts from us the people.

It means that immigrants will have free services, without being public burdens, free health, food and housing, and we citizens have to pay for Medical Insurance, and pay for our housing, meals and much more. Biden has entertained himself by making totally unacceptable executive laws, because they are not directed at his people, but at foreigners; and the press does not criticize him, nor do his advisors correct him, telling him that the people do not accept such ignorance.

As advisors to the President, they must work for the people too, but the swamp is very deep. Reading on the internet, I came across Biden's executive law and I present to you some of the paragraphs of it. Biden, in his eagerness to defend homosexuality within his cabinet, what he does is ridicule them, making them look abnormal and uneducated, and discriminating against prostitution. I differ a lot when the presidents in office erase what the previous one did because there are always possibilities of maintaining the legacy by making corrections, but in this case of Biden, I ask our President that on the first day of being in the White House he stops all executive laws and that they be changed for others.

Executive Order 14121 of March 27, 2024. RECOGNIZING AND HONORING THE HISTORY OF WOMEN. In the course of composing this executive order, they included girls later, but not in the title of the law. I decided to read it because I like inspirational stories of prominent figures in any subject because they teach us to analyze different topics from other perspectives.

Everything was fine until I got to these lines that I present to you and you can go to the White House archives and check it out.

Executive Order 14121 (some paragraphs) "Yet women's history is severely underrepresented in our National Park System, creating an important opportunity to strengthen our nation's recognition of women's role in shaping this country. This order directs actions that will strengthen the Federal Government's ability to recognize women's history and the accomplishments of women and girls of all backgrounds. It builds on the steps I have taken to promote equity and equality across the Federal Government and help tell a more complete story of our Nation's history, "The Secretary of the Interior will review previously completed topical studies and publish a report to help ensure representation of women's history at sites of national significance. This review of completed topical studies.

Should include, but is not limited to, sites of national significance focused on or linked to the stories of Latino Americans; Asian Americans and Pacific Islanders; African Americans; people of Native American descent; and Americans. (They Always Separate Us).

Lesbian, gay, bisexual, transgender, queer, and intersex; as well as American civil rights and labor history. Did the president forget that prostitutes should be in that executive law? That he has discriminated against them and left them out of social studies. Mr. Anthony Blinken must immediately correct those mistakes of the president but he must have cognitive problems too.

To put it simply, (everyone should go to the dictionary if they want). Of course, Biden is all tangled up and so are his secretaries, (I don't know if they are working with the 13% of apathetic to work) (Work inefficiency for not being rude and calling them lazy). As we know, the Dictionary is lost from our society, but the "Mata Burro" still exists, and is waiting for someone to take care of it and feed it.

It is necessary to clarify that throughout the glossary the term Gay is used to refer to homosexual man, since this type of terminology also includes a large number of words related to lesbians, transsexuals, and drag queens.

In the United States, drag queens are people who use makeup and drag clothing to imitate and exaggerate the roles and meanings of the female gender for entertainment purposes. Drag queens are usually male, but not all drag queens are homosexual. Heterosexual men and women also perform drag, and some say that about 20% of male drag queens are heterosexual.

Lesbian. Said of a woman: homosexual. Also used as a noun Gay. Gay. Sexual or romantic attraction to people of the same gender and not to people of a different gender. They can be in that law because they are women (they have vaginas). Bisexual: romantically or sexually attracted to people of the same gender and people of a different gender. If bisexuals are women they can also be in that law, they have (vaginas). If bisexuals are men, they cannot be in the law because they have a penis, and as we all know, men have it, and the law is for "women and girls," and until they are mutilated by surgery, they are men, even if they think they are women, and they have a penis. Transgender, a man or a woman. These can be from woman to man, or from man to woman, but if a woman got a penis, it cannot be in the law because it is for "women and girls" while if the transgender is a man who has had surgery and does not have a penis, he can be in it because they made him a vagina.

If a queer is a woman and wants to be a man, he should not be in that executive order either, because he does not want to be a woman. The law says it very clearly: "For women and girls." If a man is "queer" and wants to be a woman, he should not be in the executive order either because he still has a penis and the order was made to "highlight the achievements of women and girls." The ignorance in the White House under the Democratic administration of Biden Kamala on these issues that they defend or impose on society is historic!

This is unbelievable. That a Harvard graduate in Social Studies does not clarify to President Joe Biden that he is totally wrong, disoriented, without even knowing what he wants, and that these errors must be rectified before the Executive Law is released to the public? The Secretary of Government must be removed from the staff for cognitive problems as well. I have never talked so much about the penis and the vagina without being a sexologist.

Although it would have been convenient for us for Biden to stay in power until November 5, for reasons of consideration, he should not command our country, and they should have removed him under the 25th Amendment and this shows how false Nancy Pelosi was, who knowing all this, did not accuse him to remove him, the Democrats are deceiving their own voters and themselves, wanting to remove Donald Trump not because of that amendment that would have been the right thing to do but because they have already made the plot together to eliminate Biden. Kamala will have to prove that she is intelligent as Donald Trump said. Everything they have done to former President 45 is happening to the Democrats. They want to apply the Fourteenth Amendment to Donald Trump and those responsible for what happened were our entire government, for not working and letting everything get out of control. They were definitely responsible for all the crimes committed on January 6 and for dignity they should not blame others and constitutionally suspend the Witch Hunt and apologize to Donald J. Trump. It seems that we are all in Kindergarten. We have to repeat what is obvious because they do not want to listen. Nancy Pelosi received help from Trump to stop that situation and refused the help. Nobody wanted to work, but they did collect the check for the month, so to speak. This executive law shows that he does not read what is put in front of him, that his advisors do not advise him properly either. I rightly say that Social Studies teachers do nothing for the country. Neither does our Democratic government.

The ignorance in Biden's Cabinet is obvious. What is Mr. Anthony Blinken, Secretary of the Interior and graduate in Social Studies from Harvard University, doing? Another from Harvard. Biden in his diversity, has discriminated against prostitutes who are women and should be on the list, as are lesbians, bisexuals, and men who have become women, due to surgeries and all together in that diversity, not ignored in the category of Social Studies. That is absolute diversity, not halfway. The others have been included because of the hypocrisy that corrupts society, and it is not correct before the Constitution, which does not specify which citizen is homosexual, or heterosexual, or prostitutes, or who are one or the other. We are American citizens!

Biden Kamala does not know the Constitution, and that is why they violate all the laws, but their advisors do not know them either. An insult to justice! These ignorant of the laws are the ones who have programmed the persecution of Donald Trump. That the democratic people hate the 45th former president, that is their own religious moral problem, but that they hate the Justice of their country, is inadmissible. They must wake up!

Why does society have to participate in the sexual entanglements that they, under their responsibilities, have created? If it is a political party of homosexuals, then those who think the same should join it. It is not obligatory to put them in all the laws to win electoral votes, that is ugly, immoral and ridiculous. Nobody is attacking them. With this, what they do is humiliate them by making them look like ignorant homosexuals, and they are not like that, they are homosexuals, with a brain that directs them by themselves, Biden has crossed the line of human understanding, with this executive law and his Secretary of the Interior with the degree of Social Studies saved. What cannot be accepted is that if the law is for women and girls, there are people with penises. Period.

Biden wants diversity, defending all groups, but he only gives homosexuals the privilege of supremacy over prostitutes, whom the hypocritical governors in many states persecute, but none of them speak of the consensual pornography "The Porn Industry" that generates billions of dollars and the mafia controls it. Biden does not plan to confess it.

The Teaching of Social Studies aims to offer students a general vision of the society where they live; its location and development in space; its origin and historical evolution; its role in the framework of Geography and World History. Good God! If communism doesn't kill us, ignorance will. What do Democratic voters say about this? Will they vote for Donald Trump or not even if they hate him? Will we all go down in history together by cleaning up current politics? We need it!

They have made a fool of themselves, based on hypocrisy and ignorance, without first analyzing the situations of all citizens in order to correctly identify them. I am sure that any homosexual man will say, with all his reason, "Biden should get me out of there because I don't want to be a woman." Under the 14th Amendment, all citizens have the same rights as such. As far as we know, AN EXECUTIVE ORDER HAS THE FORM OF A LAW. The protection of the laws is on an equal footing in the Constitution.

Have they equated prostitutes with lesbians and bisexuals in the executive order? Does President Biden discriminate against prostitutes or not as citizens? Has he restricted their privileges to be in that law? The Constitution has a voice and we citizens do not listen to it, but the tragic thing is that our politicians and rulers are deaf and act according to their ideas, and not according to the laws that govern us. The Department of Justice must put on its apron and start cleaning the house (USA) that is very dirty starting with all the staff that works in that institution and in the White House and Mr. Merrick Garland in the Department of Justice. What destruction in four years of Democratic government! I imagine all the members of those institutions, the Supreme Court, the Department of Justice, the Pentagon, the FBI, the CIA, the President, the Senate, the Congress and the House of Representatives, who have failed us so far WITH A PATRIOTIC APRON ON THEIR WAISTS AND CHESTS, dismantling the injustices, whether racial, religious, political, etc., the persecutions of the 45th President, who served the country for free and seeking the best for the country, without getting rich in Washington D.C., defending the prestige of the USA, totally outraged before the international community. Dismantling all the trials that have been unconstitutional, based on hatred and racism, cleaning up ignorance through a new education in school curricula, dusting off the poor Constitution that is dirty, contaminated with manure and feces, that they neither look at, interpret, understand, nor respect. Hopefully those of us who are already older will be able to see it, but the future is in the hands of our wonderful children and young people who will see it. Imagine, all the people with patriotic aprons cleaning up the American government. We will go down in history together. Both Democrats and Republicans and the other political parties are fed up with so much cheap politicking that we do not deserve.

When the house is clean, we will all sing together the National Anthem that many white and black athletes have despised, wanting to impose their absurd philosophies. Wanting to compose a National Anthem for them, (divisionisms) not by white men, but by racist black men. Hating their Flag. Those who do not respect the national symbols, and likewise, do not respect others, whether they are black or white or of any other ethnicity. Parents should tell their children that disrespect for their country, for races, for those who feel different in homosexuality, is not correct, since in many schools they do not even mention it because they are afraid to tell the truth and implicate them by accusing them of all the epithets in the dictionary.

Let us hope that hope, the faith placed in our institutions, remains alive like the Olympic torch, and that we can have an imaginary Olympic torch for 2024, recovering the country in a race towards justice, and after achieving it, that it rests extinguished, but satisfied of having inspired those who try to maintain order through our government entities, regardless of the political party to which we all belong.

"During the ancient Olympic Games, a flame burned permanently on the altar of the sanctuary of the goddess Hestia; additional fires were lit in the temples of Zeus and Hera." For the ancient Greeks, the flame represented the most positive qualities of men, who were to bring out the best in themselves in the different sporting events. It would be wonderful if this fire could merge with our politicians and institutions, which have already lost the essential, to impart justice with truth and not with lies, bringing out their positive qualities for the sake of their servants. We will achieve this with Donald J. Trump in the White House, paving the way for bipartisanship, while the Democratic Party wisely restructures itself for the next presidential elections in 2028 and many of my relatives who joined that party when they became naturalized can feel proud of their political decisions, not embarrassed and insecure with a dirty and destructive party that they had to punish with their votes in 2024 with pain and resignation, seeing the light at the end of the tunnel.

We must not erase ourselves from the Democratic Party, we must wait wisely for four more years and let all the ideas shine to honor the country that protects us with its laws, when these are applied appropriately and not by dirty interests of politicians. New faces are needed in that party because the toxic ones who have governed us until now no longer know what to do to please. It is good to remember them and forgive them. Nancy Pelosi, Chuck Schumer, Adam Schiff, The Clintons. The Obamas and the Bidens are all implicated in having made their fortunes in Washington DC. It is their time and they can have fun, but far away from the government. It is time for everyone to spend their time spending their millions and enjoying life.

The damage done by the Democrats as rulers has been extreme and to restructure that situation we all need each other. This is what we have all had in four years of civic misfortunes.

THE TAKE CARE ACT

Senators Mike Lee (R-UT) and Josh Hawley (R-MO) introduced the Take Care Act on June 5, 2019. A bill designed to promote accountability and effective administration by restoring the original understanding of the President's constitutional power to remove his subordinates. Written words from one of its sponsors. "For too long, massive federal agencies have been regulating our lives and our businesses, without any democratic accountability," said Senator Hawley. "The Take Care Act is an important step to rein in these bureaucrats by returning them to the control of the elected branches of our government."

Examine these words written in the TAKE CARE Act: "In short, the bill fully restores the original understanding of the President's power to ensure THAT THE LAWS ARE FAITHFULLY EXECUTED. All the laws? Or the ones in the Take Care Act? Here we see Biden's violations of his presidency. We wonder: Is Biden complying with these laws? It doesn't matter where they are written, whether in this Take Care Act or in the Constitution. Have the Democrats lost their minds out of hatred and breaking the laws in an extraordinary way? Where is the respect for their own Democratic voters?

Said very clearly by Biden, in his own words. He chose Kamala Harris because she was "a woman and black" (in the July 11/24 conference he said he had chosen her because she was a good prosecutor and because she was qualified to be the Vive-President. He chose her because she was black and a woman, ignoring whether she was stupid or intelligent. That's how racism began in the Biden Kamala government, something that some violent black groups criticize the federalists for even in these times, associating their flag with racism and discrimination. Look up, in Washington D.C., there is more racism than in our streets with the federalist flag.

Biden discriminated against white women. He chose "black woman." What good is the Civil Rights Act if they are violated by the president of the USA himself? What good are the Immigration laws if he allowed millions of illegals to enter the country violating the laws that he must respect by advocating for open borders and ignoring them all?

The same concepts perhaps when it comes to electoral fraud and the Democratic denial of counting the votes? What can we think now? That if they edit the documents to improve the president's image, anything could have happened and will happen again.

When there is a document of that magnitude, it is not edited, it is presented to the people as the Prosecutor declared. That is the responsibility of the prosecutor, to ratify his report, not to edit it. But if Trump does that, the reporters of the liberal communist newspapers run by the Puppet Master would still be perched like vultures on him.

When it is edited, it is because they did not like something and it would harm them and in the middle of the presidential election campaign, it was not convenient for us to know the results and this was: Manipulation of true information. Whoever does not want to see the truth should remain blind, but in the future, even the blind will be harmed by the Democrats of Washington D.C., and communism allied to terrorism.

If this is not the death of Democracy, what do the American people expect to happen?

If everything Biden and other presidents have done, whether they are Democrats or Republicans, had been done by Donald Trump, he would have accumulated another 91 futuristic unconstitutional lawsuits by the Democrats. Has any Democratic judge, black or white, in New York pursued Joe Biden? Have they brought him to trial for the laws he violated? Of course not! Have they investigated his coffers, enriched by money allegedly illicit from Ukraine and possibly from terrorists, because we already know that the COMMUNIST PARTY gives them funds in their presidential campaigns? Let them have the dignity to answer the people the many questions that we all ask ourselves using truth and justice, not inventing it or preparing the questions for him to answer correctly.

Now they are defamations against Biden, and the defamations against Donald Trump are Democratic laws violating the Constitution. Many doubts, tactlessness, and lack of ethics are happening daily in our country and if the Supreme Court, which is our hope, does not act quickly before the presidential elections, putting order and sanity, and that everything returns to how it was in the past, "Democratically" then we will have to accept that we are at the doors of the political demoralization of our times, in the USA as in the third nudist or communist countries. When interpreting the laws that serve to destroy or build, we Americans are stunned and naked before it. In short.

The black or white Democratic judges without tact, accuse him of having falsified and intervened in the votes, they accuse him of everything the least and they are missing to accuse him of smiling, (for not saying what we are really thinking).

Despite the avalanche of false and senseless accusations by the Democrats, we are not going to ask God, because he is very busy, we are going to pray for everything to be clarified and the prayers are already arriving. This is a Christian, non-communist country, but we are going to ask the people to think about the country. Even God will be grateful for the help when he says: "by their fruits or works you will know them." Why don't they investigate whether this wave of judges and prosecutors accusing Donald Trump are receiving monetary bribes or favors from the Democratic Party to those who encourage them to commit these legal atrocities? Hate breeds hate. We must not continue in this direction because we will destroy ourselves!

It reminds me of the Obama era when he blamed Bush for his inefficiencies, but it must be recognized that he did not persecute anyone (so that they would not persecute him), although now he supports the persecution of his counterpart like all the previous expresidents who do not have the courage to express their opinions on the matter, or so that they are not involved, but those who support injustice will always carry it on their conscience. During Obama's term there was not the current shamelessness of bringing illegal immigrants by the millions into the country, although he was not liked by many, including me, for having closed his private information perhaps because he belonged to the Black Panthers and it was not convenient for him to be associated with socialism or communism, for the presidential elections programmed by all of them etc., but I am not commanded by cowards, with my vote and I did not support him although I wanted him to leave to end once and for all the farces of the famous racial discrimination that many use for their personal ends.

We have to recognize that he also worked with caution and we cannot criticize him for that (self-defense). His plans were different and he is fulfilling his dream of becoming a millionaire and he knew how to do it from Washington D.C., making his stories for future generations outside of politics and he is either laundering money as many say for having forgiven so many drug dealers or with his speeches charging for his work which is good, although many would not pay to hear it again, or working on series or documentaries (I saw one about animals and I liked it and Obama was the narrator) but now we see why many of us had to leave Netflix, the disastrous movies. If they are not all forced homosexuals, they are drunks and smokers. Introducing a different social way of life is not obligatory to put it on all programs. The message is totally degrading for the audience that wants to be entertained and not upset. In the movies, women are rude, drinking and smoking (so much so that they criticized tobacco and cigarettes) and now they put the same cigarettes and marijuana in the movies and episodes. If this is their great legacy as a citizen, it is better that they never run for politics again. Let them continue in their real estate business that is doing well and their contracts, but I would advise them to look for better social options.

Democratic voters must be alert to who gives them their votes. Fantastic misery awaits us all under the Democratic administration, whether with Biden or another candidate, regardless of the political party we profess. Why does the population have to continue hatred and resentment? Why deny ourselves the most beautiful thing about human beings? Love!

Biblically we have it at our disposal and you will see that in this Democratic administration they have supported hatred and not precisely the overwhelming force that moves the world, which is the love of what you defend with honesty.

Agape love is unconditional. Do we love the country in this way? Phileo is fraternal love. Do friends from different political parties love each other fraternally? Eros is romantic love. Couples divided by politics? Storgé: family love. What happens in our families divided by politics and gender? All these classified loves are part of the human essence and we must recover them. These definitions of love have been violated by this destructive policy of our last four years, full of hatred and lies, which does not resemble the past policy where we could express ourselves without the existing bad feelings and unfortunately everything comes from Washington D.C. We are Americans, and those who are not yet, should think from now on that this country is their new homeland and give it their respect, gratitude and love.

Americans are their hardworking, supportive, respectful, and Christian people, many in the most rampant misery in recent years, the so-called golden years. Older people returning to work after retirement or moving to other third world countries, in order to survive on their income, and our money in irresponsible hands.

These are the politicians who govern us. Together with the great power of the special elites that they all mention and belong to. The political, moral, religious destabilization of our times arises, and it can be said that the Biden era marked American history from Washington D.C., as the most DESTRUCTIVE ADMINISTRATION IN ALL AMERICAN HISTORY.

As the administration that harmed the honor of judges and lawyers by applying or interpreting the laws dirty, undemocratically in the Witch Hunt of Donald Trump. To the point of accusing him based on our misinterpreted laws, forgetting that the Bill of Rights explicitly says so.

This had never happened in our country, and the Democratic friends who have disassociated themselves from the party are already saying it.

The hope of recovering our country is not only in the future president, it is in the interpretation of the laws that defend us and destroy us and in our electoral vote.

Let us hope that the SUPREME COURT will do its best to apply the laws for the good of all Americans and for the lost international prestige, although knowing the thoughts of Judge Sonia Soto Mayor, we consider that Democratic corruption has infiltrated the Supreme Court and that to clean up that image, they must remove her as a judge because she is capable of contaminating evidence.

Hawley said: "The Take Care Act is an important step to control these bureaucrats by returning them to control of the elected powers of our government." In the USA everything is nice when it is written in documents, which are then forgotten and no one takes them into account, not even President Biden himself.

In this famous era of the Witch Hunt of Donald Trump, Democratic political corruption has become a tsunami drowning the American people for their hatred and bad behavior. President Biden violates them as many times as he wants with his unbridled senile irresponsibility, supported by those who really govern our country, which is not exactly Joe Biden. He should have been tried for being a traitor to his country.

He distributes oil his way. President Joe Biden's government sold 180 million barrels of SPR oil in 2022, in an effort to control gasoline prices that had risen after Russia's large-scale invasion of Ukraine. So far, the agency has bought back only 35.6 million barrels of the 180 million barrels sold. Why doesn't he drill our soils and then we wouldn't depend on anyone? Trump wanted to do that and already on the way they wanted to eat him alive defending the environment, another very well-organized story without consulting scientists. Because they have no ideas for the future, it seems that the entire cabinet suffers from cognitive problems. Power is the worst drug in Washington D.C. No wonder they released marijuana in many states so they could all smoke it together and rule the plucked chickens that allow them to and don't raise their voices.

No one is above the established laws. They tell and do that to Donald Trump daily without seeing the reality of the Democrats violating the laws and feeling above them.

Biden Kamala, they are not accountable, they are not interested in the Take Care Act, nor the Constitution, nor the Civil Rights Act. How can Democratic voters fall in love with people like Biden or any other candidate with aspirations to the White House? They have all failed the people. Because of hatred for Donald Trump? So it is true that they are denatured with all my respect.

The country comes before Biden and Trump. The difference is that Trump knows how to work and he demonstrated it in his private life and in his public life. Biden has made his fortune in bad steps during his several decades in Washington D.C. Lobbying and his private life has been a disaster too. No one is exempt from a problem, but he is the public image, not us.

I firmly believe that what Martin Luther King said when Kennedy was assassinated, expressing: This country is crazy! I would say, Our country is not crazy! It is resentful and divided by the bad actions of its politicians and corrupt press! From what we can interpret, in our Constitution and in our Bibles and in any Act that is a law in the USA, it seems that everyone can interpret any issue in their own way, not in the written or original form of the texts. Hallelujah! For those who want to fix the political disaster of the swamp using their vote, but not as Univision wants, "vote with me" because it means "vote for the Democrats." If the political evils of these four years have come from the Democrats, it is enough time to remove them from political positions.

The Univision television channel did not campaign to ask for a parole even for its Mexican viewers, but it did poison them by speaking badly of Donald Trump and well of Hillary Clinton. The Special Interests of that television channel were and are evidently supporting the Democrats. Read the book ¡Viva Trump! by Martha Magaña, Mexican author, and they will see if Univision's interests are true or Hysteria as historians call it when the people refuse to interact with the shepherds of the flock.

Who are destroying these "elected powers of our government"? Analyze for yourselves! There is no need to even comment on it, we all know it! The Democrats with their injustices and violations of the laws to continue bribing, squandering, stealing our peace, to stay in power. They even steal the dignity of their voters and they are blind as if they had bought the Democratic Party and were giving them good dividends.

Between now and the presidential elections, many things can happen, good or bad, we will have to live them, to tell them to future generations. I hope, and I highly doubt it, that the Democrats of Washington D.C., stop this unbridled race to hurt or want to kill our Democracy. Let them react positively and in a bipartisan way, and let everyone work for the common good and not forget that: "WE ARE THE PEOPLE" is a reality, not an anti-Communist hysteria or an anti-Democratic hysteria or a patriotic hysteria, it is a new rebirth! It is a cry of pain to see our democracy dying before our eyes and not doing anything to save it.

It is like seeing a human being, or an animal in a well drowning, and not seeking rescue. We offer them our hands so that they can react, and return to being decent, the Democratic politicians destroying their own party, we need their voters and you for the 2028 elections to be strengthened. As a suggestion to historians, political experts, Donald Trump's detractors, to the institutions that are there to legislate laws correctly, and above all to the American people, regardless of the political party, is that "history should keep the facts as they occurred, without makeup, without lies, not based on emotions, but on reality. Analyze what has happened from 2016 to this date, whether or not we are in a country destroyed by a Democratic government allied with communists and social destabilizers irresponsibly for having POWER

Everyone is responsible for defending their country both from outside and from within. Decisions are individual, but the duty is unanimous. We are in a war of power and communist infiltrations are stalking the moment to start governing ourselves. We need to act together, not separately. Do you consider it anti-communist hysteria? Or based on reality.

AFRO-AMERICAN

According to this information, it has given me hope that the prefix "Afro" will disappear for those born in the USA from African ancestors, but in our country, due to ties to slavery, they continued to use it in historical documents, and many took advantage of this information and wanted to impose it on black Americans without consulting them.

It was surprising for us Caribbeans, accustomed to living and interacting with our blacks as a family in Cuba, where there was also racial segregation, and never calling them "Afro," to know why blacks in the USA are called "Afro-Americans"? Something that has always bothered me personally because it is a separatist prefix. Born under slavery. The term "African American" generally denotes the descendants of black African slaves. It is also said to whites who are African Americans. Whites are called by their country names, Afro Americans. That is not legally correct because our naturalization certificates say: citizens of the United States. Here everything is violated or names are changed. For what purpose? Seeking monetary funds for groups that instead of thinking like Americans, each one sees it in their own way.

We are tired of so many violations. Martin Luther King was absolutely right when he said that he would march to Washington D.C., as an "American." The most common term, rather than the American one.

Just like the one they give to naturalized immigrants as CubanAmerican, Mexican-American, etc. Even though we have our ancestors on different continents, we will always be separated by the census, history, statistics, etc. But united in duty, responsibility, and love, and if we do not accept it, we have the right to protest.

And the Constitution is kept and not put into use in Washington D.C. Because the arrangements would be endless. The certificate of nationality calls us Citizens of the United States. So after that process, they would call us American or Americans in a more used and colloquial way.

History and censuses in the country have painted with a broad brush the ethnic division in the Tower of Babel by descent, skin color, etc. Amendment XIV (1868) Section 1. Every person born or naturalized in the United States and subject to its jurisdiction, shall be a citizen of the United States and of the state in which he resides.

The Constitution does not speak of separating us into groups, nor does it call us by the country of arrival, nor can laws be made to restrict our right to call ourselves only "Americans or citizens of the United States, which are called Americans."

Why do they divide into groups the naturalized and all those who appear in historical documents? It is unconstitutional. They do it officially and we are all in trouble.

And we do not see the logic with what the Constitution says. It says: No state shall pass or enforce any law abridging the privileges or immunities of citizens of the United States etc. The Constitution speaks for itself. It's just that for some it has been turned deaf. And for minority groups too.

As everything is up to interpretation, many of us interpret that calling black Americans "AFRO" is a restriction on their privileges as citizens of the United States. They are AMERICANS because of the Constitution, not "Afro". Each reading of the Constitution shows us that politicians do not read it or they interpret it as they please. Or the people do not know how to interpret it, but when any law student reads it, they know that what is written is literal in most cases. All those prefixes of separation between groups are unconstitutional, creating separatism or divisionism that never ends, no matter how many decrees or laws they legislate because the government itself separates us. That must change, marking the era of reading the Constitution and applying its laws correctly as it is written.

The story involves Jesse Jackson with his ideas of segregation, rather than integration. Martin Luther King marched to Washington

D.C. with white and black men, even though the black opponents did not want the whites to go to the demonstration. (The hatred of white citizens by violent groups has always been racism. That march was held because of the poverty of blacks and whites. Luther King said that as an AMERICAN he would protest. He did not say that he was of African descent. When Jesse Jackson identified black Americans as "Afro" in the Washington D.C., Department, to benefit his presidential campaign, he was violating what the Constitution says.

But since slavery was abolished and before it was abolished, they were already called Afro-Americans. It seems that he did not realize that in Africa they are still mired in repression, corruption, and social misery, with which none of them should be represented in the USA because they are Americans and not Africans. Recently, the Biden Kamala administration sent billions of dollars to Africa to help it with democracy. And ours when it becomes extinct?

Your real country USA is prosperous, although they are already destroying it economically and soon we will be like Africa, but no country will send us money. The Constitution states that those born in it are citizens of the United States and Acts that defend us from discrimination, left by Martin Luther King as a peacefully achieved historical legacy, is a violation of the individual rights of blacks that many do not want to be called "Afro". That should not have happened, and much more without consulting the 30 million black Americans with a referendum, to find out if they agreed or amending the XIV Amendment to include that those born here of the black race would be African Americans and not American citizens. Doesn't it sound ridiculous? Here the sleeping Congress that we have with two thirds of the Chambers would have to intervene. Both the blacks who do not agree with the prefix "Afro" and all the citizens who have been naturalized, they affected us by violating our constitutional rights. As long as the same government, without reading the CONSTITUTION, continues to separate us with prefixes or suffixes, we will never think like Americans, which is where we choose to live. Calling them African Americans was a political campaign manipulated from Washington D.C., although the prefix "Afro" is established in history before and after slavery. Politicians think that only they use the gift of thinking when reading history, but they do not understand it.

In Africa, the business of hunting blacks to sell them to white men as slaves was born. Separating them from their families, disintegrating their tribes, and their descendants, for the pay obtained from white men. Unscrupulous blacks and whites. That was true. History now is to erase that dirty episode and continue with the lies, deceiving Social Studies students. African blacks served as traders in those slave trades, it was true. With respect to history, it was better to remain American and not put that prefix in front, which is not exactly a seal of morality, although that happened many decades ago and it is time to move forward with the blessings of these times. Our Indians suffered similarly from the mistreatment of the Spanish and we are all related, nothing more and nothing less, than with the family. Are we all going to hate each other?

He who lives in the past does not see his present, and much less will he see his future. If I were black, I would not allow anyone to call me "colored" or any other word so as not to tell me that you are black and not be offended. Whatever race you are, we will never be able to get rid of it, it is in our genes. If we are not proud of who we are, we will not be able to understand others who are proud and shout it from the rooftops. Example: those who call themselves white supremacists. Even if it is not true.

As long as each group respects each other, they are not criminals attacking people, the infrastructure in the country, killing whoever they find in their path, we can all get along accepting each other as we are, but if they commit a crime by killing a black or white person of whatever race, then they should be judged, imprisoned and in several states they could face death row because they asked for it.

The same goes for the blacks who are killing each other in Chicago, and in our different states. Los Angeles, New York, etc. When we hear the news that is not discriminatory, it is true. If they shout that they are happily white, let them say it until they are tired. That is their right to peacefully march.

We all know that they are not, but they are happy to say it as long as they do not harm anyone, we must accept them. Where is the "tolerance" that already seems like a national anthem for corrupt Democrats? It is in the Constitution to express ourselves publicly and march PEACEFULLY. No one is prohibited from marching with their flags, federalists, with torches, slogans, pennants, etc. Nikki Haley removed her from her position in her State for fear of racial confrontations, not because of history. The Secretary of Defense of the United States, Mark Esper, prohibited the display of the Confederate flag in all military installations in this country. In a memo sent to the US Army, Esper did not explicitly mention the flag, but said that "the flags we fly must be in accordance with the military imperatives of good order and discipline, treating all of our people with dignity and respect, and rejecting divisive symbols." How did this Esper not go to the press and condemn the misconduct of the Live Black Matter? Too many ranks of US Secretary of Defense and little patriotic love to defend us from urban terrorists. He effectively prohibits the display of the flag of the Confederacy, which took up arms against the Federal Government in 1861, in a secessionist attempt to maintain the legality of the ownership of African-American slaves. The flag has been a very controversial symbol that embodies racism and in the midst of protests over the murder of George Floyd, which occurred on May 25 in Minneapolis, protesters have asked to remove it from all government institutions. So soon, we will have to uphold the Constitution and they will rule our laws. Are we governed by a government that follows our laws or by a cowardly government obeying Black Lives Matter because they complain about racism?

Isn't it racism to have a College or universities for blacks? It's not time for that anymore, leave the past behind, you weren't the only ones who were abused by society, too many decades have passed to continue with the same complaints. This litany is already tiring. Is TV shows for blacks racist? Isn't it racist to violate the rights of others because you don't like their ideas? Is taking the streets hostage black racism? Is killing a policeman in those days of unbridled riots over the death of George Floyd going against racism by committing crimes? Destroying whatever statues, whatever they are, and whatever they represent, is the history of the country and if our authorities did not have the courage to defend it out of fear, then we are showing that the communist system is the one that governs under the name of the Woke.

In the United Kingdom, they removed a statue that represented racism (according to some groups, not others) and put up one of the criminals of Black Lives Matter. Those who use violence to kill and destroy are criminals, and there is no other name for it, that is why I call you criminals, because you set the tone when you stole electrical equipment, clothes, perfumes and jewellery in the riots like common thieves, not like American patriots. Do we have to obey Black Lives Matter and their demands for not being honest and telling them the truth? Do they criticise others and they are worse?

Martin Luther King would never have done that, because he was an educated, gentle, gallant and brave person and his pacifism was not in vain. Whites and blacks remember him, we admire him and we respect his memory and his work, something that you, being black, have betrayed. That is an infamy. Martin Luther King is an example to follow in any generation, but the Black Lives Matter betrayed him and our authorities, in order to clean up their feces, protect them instead of imprisoning them. Do we have to guide ourselves or write another Constitution?

Is that a lie? It is not, but the terror imposed by official communism here has worked, but as long as I live I will denounce it no matter who falls. That is my citizen participation and let them call me what they like, they have every right under the Constitution to judge my theses, or our theses, if they think like me, which are not hypotheses nor can they change them.

Now logic has vanished from the United States, the Woke pulls the strings internationally, seeking to position themselves in governments and I am convinced that also by putting one group above another, we have returned to social racism by not complying with the laws and being afraid to apply them correctly and denounce it as I am doing in this book in my name and in the name of the people who want to join. The truths without makeup and naked. No more manipulations, everyone should respect each other, but they should also respect contrary ideas, which are valid. Amendment I Congress shall make no law respecting an establishment of religion, or prohibiting the free exercise thereof; or abridging the freedom of speech, or of the press; or the right of the people peaceably to assemble, and to petition the Government for a redress of grievances.

Blacks marching peacefully, just like white supremacists, carrying their slogans, the American flag, the flag of the state where they march, would give color to the marches and we would all enjoy them, without criticism or accusations, but with order, as Martin Luther King did, his pacifist concepts betrayed by those of his own race, with whom he has enjoyed his bad behavior since before he died. If blacks are bothered by the federalist flag, they should read history and, as such, let everyone believe in their concepts, even if they are wrong, just like you who were wrong to take the streets as hostages and kill a policeman in those days. The ideal for all those mothers is not to see their children in divisionism, violence and lack of respect for the country, their friends, etc. They would be happy to see them healthy, educated, respectful of their national symbols, that is what we all want. But if both groups do the same under violence, both groups are equal. The difference in these times of Biden is that they criticize and crucify whites and they let black criminals loose and it seems that they fear them or protect them.

What is happening in the country?

Decent, educated and uneducated blacks do not need to go out on the streets to say that they are proud blacks, to be heard, they have demonstrated it with their social behavior just like whites and Hispanics. If you do not want to be equal to others in bad things, do not do them.

We must feel "proudly black, Hispanic, Asian, white, and so on without having to parade through the streets, because then we would be in a low collective esteem. The groups that want to prohibit being told the truth about their origins, live in ignorance and not in development. They live in bad memories and not in progress. We are as we are, and all united is the best form of racial, social, cultural, political and religious integration etc. In any country. Because we humans are of different colors, and many without having descendants of the black or white race. The different races, some are darker than others.

It is a big mistake to tell blacks "colored", they are black and that is their race. The colored ones are the white ones. "When they are born they are pink, when they cry they are purple, when they sleep they are white, when they are cold they are blue. When the sun burns them they are red—Blacks do not change color, whites are colored, but hypocrisy kills other people's self-esteem. American blacks, whether they are communists or not, who hold resentments against whites, must break the link with the stories of their parents, grandparents, uncles and friends, who seek division, not out of malice, but out of resentment from the past and lack of cultural instruction, making them weak instead of strong men.

Those who broke it many decades ago are free black men, those who preserve it, continue to be slaves of their sad thoughts and attitudes. Break the chains with the legacy of Martin Luther King! And integrate with positivism. Whites today are not guilty of slavery and blacks today are not guilty of their ancestors suffering those times. In our homes, racial, social, political, and religious differences arise and are maintained. We all know that.

Violent blacks are the same as violent whites. That is not racism. It is bad behavior, lack of education and respect for one another.

Those who have broken the chains of the past are those who integrate by forgiving what whites did to their relatives during the time of slavery and remembering that they were not the only ones who suffered; many whites died defending blacks. We must be grateful.

That whites joined them in their struggles and that emancipation came from a white man, Abraham Lincoln. We must recognize and give thanks to the white man who tried to free your ancestors so that they would not continue to suffer the discrimination and abuse of that fateful era full of hatred and ignorance, which countless countries suffered globally. In Cuba, the one who freed the slaves was a white man, and I believe that because of that, our Cuban blacks integrated themselves wholeheartedly into their country, feeling Cuban and not Afro-Cuban. Celia Cruz, our singer, called herself black and when referring to her husband she called him my black, she wore blonde and colored wigs and was a Cuban anti-communist symbol in exile and in folklore and we all said "that black woman has a guts." Nobody was upset because they were told the truth. They called my father "Galician" because he had come from Galicia, Spain, and as a result, his daughters were called "Galician girls" and not "Cuban girls." We cannot live with our backs turned to the truth. These are confronted even if we don't like them.

There were racist whites, but there were white men fighting against slavery too. Those who accepted them and those who didn't. That is called integration, respect for those difficult times. What do they criticize white supremacists for? Their behavior? Black Hispanics and whites in this country have behaved badly for decades with street fights destroying everything in their path. Let's think about that. Never in any video archived in this country did they see Martin Luther King stealing a television from stores during protests. That is shameful and should not be repeated.

Good things must be imitated, so as not to be criticized, not discriminated against as journalists who detract from their own country say. The day that Black Lives Matter, Antifa, the remnants of the Black Panthers and other groups of Hispanics, blacks and whites as incorrect as so many others, integrate correctly into society, claiming their rights, but not trampling on those of others, that day Martin Luther King's dream will be fulfilled. We are tired of so many lies damaging Democracy by a corrupt press, which has forgotten the concept of what journalism is. We are tired of politicians who group us like cattle to achieve their political ends. They are the ones who spread hatred by not reporting and telling the truth about any group that acts wrong. Biden has unleashed a dirty and unsustainable racism because neither he nor Kamala will be president again. If Democratic voters do not analyze the situation, they will not go down in history as defending their country from internal enemies.

That would be deplorable. Although if Biden is punished with a trial that he deserves, but did not try, he will come out dishonorably. The Democrats have not used the laws they wanted for Donald Trump. Kamala receives what is called in third world countries "The finger pointing". Biden without the right to govern due to illness. Kamala as a woman or black although Biden wants to backtrack and now says that he appointed her because she was intelligent and could not fulfill the only task they gave her of supervising the Southern border.

Hypocrisy? Yes sir! They did not use any of the Amendments to give Joe Biden the judgment he deserved. They omitted all of them and in the plot to save the Democratic convention they chose the most opportune Kamala Harris. Is Joe Biden still walking around the Oval Office?

Anthony A. Beale (born October 22, 1967) is an American (not African-American) politician from the 9th District of the City of Chicago, Illinois, United States. American, that is how blacks born in the USA should be named, not African-Americans.

Oprah Winfrey describes herself as an American woman, not African-American. Many blacks do not agree with the prefix. Have they said this publicly? One thing is knowing where our roots come from, knowing the country of our grandparents, etc., and another is sending them a message that they will never be Americans.

This happens to all of us who have become naturalized even though our citizenship certificate says that we are citizens of the United States without the divisive classifications by the Census. We are fed up with so many invented laws separating us like animals in the pastures. When you apply for citizenship in any country, it is because you want to live there and respect its laws or have the citizenship of your parents, who are from other countries out of love or because they have lived in those countries too and it was part of their history. But in every country that grants you citizenship, it says that you are a citizen and not a string of prefixes. It is time for the American black community to stop separating themselves. They are Americans. American black citizens are as they should be. This is following what their great leader Martin Luther King wanted, integration not separation. "I have a Dream."

It is time to make individual changes that will later become mass changes, a rebirth towards the truth. We are Americans and happy to be so. Not that politicians of all parties have taken us as scapegoats to obtain electoral votes. If we are Americans, we vote as such, with the red, blue and white colors of our flag, not by skin color or ethnicity. Remember black Americans the ridiculousness of Nancy Pelosi and Chuck Schumer, when they called you black Africans and not Americans with the message of the African scarves. Your own politicians do not consider you Americans by wearing the scarves of Africa and not of the USA.

In four years we will vote again without separation of races and colors. Today is the culmination of past eras and a new dawn will return to this land and that is why I invite you to vote for the candidate who deserves the presidency for his honesty and love for the American people and that is Donald J. Trump helping us to take back the USA for the next elections of 2028 when the Democrats have reflected on all their bad actions. We all deserve or need a second chance!

The honest words of Anthony Beale, an American, in the plenary session of the council in Chicago, highlighted the disparity between the support given to illegal immigrants, and the struggles faced by legal citizens, including veterans who may be poor or homeless. He noted the irony of a city where those who have served the country can witness the allocation of such important resources to those who entered the country illegally.

This point of view is not only his, it is ours as a people, and this is happening where they have sheltered part of the millions of illegals that Biden irresponsibly allowed for going against Donald Trump. If all politicians did like Mr. Beale, we could believe the Democrats. It is time to start telling the truth as it is, not as the irresponsible want to present it to us.

The 45th former president Donald J. Trump has become a global obsession. I believe that destiny, the cosmos, or God, had it reserved for this to happen and many of us would open our eyes. Donald Trump, no matter how much they want to destroy his material interests, will always be at his billionaire level, whether it hurts those who are hurt (the envious), but not the people. And here is the concept that by destroying a man, they destroy his voters and consequently the country. Trump, under his slogan "Americans first" made it very clear.

My respect and admiration for people who are not afraid to tell the truth correctly. To Mr. Beale, for recognizing the situations that can cause us serious problems when citizens lose their rights for the sake of illegal citizens entering the country, and receiving generous aid, which is denied to American citizens and with the consent of President Joe Biden and our veterans sleeping on the streets just like in California, with the inept Governor Gavin Newsom, who was elected by the Democrats for going against the truth, not for his knowledge. We who are immigrants are not against immigration, we are against disorganization and violations of the laws affecting us all.

Social justice is achieved when we all recognize our serious mistakes. There is no social justice doing what Joe Biden does, taking away the rights of legal citizens, those born, and giving them to those who violate the laws. That is unfair and lacking in common sense.

Not only does it violate existing laws, but also the moral laws, by which those who claim to work for the people must strictly abide. The Biden era marked American history as the worst President in the country. A witch hunt for a former president who worked for free for everyone. It must be repeated!

This saying is widely used by parents and grandparents in different cultures. "A beacon for the street and darkness for your home." It means: you help those outside and not your home. Buying power is easy, but holding it without morals is not easy either, and we are seeing how the Democrats' plans are falling apart.

The archives of the Library of Congress will keep for future generations what has historically happened, as the worst demoralization of the Democratic political party by its own members. Joe Biden's racism has been the most ridiculous thing that could have been impartially observed. You don't praise one group over another, you don't employ Hispanics, blacks, homosexuals, or whites to prove that you are fair, because in itself you are proving that you are not criticized for being racist. You don't employ incapacitated people for the positions they apply for. Homosexuals, blacks, Hispanics, don't need that circus. Races don't distinguish between good or bad knowledge, but rather what we demonstrate with facts of what we are and will be without further divisions in schools for blacks, television programs for blacks, chambers of commerce for blacks and successively also involving Asians and Hispanics in an era in which separation is not worth it, but integration.

If they do not know how to get out of racist creeds and dogmas, they should ask for help or understand that what they criticize should not be done. Jesse Jackson said: "We will never be satisfied as long as our children are stripped of their being and robbed of their dignity with signs that say: 'For Whites Only.'" If blacks do not want signs that say "For Whites Only" we assume that whites do not want to hear about Black Chambers of Commerce, Black Universities, Black TV Shows. Please let us not fall into ridiculousness. There is a golden rule that says Luke 6-31 "Do also to others as you would like to be done to you.

Each group has to make its own decisions about this, whether they want to integrate or continue being the scapegoats of a dominant group – the politicians or Big Tech! a digital socialist agenda, a Digital Technology Deal (DTD), centered on principles of anti-imperialism, class abolition, reparations and degrowth that can take us to a 21st century socialist economy. It is based on proposals for transformation, as in existing models that can be expanded and seeks to integrate them with other movements that promote alternatives to capitalism, in particular the degrowth movement and the American people already want a good economy and for everything to continue flowing normally, without shocks and anguish, but to share with the family each one according to their social status. Jesse Jackson, due to his bad political actions, imposed the Afro without taking into account all the blacks in the country. In 2005, the Federal Election Commission ruled that Jackson and the Democratic National Committee had violated election law and fined them $200,000 (equivalent to $299,900 in 2023). Also being a clergyman, he made the mistake of embezzling his fundraising platform for donations from his followers by giving himself the sweet life. He not only betrayed his voters but also his religion. It is not good to follow crowds without reasoning first.

Despite the good things he did as a Civil Rights leader, people have light and shadow. A clergyman accepting gay marriage when Obama approved it in 2012 is a betrayal of any religion that Jesse

Jackson professed. In no Bible is it stated that Jehovah allows that. It is better not to be religious and to be able to express yourself freely without betraying, and if you are a clergyman and you betray your religion you are doubly hypocritical. History sees what suits it and politics Also, when in the politics that has always existed we see how true stories are made up to give a false image and make it seem true, that is when the disappointments come alone. Jesse Jackson was not exactly the leader he proved to be. Jealousy of blacks and whites, lies and betrayals, were creating what remains of him. It does not matter that he supported Hillary Clinton's candidacy, because both were Democrats. Many blacks resist being called African Americans and they have every reason. They are Americans by birth.

In 1988, the Reverend Jesse Jackson urged African Americans to eliminate the adjective "black" and replace it with "African." Jackson argued that "black" no longer described "our" situation in the United States. The term African American was used for decades. I differ with Reverend Jackson because the Afro is the one that does not describe black Americans. The fact that his ancestors of several generations go back to the time of slavery is not correct. That's where the prefix "Afro" comes from, with the connotations of slavery that has nothing to do with them at all. The same thing happens with naturalized people, calling them Mexican-American, Cuban-American, etc. We're already sick of so much separatism or whatever you want to call it and having to repeat it many times for them to assimilate it. Use logic and not emotions!

ALEXANDRIA OCASIO CORTEZ

Representative Ocasio Cortez is not only a member of the group "The Squad" but of other communist groups, DSA, social democrats, progressives and all "pathological liars". Not to offend (mythomania). Sadly hypocritical in their concepts that they want to expose, and their behaviors denounce it. Alexandria OcasioCortez. Born on October 13, 1989, also known by her initials AOC, is an American left-wing politician and activist. Ocasio-Cortez is a member of an informal group of progressive members of Congress called "The Squad", along with Ilhan Omar, Ayanna Pressley, Rashida Tlaib, Cori Bush and Jamaal Bowman. Look for information on all of them.

In January 2024, the United States and other countries cut funding to the United Nations Relief and Works Agency for Palestine Refugees in the Near East (UNRWA) due to intelligence reports that certain UNRWA staff members supported Hamas during the Hamas-led attack on Israel in 2023 by participating in the attack.

On January 29, Ocasio-Cortez acknowledged the reports, but also said that cutting funding to UNRWA was "unacceptable" and that the United States "should restore aid immediately." These are the politicians that the people of New York vote for without knowing who. This Ms. Ocacio swore an oath under the Constitution and wants our money to go to terrorism. She defends the Palestinians and Hamas more than her own people, forgetting that the Twin Towers and the more than three thousand American deaths are due to terrorism. We also owe it to the Clinton family because by enriching themselves with all their lobbying they forgot to put the Department of Justice and Counter Intelligence in order.

That means that the Woke has been running the Department of Justice for many years and that is very serious. Or does the Ocasio Squad have its tentacles inside that Department already?

The communists are not honest, and Mrs. Ocasio is always defending the proletariat and I do not criticize her, that she wants to look like a princess, when she attended the Met Gala 2021, which had as its theme "In the United States: "A lexicon of fashion." That the cost was $35,000.00 dollars per person and she got it for free, as a guest and that is what the communists take advantage of, who talk about poverty, but look for "millionaire men" instead of looking among those who clean the House of Representatives, who are actually the "proletariat" that they defend. The millionaires are Opulent. But communists end up being millionaires or bourgeois and the people in misery. I am not against millionaires, on the contrary, but I am against millionaires with the suffix or prefix "communist" like those we have in Washington D.C.

They should marry the poorest, because it would be an irony to defend poverty and for her to live in the luxury that they criticize others for. They are so hypocritical that it is embarrassing to even know it. They want to distribute the millionaires' money among the poor and they sit without working watching TV. They dress in expensive fashion designers, surround themselves with the bourgeoisie and want to marry millionaires, not the poor. What theory do they defend? It is better that they keep quiet, but even if you don't believe it, the communists make millions, and they live a bourgeois life, because they are supported by the fools who follow them and donate money to their causes, or they expropriate their businesses as happened in Cuba, Venezuela, Nicaragua and in Europe etc., without paying a cent to the owners affected by the theft. Do the voters want to continue supporting them?

That is the double standard of all communist, socialist, radical politicians or whatever you call them, who want to govern us and we all know the reality, except for the young people who come out of our Universities, and their professors who confuse them daily, those who come out of social networks supporting the first one who says that poverty should end, and reading without confronting the facts, but socially and lovingly related to millionaires. From Capitalism to Communism it looks good.

Capitalism is wonderful. Defend it for the sake of the democracy we have. The voters who are part of the Stalin metaphor because they settle for false promises and re-elect them to their positions should think before giving him their votes that are sacred.

Fantastic our politicians of the House of Representatives who were the very well-led women in Nancy Pelosi's flock and the disguises of repudiation of their own government and we can already imagine how "The Squad" prepares to attack the country, not to defend it. It is shameful that Alexandria Ocasio has formed a squad to attack her own country? Who says that communism and terrorism are not within our government? Ocasio should go out and fix the miseries of New York, that is her job and she does not do it, or that they should not vote for her. No more democratic communism. We want capitalism. Progress, a future for the new generations, not social miseries. Men also support all those beautiful theories along with Ocasio. Will it have connotations with The Squad with the guerrillas? Ocacio should clarify her situation and tell us the intention of that famous Squad but it is no longer necessary because we will take her out in the elections of November 5.

I think that if they do not read the Constitution, our Democratic politicians will not read history either. It is better and more patriotic to change the name of "their group" or to be honest and add the words that are missing. "The Squad" of the Death of the USA. Maybe the FBI, when they restore the miseries of the Justice Department, will have some free time, starting to investigate them all, but we doubt it for the moment while they rot in social misery as traitors to their institution. Or let's hope that the Democratic people of New York will open their eyes and not vote for Alexandria O.C., joining the Republicans to vote in a great red, blue and white wave, saving the country from communist scum together.

KATIE PORTER AND ADAM SCHIFF

You might wonder what these Democrats are doing here? Simply seeing two Democrats with different options. One destroying the country and a Harvard graduate, the other defending it and both in the same political party.

Schiff's campaign has 32 million dollars in the bank. Porter 12 million dollars and Lee, 1.3 million dollars. Data that we no longer know if everything is a lie, or everything is true, since the Democrats are in power everything has been lost more and more. (Journalistic dignity). Mrs. Katie Porter and Adam Schiff. They ran in the California primaries seeking the Senate.

Words by Schiff. "I don't think Representative Porter has been entirely clear about her history of accepting thousands of dollars from people in the oil industry, thousands from Wall Street bankers, thousands of people in the pharmaceutical industry," Schiff responded. Where did this idiot at the bank get the $32 million from? "The problem with purity tests, as Representative Porter would like to establish, is that invariably the people who establish them don't comply with them." And Adam Schiff knows about that because he doesn't comply either.

Ms. Porter's words. "My colleague Representative Schiff says, for example, that he wants to reduce the cost of child care. But it's not in either of the two major Democratic bills that would do that. It's not in a bill to provide rental assistance to people, although they were all part of the plans. That's the gap between Congressman Schiff and candidate Schiff." (12 million)

But we voters do know where Schiff is. "Wanting to make another trial of Donald Trump." With all due respect, but this man is sick with it. Is he secretly obsessed with Trump, like all those who persecute him?

The Democratic politicians who would have come forward to denounce their party, for everything that happened to Donald Trump, would have been the pioneers in putting things in order and restoring the bad image that their predecessors, mentioned above, have left behind the dirty footprint of their actions. They would be the ones who would restore the prestige of a party that was as correct as any other in the past, or as corrupt as any other in the present. Because in this present of 2024, we have seen corruption of all kinds and "sizes" (metaphorically, coming from the Democratic Party more than from any other. It is as if they wanted and felt the pleasure of destroying their own country from within. Are they all sick, or have they taken off their masks?

Reading the Statements of the Democratic candidates (United States Senate - Partial Term Unfinished. I wished that Mrs. Katie Porter was elected to the position of Senator by the Democrats, so that there would be someone who wanted to serve her people in that party with righteousness and decency, but for so many years living in California, I have always thought that the Californian Democratic people do not read the information, but rather, they vote for the face of those they know, because they think they owe them favors, and not those who have destroyed the party and do not want to understand it or because in hatred towards Donald Trump it was sweet revenge to vote for Adam Schiff the persecutor, but the inept jurist because he could not condemn Donald Trump. Do not vote for inept people in both parties.

They voted for Adam Schiff who persecuted Donald Trump and wants to continue doing so, like a mediocre comedy that we have to watch again.

We must hurry up in building hospitals for the mentally ill. The millionaire California Democrats intervene in supporting those who suit them in Washington D.C., and in this case the support was for the "Resounding failure in the trials of Donald Trump while serving the people" Mr. Adam Schiff, a Harvard graduate. Katie Porter's words were in the Candidate Statement among many others: "In Washington D.C.,"

The powerful special interests have too much control, while Congress is bogged down with endless bipartisan battles.

A reality. Something that took out of context the millionaires who suit the swamp of Washington D.C., and consequently Mrs. Katie Porter, sought the same reaction when Donald Trump denounced the great swamp of our government. By saying "too much control" is what the American people have come to know until these days of 2024. She represented a threat to her party, wanting to clean it up. Results: defamation of her campaign and putting a foot in her way to make it fall. We who have lived in third world countries know about these maneuvers without being told.

The millionaires or the Democratic Party paid for her televised advertisements against the only person in these times who wants to clean up the party and the Californian people did not support her in the primaries. (This is common in California). The Democratic Party members do not like to be hindered in their actions, and they pay and join those who want to maintain the swamp. Perhaps there is hope that this lady will reach the important position of Senator to try to correct what happened to her party.

The inefficiencies of the FBI, the Department of Justice, and black and white judges who "go for Trump" and not for "justice and truth," persecutions of all kinds, are what have undermined the country. They are all falling little by little. The rape trial was revived by the Democrats to attack Donald Trump. Discrediting him before voters as a rapist is already the ultimate extreme of social and political shamelessness not contemplated in any book on criminal justice. Since there is no law that dismisses cases where women have waited years to report a rape, women will continue to take or try to take money from public figures with whom many slept when they were not. Most do it, not for love, but for monetary interests.

Until there are laws that protect men and women from accusations that are mostly false, because these types of raped women, who charge large sums in court or outside of court, are the ones who sleep with millionaires to see what they get, not for rape, but seeking to obtain benefits. If a woman is raped, she must immediately report it and present proof of "semen", if she was beaten, a medical certificate, and when and how the events occurred (witnesses).

Many women report their aggressors for rape when it was consented by both. When they do not get what they expected, these cases occur. Not all women are raped, nor are all women decent or indecent. When having sexual relations, they must also have the dignity of discretion and responsibility of adults. There are many of us who know that there is "too much control" that has caused all these phenomena of corrupt politics and incongruent laws.

Bill Clinton, Donald Trump, Brett Kavanaugh, Clarence Thomas, etc. Accused of sexual assaults, several years ago. If they did it, that remains on their conscience, but accusing a person wanting to gain fame or money, or destroying his professional or private career with his wife-or-husband, is an unacceptable way of acting. Even prostitutes benefit from these lawsuits, when they have not been raped, but taken advantage of and paid for the service.

All this can end, by making laws that benefit those who are truly slandered and the women who are abused. (Time limit for filing complaints) not 30 years after having slept with the individual in youth. That is ridiculous. Instead of asking for belated justice, women should behave with dignity towards men. And if they are going to have these relationships, they should do it for love, pleasure but responsibly. Today men and women talk about their intimacies. Prudence has disappeared from the dictionary. They should not provoke sexual conversations, they should not flirt with their coworkers, they should respect themselves, so that they do not have to accuse individuals when they respond to their flirtations. "The man proposes and the woman disposes." One thing is having sex looking for monetary interests, and another to have it because you like it or because you feel attraction or love under a code of respect and silence of the couple. Discretion has been lost, both for men and for women.

It is true that at a global level there are cases of sexual and all kinds of violations. No one denies that. But sexual responsibility is part of society and we are tired of those stories that come to light when the individual gains power and money. No one escapes. Judges, doctors, teachers, lawyers, program presenters, businessmen, etc., have gone through these problems, but these women do not sleep with gardeners, pizza sellers, or home maintenance workers, because none of them have enough money that they hope to obtain through sex.

Prostitution? If they do it with them, it is for the pleasure of sex. These women come out to give their testimonies, paid doubly by the detractors of those who have suffered these sexual scandals. In Secondary Schools, Colleges and Universities (we all know what happens). The girls mostly celebrate feminism by sleeping with their schoolmates, smoking and drinking until they get drunk. Those who have had these famous school parties are responsible for these situations if they suffered them. If they get drunk with drugs or alcohol, they lose consciousness of what they do, whether it is correct or not, and then they say they were raped. If they were responsible, educated, moral young women (values that have disappeared in all societies) they would not be at parties where drugs, smoking and alcoholic beverages are everywhere and they all know what they are going to. They hope that those accused people will have a relevant position in society to attack them for what they allowed and did not accuse their offenders at the time. They waited 30 years to denounce and make international movements like Me Too. Who do they believe them? It is better that they meet watching You Tube because they will learn something good if they look for the good because there are so many videos of liars that they should all be removed.

Those who accuse immediately and their corrupt countries forget the laws and do not take the correct measures are those who can raise their voices as happened to the young Pakistani Khadija Siddiqi, a law student in Pakistan, stabbed 23 times in 2016 by a classmate, after rejecting his advances. The aggressor had good contacts and was acquitted by a judicial system that usually excuses perpetrators of violence against women. Khadija refused to remain silent and over 2 million followers used the hashtag #JusticeforKhadija to plead her case on social media, ultimately helping her win her appeal. Khadija said that day: "Today is a day of victory for all women," she defiantly told reporters from the steps of Pakistan's Supreme Court, after more than two years of struggle.

These are the admirable women in any situation in any country who denounce their aggressors properly and in time, not waiting 20 and 30 years to bring their case to light and form movements about the violence that has always existed and now thanks to social media (not everything is bad nor is everything good in them) cases can be reported internationally. This young woman demonstrated her vocation for justice. She used it to her advantage. These are the future lawyers who will serve as an inspiration to law students and graduates who discredit their profession. As is happening in the USA under the Democratic government, they should be investigated and their licenses removed until they return to justice seriously.

Katie Porter aroused a feeling of sympathy, not because she is a woman, nor because she is a Democrat, but because she is a good American citizen, because of her affinity for the right things. If she had been a Democrat, my vote would have been for her, for seeking justice and truth under her so vilely outraged Democratic Party. I was surprised when I read her next words. "I am one of only 11 people among the 435 members of Congress who reject contributions from federal lobbyists. In my lexicon I would say corruption. Mrs. Porter says: Instead, I am leading the fight to prohibit members of Congress from trading in stocks. People like her are the ones who should defend the Democratic Party, not Adam Schiff who wants to destroy it with his bad actions.

This was when the Democratic Party reacted by removing her from power. Should Congress trade in stocks? If all or almost all are "wealthy" both Democrats and Republicans and all the politicians who walk the halls of Washington D.C. Using their jobs for personal enrichment, not for the people. It is worth mentioning that Donald Trump did not make his millions in Washington D.C.

Nancy Pelosi, Chuck Schumer are irrefutable examples of their fortunes obtained through contacts, lobbying or government information. Mrs. Porter, similar to Donald Trump, had the same thing happen to her, wanting to touch the claws of the crocodiles. The Californian millionaires in favor of Donald Trump's persecutor Mr. Schiff, saw the danger of Katie Porter winning, and went into the ring to fight not with a bull, but to defend the Democratic government corruption that is worse than Satan.

I think that Mrs. Katie Porter will have to redouble her efforts to ensure that in the halls of Washington D.C., individuals are not enriched as it has been until today and that Californians open their eyes to what is happening. The donations that politicians receive are the cause of discussions in the primary or presidential elections by many. Fundraising is necessary for propaganda and other things that do not always work for good and sometimes for bad.

They come in talking horrors about the rich, defending the poor and everyone gets rich, but they are not affected by the "interpretative" laws of our Constitution, nor by the judges and prosecutors who persecute a single man in the nation, showing the world our corrupt political and human weaknesses. This filth must stop so that our Society can advance.

Another traitor to the American system is the Democratic legislator Ilhan Omar. This Representative hates Israel, has a dark past of having married her brother violating immigration laws (according to comments in the press and not corroborated by official investigations that refrain from informing the people, to find out if they are true or not). She has spent money from her campaign for personal purposes according to the Internet and none of this has been clarified by the Democratic FBI so that we know if it is true or not, what the corrupt or honest press says. They no longer investigate corrupt officials, let alone share this information with voters so that everyone knows who they are voting for. Is that over in the US or are they taking a break?

Ilhan Omar was expelled from the US House of Representatives Foreign Affairs Committee for anti-Semitic statements. Anti-Semitic acts are considered crimes at the time of their criminalization (for example, Holocaust denial or distribution of anti-Semitic material in some countries). https://holocaustremembrance.com/resources/working-definition-antisemitism.

She knows that talking about discrimination is a clear and convincing passport for the weak who hide behind that concept and use it saying that they discriminate against her because she came from Africa. It is not discrimination, it is incompetence, it is treason and support for terrorism. The immoral use any weapon to attack the enemy, and the enemy of this representative and many others is the USA and Israel. We can no longer demand that those who claim to be public servants be investigated.

The Democrats support them. That is how corruption works. Her daughter has been seen supporting Hamas in the riots in favor of terrorism.

It would have been an honor for the California Democrats to have voted for Katie Porter and contributed to American history in these difficult times of insane persecution. "False Prophet" Adam B. Schiff, complicit with lies and false evidence in the first trials of Donald Trump, chosen as "forceful" by Nancy Pelosi, along with Schumer and Republican traitors for the media show, was the choice of voters who have not read the Stalin metaphor in the California primary votes for Senator.

He already wants to organize another trial for Donald Trump. Does Adam Schiff feel like a Roman emperor? Since he does not pay the money to the lawyers, he spends it lavishly. Katie Porter's words agree with what the people know they think. Katie Porter has openly criticized the amount of money that special interest groups and wealthy donors were spending against her. Thanking her supporters, she said: "Thanks to you, we had the establishment scared, enduring 3 to 1 in television spending and an avalanche of billionaires spending money to manipulate this election."

"Rigged" means manipulated by dishonest means. A few billionaires spent $10 million and much more on attack ads against me, including one ad rated "false" by an independent fact-checker," Porter said. "That's a dishonest way to manipulate a result."

But the Democrats sacrifice their members and don't even stop with this Katie. First comes the swamp and then comes the rest. We all know that.

When Katie Porter says she has not "undermined the vote count and the electoral process in California that are beyond reproach" she is lying or misinformed and it takes away credit from her but we have to recognize that she belongs to the Democratic guild.

How old was Ms. Porter when the electoral fraud was committed in California, where dead and illegal people went out to vote when Loretta Sanchez? And that there was no vote recount because there was no money to pay for it. Does Ms. Porter know that in California they stopped counting thousands of ballots and the press did not emphasize that, because they are all corrupt? California voting has never been blameless.

Let us remind Ms. Porter that Donald Trump suffered on a large scale what was done to her on a minor level. But as a good Democrat she has to follow the establishment of her party emphasizing that Donald Trump undermined the vote count.

She emphasizes: I said: 'rigged billionaires' and our politics is, in fact, manipulated by large amounts of dark money. Is she learning from Donald Trump? I hope one day she switches to the Republican party, where she will do better. If Abraham Lincoln did it, why not any voter? But Mr. Rick Hasen, a UCLA law professor and expert in electoral law has wanted to manipulate the truth that she expressed. Is manipulation essential at UCLA? The people know that there are crocodiles everywhere and that UCLA may be learning to swim or has been swimming for a long time among all of them. This gentleman thinks like a Democrat, not as an American citizen, when he said that Katie's comments can be taken out of context (which has always happened with Trump) that she is as bad as Donald Trump by saying that the electoral system is unfair and this will make more people doubt the integrity of the electoral process.

The comparison of how bad Donald Trump is could be summarized, it is not that she is bad, it is that she forgot that you cannot tell the truth. Mr. Hasen, we do not doubt it, we know it, and you do too even though you want to disguise the truth. Why do Democrats not know how to deal with the naked truth? According to Ann Ravel, former president of the Federal Election Commission, she is not wrong about domestic spending, but she considers "Mrs. Porter's choice of words" worrying. All this reminds us of the Moral of Truth and Lies. Which we dedicate entirely to the politicians of Washington D.C.

MORAL. TRUTH AND LIE.

Legend has it that one day Lie and Truth met in a river. Lie said to Truth: -Good morning, Mrs. Truth. Truth did not trust her new friend very much and replied -Good morning, Mrs. Lie. Truth confirmed that it was actually a beautiful day. -The river is even more beautiful today, said Lie. Truth looked at the river and was convinced of its beauty by touching the water with her fingers, checking that the water was cool. Lie, running towards the water, said: -Let's go swimming! The water is much more beautiful! Truth decided to believe Lie and follow her. They both took off their clothes and jumped into the water. Truth and Lie swam naked for a while, very happy, until Lie came out of the water and put on Truth's clothes. Truth, unable to put on the clothes of Lies, began to walk naked through the streets and everyone was horrified to see her.

NAKED TRUTHS

Democrats live horrified to hear and see naked truths. We are going to have to ask the government to make us a statue (replacing those that Black Lives Matter destroyed), representing naked truth in the special room where the symbols of the Supreme Court are. And for the Democrats to understand us, we have to cover up the truths or speak to them with lies, but like Moral, we refuse to put on the clothes of Lies. Good God, that's why we are so bad socially.

To muddy the Senate as well, Adam Schiff has started the race for Senator. The former Democratic leader of the House of Representatives, Nancy Pelosi, chose Adam Schiff instead of Jerry Nadler, chairman of the Judiciary Committee, to lead the impeachment process against Trump. It was not impeachment, it was a COUP D'ETAT disguised with our own laws. He was saved from not being elected to American history in that dirt even if he supported it. Pelosi said: Schiff is "logical, linear, measured but forceful. Now we know after having lost the trials against Donald Trump, that Nancy Pelosi was wrong in everything. Adam Schiff was not logical, he was stupid to let himself get caught up in the fabricated lies of all of you. He was not measured, because by saying that Donald Trump was a mobster or a corrupt politician, he showed that he was not a measured or ethical person. (False evidence because he had to prove that Donald Trump was a mobster) and he went beyond logic, by saying that Trump was a politician. Defamations from the government. She was not forceful, because to be so she had to work with Truth and Justice and she worked with gossip, from all of you basing your accusations on whispers, within the dirty corridors of Washington D.C., where the first persecution of Donald Trump was carried out along with the other Democrats and Republican traitors.

Nancy Pelosi is an expert in making mistakes with the people. Who do they want to fool? It must be repeated until exhaustion, Donald Trump came out free of all the stains that you smeared on him. Only a desperate person trying to win a lawsuit demonstrated his inefficiency in his career, and if we go beyond the conspiracy against Donald Trump, the Universities that graduate lawyers like Adam Schiff should withdraw his license until they take classes on work ethics, where Justice was the priority. Rudy Giuliani has his license revoked and they want to destroy him for being a friend of Donald Trump? Is this how the judges we have are? This bad behavior of Adam Schiff discredits his Harvard University and his classmates who graduated together. His classmates will be less famous than him, but honorable.

Bad practice in any profession must be addressed by an ethics committee and evaluate the consequences that this brings to the guild and the country in these cases. Adam Schiff, desperate because he knew he would not win the case, said: "Americans will hear directly from dedicated and patriotic public officials, how they realized that the foreign policy of the United States had been subverted for the benefit of the personal political interests of the president." Why if Adam Schiff and those public officials he mentioned who were so patriotic did not investigate Biden and his son in this era? The one who said that Biden was involved with Ukraine in dirty money dealings, is now the scapegoat of the famous Series, Biden-Son. I continue to insist that they should consult a Professional Hollywood Screenwriter.

Adam Schiff, the Democratic head of the investigation against the president of the United States, Donald Trump, should have stayed as an actor in Hollywood, since that was his dream, repeating the scripts of the professionals of that company, because the script that led to the media trial against Trump demoralized him as a lawyer, prosecutor, actor and creator of scripts for cheap circuses, because the good guys would never have hired him, not even for a good movie. By creating an incoherent script, based on evil, and not on Truth and Justice, it was demonstrated how cowardly and inept he was.

Does he want to smear the Senate too? (His new political aspiration) so that he can lie every day to the skimmed chickens that follow him without investigating how he behaves. The vote is sacred and through it we can solve the problems by wisely and emotionlessly choosing those who will represent us in Washington D.C., regardless of color, race, and religious beliefs, but if they all converge in honesty, so that all this never happens again. They are not the only ones to blame, it is us who in moments of hatred, rage, or political ignorance, become those famous "plucked chickens" so many men and women that all politicians are fascinated by.

The Senate, if Adam Schiff gets there, will have to speak to him clearly and honorably, that at the first attempt at lies and dirt, they will send him to the ethics school that many need so much, including Bob Menendez, a lawyer, who studied at Rutgers University. Coincidentally: Are they all Democrats? The Senators who wish the best for the country and its people must begin to be scrutinized and with this we lend a hand to Jesus Christ, while he does not arrive.

As Chairman of the Intelligence Committee, Mr. Schiff demonstrated in his failed plot against Donald Trump, by losing the trials where all were involved, that they were not trustworthy to Democracy. What kind of Intelligence Committee we have in power!

They could not prove that Trump violated his oath of office and the law by seeking help from Ukraine for his 2020 reelection campaign. Trump's request for a "favor" to Ukrainian President Volodymyr Zelensky reflects "a typical scam by a mafia guy to a foreign leader," said Schiff. If Schiff calls the president to whom he owed respect a "mafia guy," it is not what Nancy Pelosi said about him lying to us all.

What can citizens expect? Although citizens have reacted to all the chaos caused by Democrats defending Democracy, Truth, and Justice, which they all want to destroy, we are highly criticized and misfits by a fanatically involved Democratic people.

Adam Schiff is nothing more than a very weak lawyer or prosecutor. What could you say to him? If the Ethics Committee did not see this, it is because everyone is complicit in Washington D.C. "This is how a mob boss talks: 'What have you done for us?'"

Now tell us Mr. Schiff, what have you done for us? If not enrich yourselves, defraud American justice, lie, conjure like the witches in the stories, plots to destroy and could not achieve it. They proved that the plot was genuine, but without evidence, because they could not accuse President Donald Trump and failed in their dirty attempts. What kind of lawyer is Adam Schiff?

All the conspirators in these trials demonstrated the political ineptitudes involved in the plot and unfortunately they are the ones who lead and govern us. Trump responded that Schiff fabricated his words, and now he does not miss the opportunity to label him, (according to the information) without any proof, as a "corrupt politician." This is what the defenders of the Swamp write, saying that Trump labels him as corrupt, it is not a label, it is a Truth. Do those who defend political corruption also want to change the name of the truth to "label"? In an X Trump said that "Schiff must testify why he fabricated a statement of mine." He also said that "the corrupt politician Schiff should be investigated for fraud!"

Mr. ex-President, you are not the only one who thinks that this overwhelming failed jurist should be investigated. We as a people are crying out to the Department of Justice to investigate, but since everyone is involved in one way or another, they would only remain investigations and not consummated trials. It has now been proven that the Justice Department, headed by Merrick Garland, has been involved in several judicial disorders against Donald Trump. Every day, Americans lose confidence in their own laws. In the case that Judge Aileen Cannon is in charge of the proceedings for the classified documents from Mar a Lago, lies from the FBI and others are involved. Democratic politicians are investigated to silence the people, but only Hunter Biden has been prosecuted at the convenience of the moment.

The President's son did not fall into disgrace, he was and has always been in disgrace. He is condemned "opportunely" so as not to affect the father's presidential elections. (That the communist Democrat plot could already get him out of the way.) The people had to be shown that justice has not died and they sanctioned Hunter. President Biden and his son are examples of political corruption,

Hillary Clinton, Obama now buying mansions in Real Estate, competing with Donald Trump, Nancy Pelosi, Chuck Schumer, and the list is long of corrupt people enriched from Washington D.C.

If they had made their money working it would be a blessing for the American people to have had them in our politics, but they have been and are corrupt. What did Donald Trump lose money while serving us in power? Yes, even in that, he is different from the accumulators of dollars who have passed through those halls. Let us open our eyes, let us inform ourselves, to be able to vote freely and rescue the country from democratic communism. Let us analyze the past, and compare the present and it is enough to make the right decisions, Do not hate, love. Do not follow the Democrats until they restructure and return to the path of truth and justice.

The Department of Justice believes in them and they will not be investigated because we already know that this Department is corrupt. This shows that the swamp is much bigger than what was reported. The relatives who have had members investigated or sentenced by Adam Schiff, should ask for a review of the cases, because the way he acted with the former president, what would this forceful failed jurist do for fame? At the end of the 1980s, when he had not long left Harvard Law School, he prosecuted the first FBI agent imprisoned for spying for Moscow. Perhaps he is innocently celebrating his birthday and is part of those dirty statistics.

That is why Nancy Pelosi affiliated him to her plot, because she knew he had no ethics whatsoever. A jurist without professional ethics is a bomb ready to explode against the accused. These are the Senators nominated in these primaries in California, which has always shown that they do not elect their representatives for their agendas, but for their corruption and hatred to achieve the power that Nancy Pelosi has desperately used to destroy Donald Trump and who is a goddess for the Californian Democratic voters who re-elect her always knowing that she never fulfills her promises and the voters with low incomes or her elderly with a miserable social salary do not protest.

Nancy in San Francisco has our heroes on the streets as homeless, dirty, deteriorated, years ago instead of taking them off the streets and rehabilitating them they gave them syringes and drugs. What kind of person is this? Politician or opportunist? Everyone in Washington D.C., needs a time limit. So that they are not political burdens, making money like machinery in the corridors with information obtained in Washington D.C., Wall Street, the Pharmacopeia and much more and they all know it.

These are not slanders, they are realities. They are toxic politicians and voters do not realize it, or do not want the situation to change for a handful of wheat thrown at them from time to time. They are famous, and their earnings appear in the magazines, where they publish them and the people find out, and do not make objective comparisons with how much they came in to serve the people and how much they left. What benefits did the citizens obtain? The figures do not lie.

Just as the Democrats also know that Donald Trump is a great danger to them, or just as the Witch Hunt was to Christianity in the past. However, when Schiff described the call that Trump made to Zelensky, he made it clear that he was outlining "the essence of the president's communication" not his exact words. How poetic the blunt failed jurist came out! "The essence of the president's communication, not his exact words." The sense of smell, or the mind of the slanderer is wrong, not distinguishing the essence of honesty and justice, but confusing it with his own corruptions, is a sign that he should go to elementary school or receive treatment in the first mental hospital that Nikki Haley wants to be built and so do we.

Poor Adam Schiff, with his past traumas, because he could not be a movie actor, has made a script in his own way, inspired by the scum or the Democratic leadership behind that show, which they showed to the American people with the title The Plot Against Donald Trump Did Not Work in its first part, because in the second, the title is The Witch Hunt Accusing Donald Trump. How many ideas have occurred to them in Washington D.C., to not leave the path of corruption free and to be able to bathe quietly in the swamp of Washington D.C. Please find a professional Screenwriter to write your scripts!

With all due respect to Harvard, I don't know if Harvard teaches lawyers to be like Adam Schiff, to win cases. Why didn't Mr. Schiff investigate the FBI agent who lied blaming Donald Trump for what he never did? Why didn't he prosecute the hoax invented by Nancy Pelosi, Chuck Schumer, and many others? Do you know why? Because it was all false and with bad intentions.

Mr. Schiff, your background led you to the House Intelligence Committee, for having investigated in recent years how the Russians helped the 2016 election campaign, everything being a lie, and by stirring up the waters wanting to blame Trump, the dirt on all those involved with the Russians, who were Democrats, came out. The saddest thing is that the people saw what you did wrong. If you were as good as a lawyer, you should have investigated how you all enrich yourselves with the pharmaceutical companies, the corporations and the millionaires who donate to you to achieve your objectives, which American citizens know and among them you. It is not just like you said about Katie Porter.

The international community saw the same thing we saw, how the Democrats invent dramas to sustain themselves in power. What kind of lawyer are you who lost the case to remove Donald Trump from the presidency? Nancy Pelosi's epithets about you led you to legal failure. Congratulations to the University that turned you into a lawyer to defend Justice, and you did not succeed. For the sake of dignity, Adam Schiff should return his law degree and go to the carpentry shop or Hollywood. There he would be received with honors by Donald Trump's detractors and envious people.

Can we believe that the FBI agent you sentenced did not fabricate the same tricks that were used against Donald Trump? When laws are broken, anything happens.

The family of that agent sanctioned and investigated by you should reopen the case if he is still in prison, because whoever did what you did in Washington D.C., was political complicity, not a legal process based on the Constitution, respect and morality.

It is a shame that there are lawyers with mentalities like yours practicing the profession and interpreting our laws. The desire inherent to all corrupt people is to excel and be famous at the expense of the deviations of Justice. This is how we are living in our country with Presidents, judges, lawyers, politicians, and all kinds of situations, where the truth is covered up so that the people do not know it, and they do not comply with their lies and deceptions. We are already exhausted from hearing so many lies and legal inefficiencies.

The Department of Justice needs to wake up and start working replacing those who want to destroy Democracy. But if the head of the Department of Justice does not cooperate with justice, we are totally unarmed. To everyone in Washington D.C., do not forget that we have every right to express ourselves and not hide the negative things about others to look good, and that is called Freedom of Expression, the same that you use to destroy and defame people! But the people do not defame, they denounce, what you do wrong before our eyes. You are a political disgrace, but you are in the right place to run, because California is a branch of the Washington D.C., swamp, politically speaking.

Even if voters continue to go to the polls for the image of the candidate, and have not read the political agenda in how many injustices they have been involved in, we will continue on the path to not drain the Swamp.

Poor Mrs. Katie Porter would have to do magic to achieve what decent politicians want, to reform in Washington D.C., her party affected by the misery and violations of the laws, but until the Democrats meet and analyze the harmful impact caused first to their Political Party, to the prestige of all of them as public servants, and to the people in general, apologizing and stopping the persecutions and the 91 trials of Donald Trump in an effort to keep the party undefeated, they will have to bear the bad image left to the history of the United States, as the demolition of democracy.

Californian Democratic voters have distinguished themselves by their great political mistakes, but this can change. Changing political parties is not a disgrace, it is a challenge to keep democracy in place or wait for the party to restructure itself. Together with Republican voters we can at least lower the level of the putrid waters of the swamp. Together we can do a lot apart, we will not destroy each other. Not knowing how to choose your candidates by decency, but by their bad actions and well-sponsored propaganda, to impress them and following hate-filled crowds, ending up all in churches praising the Lord on Sundays and hating their neighbors, will hit rock bottom.

This is how communism works, no matter what the Democrats call it. Nancy Pelosi is a great example of these bad government situations and residents of California, where voters give them their votes without investigating them, these events will continue to occur. San Francisco converted into a Sanctuary City, buying the votes of Hispanics, but be aware of the consequences. Hispanics also think. But rest assured that: "Evil will not escape justice."

We will not lose the hope of working together DECENTLY AND IN HARMONY. It is not only a dream of many, but a reality that we all desire. Let us hope that the Democrats of Washington D.C., mainly you Mrs. Nancy Pelosi, and the repetitive elite Chuck Schumer, should not receive a single vote from their voters, since they have betrayed them from times past. It is time to save the country from all of you with your evil thoughts and actions. DEMOCRACY belongs to all of us, and if you decided to destroy it, we have already decided to save it. A grain of sand from each one, according to your efforts, will form "Mountains of social stability."

Leave your unbalanced attacks in the past. Retire to enjoy the illgotten money in the corridor negotiations in Washington D.C., rest, because with the age we already have, there is not much left. It is time to work in the present with justice, truth and respect. That would be truly wise!

By losing faith in government institutions, Democracy is destroyed, and the concepts of education, tolerance and admiration for the work they do are lost. Love begets love, and it is heartbreaking to live hating one another. These are not the values of the American people or of any civilized society, and a sacrifice by voting can give us the guidelines to follow.

CROCODILES IN THE SWAMP. CHUCK SCHUMER, NANCY PELOSI, HILARY CLINTON, AND MANY MORE BECAME THE INTELLECTUAL AUTHORS OF THE WITCH HUNT AGAINST DONALD J. TRUMP

You don't have to be religious if you don't want to, since the only one who can judge us is God, but since we are living in a world governed by Satan we have the right to denounce what is politically incorrect before our laws until the divine government arrives.

Proverb 14-15 "The naive believes everything they are told, but the prudent considers all their steps." The naive are the voters, but we prudent voters have the right to denounce political abuses looking for new horizons for our country and this is "measuring our steps well."

Nancy Pelosi, Senate Minority Leader Schumer, and a group of the country's representatives from the Democratic Party knelt to pay tribute to George Floyd, but never before when a black man has killed a police officer, regardless of race and color, they had such demonstrations of solidarity and that is when the American people, whether Democrat or Republican or Independent (I leave aside the communists because they are the social plague in any country, although the Americans approved that party for the sake of Democracy that today attacks them from every flank) must wake up.

They did not kneel for Floyd, but for the legislative package presented making police reforms. Those dozens of Democrats who accompanied them to the media circuses are the accomplices of those who want to kill the country from within, thinking that the American people ARE IGNORANT. It took them eight to nine minutes to cover the media scene, but they didn't have a single minute for the police who defend us, and are killed by blacks, Hispanics or other ethnicities. Here we see the great political hypocrisy of the Democrats in Washington D.C., where they are perpetrating PLANS to obtain the votes of the black communities. What these politicians don't know is that: blacks are a more intelligent group than they are, but with less power, and they don't let themselves be fooled. They are already tired, like all the groups that choose us for their political games.

Many blacks have abandoned the Democratic Party because it is not the one they joined decades ago, when the voter was respected, without dirty politics. The Democrats who lead us, with their bad actions such as lies, slander, and envy perpetrated against the 45th former President of the United States, have destroyed their own party, and they want to destroy our country and it will cost them, because we are going to defend it from both internal and foreign enemies, simply by voting and telling the truths that they hide in this historic 2024.

All Americans agree that police abuse should not be allowed, but we must educate the people that when the police stop, we must obey them, and criminals do not do so.

We have been criticizing these behaviors of criminals for years and no one listens. The American people agreed that police who kill for pleasure, or for negligence at work, should be punished, and the case of unarmed George Floyd was a criminal act by a Minneapolis officer, kneeling on his neck, but not by the police force that Nancy Pelosi wanted to take away monetary funds from everyone in the country, and then in San Francisco, California. The police saved her husband. Moral of fate. She destroying democracy with her dirty hammer, and the police in San Francisco, defending her husband from the one who had another hammer in his hand, trying to kill him. TWO HAMMERS IN ACTION. BOTH SINISTER.

We cannot forget that George Floyd, with respect to his family, was a criminal, but even though he was a criminal, no one has the right to take his life, but to bring him to justice, which is what the laws are for (although in these times they are not enforced by many corrupt Democratic judges and governors). When Pelosi said: "Do you see how long he had that knee on my neck"? Never before did she say "do you see how black people kill white people, police officers, and themselves in a minute"? This is the hypocrisy of the Democratic government that does not want to confront the truth.

Here is another hypocrisy of Schumer when he said, "It was very painful to even have an idea of how this man and so many "black" Americans have suffered for so long." He meant that they have suffered from police mistreatment and not from the disobedience of criminals. He missed that and kept quiet. Schumer forgot about white citizens, a violation of the Civil Rights Act and that is the racism and hypocrisy I am referring to. They have those positions because voters are apathetic and re-elect them, but even so, they must work for the people, and not for their dirty interests. Many white citizens have faced problems of all kinds under crime and police forces, as well as blacks, but it is necessary to say that only "blacks" have suffered those episodes to obtain the vote of the black communities, it is reckless and immoral, thinking that all blacks are ignorant. BidenKamala have an internal racism and politically demonstrate another. The conduct of the police is judged, but the crime that does not obey or comply with the laws, Hispanics, whites or blacks, is hidden and they cannot subdue them because they are murderers.

That is the cheap politics that we have with the Democrats in Washington D.C., who have not visited Chicago to see blacks and whites killing each other, and I am referring to the criminals, not to the decent people of the black and white race who live ashamed and terrified by what these liberal, fascist, communist, and ignorant criminal groups do in our communities, affecting us all.

Many black and white mothers have lost their children in Chicago, where Obama came from, and crime still continues to take over the streets and they keep quiet about it, and they never knelt down or did anything to end that street pain. Who did they want to impress by paying homage to George Floyd?

His memory and his family, who are not guilty of his crimes, must be defended and respected. What is unacceptable is that Nancy Pelosi, Schumer and their puppets in Washington, D.C., used African scarves, sending a separatist message to the blacks they "defended" by telling them "you are African blacks, not Americans." Do you see what the prefix "Afro" causes? It is the one that has connotations with slavery when they were sold to slave traders. Not to the American blacks born in this territory, and from Washington, D.C., they are still discriminated against by making it seem like they are defending them. If Martin Luther King lived in this time, he would say again "This country is crazy."

That was an insult to the black American communities. They should all have worn the American flag scarf, a symbol of respect and unity, defending black Americans, wherever they came from, all with the same rights and duties. Although if there is something that is violated in our country, it is the codes for the American Flag. The message was so hypocritically subliminal that when we saw them on TV, we wanted to become Fairy Godmothers, changing their scarves for the colors of our flag, in equality and solidarity with just causes, but the cheap hypocrisy they used impressed the generous American people, who see images, but do not see the purpose. We all sin in the same way. We have to see the reality to fight it. Through a broad legislative package, they orchestrated the separation of black Americans and Africans through the media, which included several proposals from the Congressional Black Caucus, among many others, the prohibition of the use of chokeholds, and the use of a national database to track police misconduct, but they forgot about the database to track black crime, and any ethnic group that wants to destroy the country and its laws.

We should tell the Democrats that in First Corinthians chapter 10: verses 23 and 24 they must apply these biblical rules to American society.

23: All things are permitted, but not all things are beneficial. All things are permitted, but not all things are edifying. 24 Let no one seek his own benefit, but that of others. As a people we have the duty to criticize, participate and work together for a common good, the prosperity and freedom of the United States, but not by keeping quiet about what happens, because then we would be accomplices of political outrages.

Let the Democrats remember that we cannot judge each other, but we can work honestly for a common goal. Not to kill our own country. As Romans 14:10 says, "But why do you judge your brother?" 149 They wanted to destroy the 45th President of the United States who worked for the people for free, something they have never done. Or why do you also despise your brother? They despised, slandered, and invented lawsuits of all shapes and colors, to destroy the President who denounced government corruption, and they forgot that in the end we will be together as this verse says. "For we will all stand before the judgment seat of God." And how much it is needed, especially for corrupt judges, lawyers, and prosecutors.

To the Democrats we say in Ephesians 5:15,16 "So be very careful not to behave like fools, but like wise, making the most of the time, because the days are evil." And we confirm, yes, the days will be bad for all of them when the American people forget about the political parties and analyze which candidates offer more reasons and opportunities for DEVELOPMENT to support them in governing our country, since for more than four decades they have not done anything sustainable to give them the vote again and I am referring to the Democrats, who have been in Washington D.C., for that long making their own money.

Just as there were irregularities in the presidential vote story and they did not want to investigate, similar episodes will continue to occur. The people have the vote, let them use it wisely. Deuteronomy 32:29 If only they were wise! They would reflect on all this. They would think about how it will end. God has the wisdom to tell us what is right and what is wrong. We the people, with earthly laws, also have the right to help God with the terrible burden, denouncing the bad situations in which our government institutions are.

In Romans, Jehovah (although many do not like that name and continually change it tells us: "Welcome the one who has weaknesses in his faith, but do not judge matters of differences of opinion." Therefore, both Democrats and Republicans as a people, we respect religious, political and social differences, but we all have a common right, and it is to criticize the bad things of both political leaders looking for better situations for a common good, which is our country, and to identify the lies, slander, and political filth to denounce them because we are not yet living in Paradise. Bottom of Form

I have received all the emails that Nancy Pelosi and her team send to their candidates, I intended to delete them, but I reflected because you have to know the enemy before judging him, and I present them to all readers. They are boring but you need to see how they poison with hate.

NANCY PELOSI EMAILS. THEY ARE NOT IN SEQUENCE OF ARRIVALS.

This was one of the first. Another new email. Nancy asks for help to continue lying.

Alila, I need your comments as soon as possible! That is why I am launching my FIRST Election Priorities Survey of the year, and I personally selected you to be one of the FIRST to take my survey, share your ideas with me, and help me build an UNBEATABLE Democratic strategy. I cannot overstate how much I rely on your comments in these first vital days to shape our plan and help lead the Democrats to a historic victory. (Of course it's going to be historic)

I need 50,000 of my top supporters to complete my survey to get an accurate sample size, OVERCOME the Republicans' plot to expand their majority, and TAKE BACK the House for our Democrats. Will it take you 30 seconds to complete my Election Priorities Survey before midnight? This means a lot to me.

Alila, I'm launching my FIRST Election Priorities Survey! I can't tell you how much I rely on your feedback to OUTRAGE Republicans and lead Democrats to victory during this critical chapter in our country's history. I've personally selected you to be one of the first to take my Election Priorities Survey and help me shape the Democrats' path to victory. Can I count on you to take my survey before midnight? I need 50,000 of my top supporters to share their insights to help me get an accurate sample size and help me build an unbeatable Democratic strategy. This is the most crucial election year of our lifetimes and I know Democrats cannot succeed unless they have a seat at the table. I count on your feedback more than you know. Name: Alila Barreras.

I don't say this lightly. We are on the brink of the most crucial election year of our lifetimes. So much has happened that I need to reach out to my best supporters and get your feedback on how we move 151 forward. That's why I just launched my FIRST Election Priorities Survey of the year. I personally selected you to be one of the FIRST to take my survey, share your insights with me, and help me build an UNBEATABLE Democratic strategy. I cannot overstate how much I rely on your feedback in these vital early days to OVERCOME the Republicans' plot to expand their majority and ensure we restore our Democratic Trifecta. I need 50,000 responses by midnight to get an accurate sample size. Will you complete my survey by midnight? I need your feedback to be among the first I hear from. Democrats shocked the nation and ended a Republican "red wave" in the midterm elections. But now Republicans are plotting their revenge to DEFEAT our Democrats in the next election and exert ALL power over us. As you read this, they are raising millions to expand their majority. They are threatening our Democrats for simply doing their jobs. They are spreading hate, lies, and division to sabotage us. And they are conspiring with the former president to take back all power and destroy the lives of millions.

Hear me loud and clear: I will not allow Republicans to expand their majority and regain full power if it is the last thing I do, but I absolutely need them to have a seat at the table to ensure a Democratic victory. I need 50,000 of my best Democrats to take my FIRST Election Priorities Survey of the year, share their opinions with me, and help our Democrats during this critical election year. I can't tell you how much that would mean to me. I look forward to reading your responses!

ALILA'S EMAIL RESPONSE

Simple: Nancy Pelosi. The answer of any citizen and mine is that for so many decades you, Nancy Pelosi, Chuck Schumer and Adam Schiff, the Clintons, the Obamas, and the Bidens and all those who have practiced bad practices in Washington D.C., destroying democracy with lies, political stories at election time, have already tired the American people, specifically us Hispanics, homosexuals and blacks who always use us for their political campaigns. (Although Biden in his administration has demonstrated reverse racism, and we all know that he has done it hypocritically. We do not forget that he chose his vice president because she is a woman and black and not because she is intelligent.) I repeat this as many times as necessary because these events are quickly forgotten. A very clear message for whoever wants to interpret it.

It is time to vote for other politicians giving them the opportunities that we will all see in the following years, no matter if they are Democrats, from other parties or Republicans. That is Democracy, but seeing all the bad things the Democratic Party has done in order to destroy that same Democracy, they are going to have to think seriously about it.

According to Nancy Pelosi, the Republicans are spreading hate, lies and division to sabotage them. Those are her words. Have you ever known of a case in which the Republicans have wanted to remove a Democratic candidate from the ballot or threatened to do so? That they want to take away the people's right to vote? Who has such extraordinary persecution in this era full of hate, lies, and divisions among Americans, that does not come from the Democrats? The trials that were carried out against Donald Trump while he was exercising his presidential mandate were with the clear and direct intention of removing him from the presidency at any cost. Did any

Republican make a plot to persecute Bill Clinton and Hilary? To persecute Obama and take away everyone's immunity?

UNCONSTITUTIONAL PERSECUTIONS ARE MADE BY THE DEMOCRATS. Seen and proven with the persecution of Donald Trump, and many of his followers.

How can Nancy Pelosi say that the Republicans are based on lies, hatred and much more, if it is not with the purpose of continuing to use power to harm the citizens, as we have already seen. The Democrats have no respect for themselves, destroying the party that the American people chose as good, to be represented in their government.

Upon receiving these emails from Nancy Pelosi's campaign, fortunately arrived on my computer, when reading them, hundreds of questions arose that cannot all be answered or written in this book. The first one that occurred to me was Why didn't you make all these promises a reality before 2024?

Nancy Pelosi's Plan.

"Reducing Costs for Families. Reducing Prescription Drug Costs that Save Lives. Creating Well-Paid Jobs. Protecting Medicare and Social Security. Supporting Comprehensive Immigration Reform. Increase Funding for Public Education. Make Higher Education More Affordable. Fight the Climate Crisis. Defend and Protect LGBTQ People. Introduce Common Sense Gun Safety Legislation. Support Our Veterans."

Immigration. Our laws have been violated by all of you, allowing 10 million illegals to cross our borders seeking the votes of their relatives. Medicines. Their prices are very high, which we cannot pay after we run out of the budget that the insurance companies give us. Jobs. They do not create jobs, they give bonuses and aid for social assistance, leaving out illegal Mexicans for the sake of the 10 million who came in, giving them monetary aid and the right to everything. Medicare is being scammed in all states by medical institutions and by criminals as well. Funding for education. What education? The one that the Democratic governors want to impose, violating the rights of children and parents? The climate crisis is the best invention to steal the people's money, or embezzle it, which is almost the same thing. Defending homosexuals and all those included in those groups, leaving out prostitutes who also deserve a place in the society that you want to defend. Weapons? That is the first thing that communists take away from the people. Put down your weapons as the Constitution says, which you all violate daily because in your eagerness to enrich yourself, you have not had time to read it.

Amendment II Being necessary for the security of a free State a well-organized Militia, the right of the people to keep and bear arms shall not be restricted. The greatest shamelessness of yours Nancy Pelosi, is to speak in this 2024 about the veterans in your city of San Francisco (your city) and throughout California, our veterans, whether due to drug addiction, mental illness, etc., you have them on the streets full of filth, lice, bedbugs, without having helped them recover, giving them alcohol and drugs when you distributed the syringes. That was the help of you immoral Democrats not to find them a suitable location.

Naturally, never in those promises has she proposed anything so that the elderly, both Democrats and any other political party, have more monetary resources on the misery that the American people receive after so many years of work. (I am or we are committed to ensuring that the American working people receive what they need to live on before sending our dollars abroad.) Those who have no common sense are all of you and that was my first thought. The Veterans in San Francisco (where you live) and throughout the state of California are the homeless in a developed country without help from the Democrats. Those who at one point offered their lives to save us all. The Republicans along with the Democrats will have to prioritize them in the new government when Donald Trump returns to the presidency.

Analyze how many years in power, and they did not do or solve anything at all, neither with medicine for the poor, nor with the entry of illegal immigrants into the country destabilizing public aid programs for settled groups, and for American citizens. All this that you want for 2024 is what all the Democrats should have done many decades ago. Why didn't you legalize the millions of Mexicans and other illegal groups in the country like a Republican Ronald Reagan did before allowing the wave of more than 10 million illegals entering through open borders?

Why didn't you give Mexicans illegally living in the US for decades even a parole that would have helped them work, receive public aid, and integrate into the American system like you have done now? The motto of all of you Democrats in Washington D.C., was Open Borders! The consequences are what we have seen in the Biden-Kamala government and all of you immoral accomplices.

Now, after so many years, and using us all as guinea pigs for their dirty, cheap politics, they want to transform the swamp into a blue lake with white swans, while below there are still lurking crocodiles that are all of you, in the company of Judges who perhaps studied under Affirmative Action SWIMMING TOGETHER. (Although many professionals who studied under this discriminatory program have turned out well. In the Lord's Vineyard there is everything, as the saying goes.

That is a fraud! Donald Trump worked very well for all of that, and you constantly persecuted him out of envy and hatred. Don't fool us, you only want money and power. You have to be honest, because for many decades the American people were waiting for all this that you and the other Democrats never did and now you are promising because the one who spoke about all this was Donald Trump and he always said that "America First." I have liked receiving your campaign emails, because I could know that you are not correct, neither in your plan that you offer, nor in your political life, and you criticize Donald Trump RUDELY, for the same thing that you and the others do behind the press. Supporting Donald Trump means Mrs. Pelosi, taking back the country that you have all destroyed with your deceptions and lies.

Another of your emails.

"I need to be perfectly clear, Alila. FIRST: Mike Johnson voted AGAINST reducing health care costs and prescription drug prices. THEN: Donald Trump promised to ABOLISH the Affordable Care Act. NOW: A new poll shows WHY we MUST take your threats seriously: Republicans are ahead by TWO points. Alila, I refuse to sit back and allow Republicans to take away health care from millions of Americans."

We know from your emails and from what has happened in the country that you have not sat back, that you are here and there, working on the plot to destroy Donald Trump, and that has meant something deeper than destroying a person. You and your "collaborators" have destroyed our morality, democracy, faith in political parties, faith in whether or not laws are followed. The same thing that corrupt communist millionaires do and possibly Soros is advising you, because your brain in so many years has shown us that your neurons do not work well for the people, but for yourself.

The thinking of millionaires varies on money and that is the basis. I hope that you help those of us who seek just causes because those actions will multiply your dollars (Cause or Effect) (Dharma and Karma) and in the process you will have the beautiful memory of having saved your country. When the Accountant tells you that you have to get rid of X dollars before fixing your taxes, donate it to just political or social causes. Don't do as they say Soros does. Destabilize countries and governments by increasing your billions now with Democratic help.

Mrs. Nancy Pelosi. You and all the Democrats in Washington D.C., for more than four decades did nothing for the health care of millions of Americans until Obama took power and made it a political issue. It is time to expose to the people the pros and cons of this program. Go to Appalachia for example and investigate why that population does not receive the health insurance you talk about and live in great social, medical and political needs. With transparency, people will understand the situation and you and the Republicans will work for that, because if everyone sets their salaries, establish your commitment to the people who put you all in Washington D.C.

Nancy continues.

"This is our most important battle since Democrats enacted the Affordable Care Act, because 40 million Americans would be deprived of their health care immediately, and life-saving care for 140 million Americans with pre-existing conditions is at stake. I will fight with everything I have to stop Republicans from winning this 157 election and repealing our health care, but I need to know that you are with me. If another 1,002 Democrats rush $15 before midnight to renew their Team Pelosi 2024 membership, we will outpace the Republicans, take back the House, and save our health care – again! Will you step up and make Republicans regret the day they attacked our health care?"

Shame on you, Mrs. Pelosi, that in your soul there is no peace, respect, and harmony, for everyone to work for us the people. In all the emails received from you and your employees who help you in this task of presenting what you did not do many years ago, hatred, division, dissatisfaction, and regret are reflected, for not having done something for the people, blaming now the Republicans for the lack of ideas of all of you.

We understand that your frustrations are justified, if you did not do it before, you will not do it now.

The constant attack in your emails of 2024 is not deciphered by journalists and is not presented to us, because all the corrupt ones are helping each other. (The correct press is excluded).

This unfortunately, everyone in power in the American Democratic government and their followers are the builders of the terrible evils that we have in this new society, and I say new, because we have never seen before what we have all witnessed nationally and internationally in the Biden-Kamala government, we did not even see it in the Obama-Biden government, that Witch Hunt against a former President. The Republicans never went after Hillary Clinton for all her bad actions wrapped up in her scandals about her foundation. They did not take away immunity from any president to devour him with civil lawsuits. You did, you are doing it and you want to continue doing it, but the American people are not made up of idiots, but of intelligent men and women, tired of all of you, and we will show you this in the next presidential elections.

Some for following the crowds, others for keeping quiet, thinking that nothing will affect them, others for the apathy caused by going out to vote, others for not reading the political platform that is offered to them and voting for the wrong candidate, and so on, our American people are on the edge of a deep precipice, and with just a little push from Soros, from the Democrats in Washington D.C., and from the Woke of all of you as allies, who for punishing a man, have punished the American citizens, we will quickly fall into the abyss. Democrats, left-wing radicals and criminals in the front line are all teetering on whether we fall off the cliff or not. No one will escape the fall if they do not act correctly.

ANOTHER ONE OF YOUR EMAILS.

"I am stunned Alila. The New York Times just reported that Trump raised a whopping $45 million (!!!) last quarter.

Alila, that is the most he has raised so far, I hate to alarm you, but this is the kind of money that could buy the presidency and destroy our democracy in the process. I will fight tooth and nail to ensure that this defeated, impeached, disgraced, election-denying thug and his band of Maga extremists never set foot in the halls of power again. But I can't do it alone."

Ms. Pelosi, your hate-filled words like Defeated, Dishonest, Election-denying Bully and His Band of Maga Extremists (we are the American citizens with the right to vote for any party we want), Do Not Set Foot in the Halls of Power. Thanks to all of your hatred, he has become the persecuted one, the one you try to kill to eliminate him from the halls that you defend, the one against whom you have made so many trials that it gives us the impression that with so much hatred and persecution you have plotted the murder. Why is the evidence not coming to light? Because you are waiting for tempers to calm down in order to give false answers. This is how the people think of all of you, regardless of which political party you profess. Have hatred and envy driven you mad, violating all possible laws?

Unfortunately, for your information, Mrs. Pelosi, the halls of Washington D.C., are not only yours, they belong to all of the citizens of this country, regardless of the political party we profess, even if we do not visit them. There are the politicians who must serve us, the people. Do not forget it.

1-DEFEATED BULLY: No, ma'am, Donald Trump has not been defeated, he is fighting with a two-edged sword to finish off all of you who deceive us daily to remain in power. Our enemy was defeated: The Pentagon confirmed that it carried out the attack against Quazem

Soleimani "on the orders of President" Donald Trump. (As far as we know, he only ordered the killing of our country's enemy, and therefore, all of you in the government have some responsibility for his death. Neither Donald Trump nor the Pentagon are isolated cases in our government.

2- ACCUSED. Yes, ma'am, as we all know, you were the first to accuse him several times while he was in power, because of your envy and fear. Trump has been accused to get him out of the way of the Democrats and you, along with Adam Schiff, an inept jurist, Chuck Schumer, part of the corrupt elite, along with the puppets they used to make the comedy more beautiful, forever stained his reputation with a bad script.

3- DISHONORED WHO DENIES THE ELECTIONS. Yes, there was electoral fraud and you all knew about it. You did not agree to count the votes democratically in front of the people, fearing that the great betrayal of democracy committed by you would come to light. Therefore, I denounce you all for being the intellectual authors of those street riots. and for the Capitol Riot, for not having been honest with the American people counting the electoral votes as happened with Al Gore and Bush and the other challenges that history tells and you without reading it. His responsibility was to take care of the Capitol and he did not do it despite Donald Trump offering him help.

4- HIS BAND OF MAGA EXTREMISTS. We are not extremists, Mrs. Pelosi, we are PATRIOTS defending our country from the internal enemies that you all are.

5- DO NOT RETURN TO THE CORRIDORS OF POWER. Do you know why they have made so many trials and accusations against Trump? Because that is how internal Democratic communism works. You are allied with the communists. In all communist countries there is only one leader, there cannot be more. Since the USA approved the communist party for the sake of Democracy, that is what it is collecting. Divisionism, lies, fraud, and illicit enrichment of their leaders who came in poor and are now millionaires, who have never been investigated by the FBI for their lies, slander, etc. Are only Democrats immune? In some cases they denounce and punish them to give the image of respect and justice, such as the case of "Jesse Jackson" when he defrauded his followers and their religious beliefs by appropriating their campaign money. He has not been the only cheater, but he should be the one punished by the Democratic authorities to give an example that they are not corrupt. In Latin American countries this could be translated as "the black man paid the price." In Hispanic street slang, this means that the black man is always discriminated against, being blamed for everything but in a jovial way or as a black joke without any intention of offending him. Cultural issues that many do not understand.

If they investigated honestly, we would be asking for Representatives, Senators, Congressmen, and Presidents, in the yellow pages or in the classifieds of the newspapers, and not in bipartisan elections. So that Donald Trump does not return to the halls, you with the participation of the Department of Justice accuse him, imprison him, with illegitimate evidence, defamations, bringing to the immoral forefront of all of you the trials that had been dismissed of women who sleep with anyone and then demand payments without providing evidence of rape, you violating the Constitution have fined Trump 450 million and even if you reduced the figure it is excessive according to the Constitution where you all wash your hands with the desire this time to say a nonsense that we all know, but it is inadequate. You will pay for your abuses one day and that day is November 5, 2024.

The important and certain thing is that the corrupt machinery is working perfectly well, but you will have your Achilles' Heel sooner than you think. We, the "plucked chickens of Stalin", have put the corrupt in power in their positions, but many are already changing political parties, distancing themselves from the dirt. If Abraham Lincoln, the first Republican president, did it, why not his voters?

Republicans and Democrats have enriched themselves with lobbying, using the people's money in the halls of Washington D.C. That you have all defiled. Donald Trump sweated them out of Washington D.C. Now it turns out that those guilty of the mismanagement of the electoral votes of 2020 were the Republicans. It is common when corruption is great, dead people appear, tried when they are innocent, they have to confess that they are guilty, fearing for their lives in prison, and they confess to what they really did not do, the same thing that happens in third world countries. That is how we are.

6-I CANNOT DO IT ALONE.

In that you are right. You have not been able to orchestrate the WITCH HUNT alone. For that you have to have intelligence, and they say that: George Soros has had to help you correct your mistakes, the Woke and the Obama gang. The billionaire is not a fool, he is not a fool, and he knows that with the WEAK DEMOCRATS he can achieve his objectives and lead you like CIRCUS PUPPETS, because you do not use common sense and he knows it. He has not made his billions for fun, he knows where to place them to destabilize countries, increasing his billions to buy weak corrupt people like all of you.

You have proven to be more corrupt than George Soros, because he is a naturalized immigrant and possibly did not feel the patriotic love that is expected. But you? Are you not ashamed? You have needed Governors, Senators, Representatives, Judges and a Cabal of Dishonest Destabilizers of American Democracy to be able to stop Donald Trump in those halls of Washington D.C., by constantly pursuing him as if he were a criminal. We even suspect that you want to assassinate him.

You are terrified (since you did not want to count the votes and it would have been the right thing to do, because then we would know if Donald Trump lied, or if you were the liars). That was an opportunity to demonstrate what you say about him. We would have known how much of a liar he is, that is why we know that you were the liars. Who lost their morals?

But the people knew the truth. The theft in the presidential elections that we have experienced in third world countries does not surprise us, because if they do it once, they will repeat it successively.

The plot began when Hilary lost the presidency, the trials came while the President was working and you were slacking off and by stealing the elections it was easy for you and the Witch Hunt continued with another poorly written script. A president was accused, his own government discrediting him, countless invented trials, incitements to political divisions in society, black and white judges together, not to create a bipartisan society but to divide us for the sake of a modern Ku Klux Klan.

The halls of Washington D.C., you have smeared them with... lies, blasphemies, slander, by not being able to find a single crime against Donald Trump while he was governing, and for many, that was an attack on power without weapons, to give him a good Coup d'état by removing him from the presidency, permitted under our Constitution. Something that they have not done to Joe Biden being guilty of violating our laws and of being sick to govern. Hypocrites!

This must be repeated until we are tired, because we are fed up with so many lies in all directions without any justice appearing for the Republicans. Although many of us do not like the laws of Interpretation, it is what we have in our Constitution and we must accept it and respect it or change it. But we will always remember the failures of all of you in those media trials, by not being able to prove that Donald Trump was guilty. Many of us consider that Justice run by corrupt people can die, and ours is in Intensive Care. It is time, Mrs. Pelosi, for the harsh words directed at Donald Trump to be said to the press, so that they do not only accuse Donald Trump of being rude, and you reform again, seeking the common good. The people can speak rudely as they want, but their leaders cannot, and they all do, that has always been the battle in all primary or presidential elections in the USA. Erase the word hate from your mind, because it is making you senile and much more, you are inciting the American people with your insane epithets to political division and loss of peace, something prohibited under the Constitution that is not read.

Something that Donald Trump is criticized for, but the press and your famous judges do not criticize, persecute or punish you. The fact that you are an old woman does not give you the right to use a rude and underhanded vocabulary hidden from the press, because in front of the television cameras you are one, and in your emails you are another. That is called HYPOCRISY Something that Donald Trump does not do. He says them no matter what, whether you criticize him or not. That is being HONEST and let all his followers and detractors know it. Mrs. Pelosi, they see you as a meek sheep, and you are a fearsome ravenous wolf.

Matthew 7:3-4

"You are all the same, you see the speck in another's eye and not in your own. What does it say in Matthew 7 15? "Beware of false prophets, who come to you disguised as sheep, but inwardly they are ravenous wolves." "You will know them by their fruits, for grapes are not gathered from thorns, nor figs from thistles. Likewise, every good tree bears good fruit, but a bad tree bears bad fruit."

We should not only apply it to religion, but to politics as well, although Jehovah does not like or accept politics. Never again make the sign of the cross, or visit churches, because time can take its toll on you, no matter which churches you visit. Repent and go back to your roots, and we will forgive you the money you earned working for the people.

Mrs. Pelosi. Donald Trump uses that vocabulary that you call offensive, to defend himself from the hatred of all of you, and from the corrupt press, which instead of destroying him as they want, make propaganda for him totally free, so that we see his qualities and your miseries.

That is the envy of all of you weaklings, to recognize that Donald Trump is in first place by both friends and enemies and you are in the bottom. You use it to offend and destroy him. (Dirty games of all political parties). The 45th president of the United States was very close to being shot in the public square of any state, simply for having shown us how big the swamp was.

You say that with the money raised by Donald Trump's campaign you can buy the elections. You don't need to buy them, Mrs. Pelosi, we "gave" them to you, and you "stole" them from us in 2020.

Your thoughts show what kind of people you Democrats are, and we don't charge or pay to vote, but since you think badly, you think we are all equal, and to be on an even keel, we can think that: you pay to find people who defame Donald Trump to publicly discredit him even with civil lawsuits saying that he was a rapist. All very well orchestrated. We all have the same right to think badly of one another.

NANCY PELOSI EMAILS.

"Here's my plan: I'm putting together a historic response — 5,000 Team Pelosi memberships before midnight — to completely outflank Trump, prove that every single democracy-loving American is ready to stop him and the Republicans, and deliver the most humiliating defeat of his lifetime.

I know we can send Trump a message he'll never forget. Democracy will win at the ballot box, but only if we usher in a momentous response. Will you plunk down $15 before midnight to renew your Team Pelosi membership and prove that Democrats are ready to keep Donald Trump and the MAGA extremists out of power and save our democracy, no matter the cost"?

NAME: ALILA BRRERAS ID: 119474065. PENDING

Mrs. Pelosi. We are not bands of extremists, we are kindly American Republican citizens who wish the best for the country, not like you who want power to fill your coffers and continue swimming in the swamp that Trump informed the American people. If you see your people, whether Democrats or Republicans or from other parties, as BANDS OF EXTREMISTS, how would others see the terrifying behavior, seeing how all of you since Donald Trump said that the government was a swamp came out to devour it? The trials that were brought against you, Chuck Schumer, Adam Schiff, an inept jurist, like many others, went down in the annals of American history as one of the most significant shames in the country.

They wanted to remove him from the White House at all costs, but since they could not, they worked on the supposed plot to steal the elections from him, even though the judges and all those involved say otherwise. According to your emails, you are the Democrats who destroy democracy and insult the people, whom you should serve, whoever we are. Your duty and that of all of you in Washington D.C., is to serve the citizens and because of hatred for one man you have forgotten that.

You are right, Mrs. Pelosi. Not only Trump will be able to forget the Witch Hunt of all of you politicians, judges, lawyers, the FBI department, the CIA, the Department of Justice who seem to be on sabbatical years and others in the international community who have seen and are happy about how the United States is falling apart, because of the evil and the money that you have all used for destruction, to make money in the stock market, as many of you have done with the information obtained in your positions and that is corruption. You talk a lot about the COST and we have already seen it. A country returning to racism, without justice, immoral, etc.

In the US, in the same state of California, it happened several years ago with the election of Loretta Sanchez, where dead and illegal voters appeared as voters, but because there was no money, the votes were not counted. The same for Democrats. If it happens on a smaller scale, and they placed her in her political position without counting the votes, what could we expect from the 2020 presidential elections?

Finally, at that time, they had to vote for a Democrat, Kamala Harris, in order to remove Loretta Sanchez, a Democrat who accepted these corruptions, from her chair. Many regretted having voted for Mrs. Harris. Whoever publicly declares that they would choose a woman and a black woman is violating the Civil Rights Act, discriminating against white women, and that is racism in the US, in China, and on any continent. The Civil Rights Act that the President of the nation, Joe Biden, himself, wiped his hands of. Pontius Pilate was small in history!

We all know how the Democrats work, but we are the opposing group, who do not consider ourselves sheep, nor plucked chickens, we are the chickens who still have our clothes intact, those who remind you of the truths. What are you complaining about?

What is now a big surprise for all Americans regardless of the political party they profess is that: The money raised by your employees for the electoral campaign and the donations from corrupt millionaires you have used to buy the presidency of which you accuse Donald Trump?

Those who are destroying democracy are not precisely the Republicans, not even the communist party that corrupts everything in its path, but this time it is you Democrats. Calling Donald Trump a BULLY is not only a form of vulgar expression on your part, it is an incitement to hatred and the merciless violence that you have against him and the defamation by criticizing him and you not recognizing his faults. **Mrs. Pelosi, you call Donald Trump a bully. We can tell you that Bill and Hilary Clinton have committed suicide, along with a long list of friends who have committed suicide.**

In third world countries they call them "**invisible murders.**" Thanks to Donald Trump, Hilary could not be the president of the USA. We would say that we are facing the greatest corruption of the Democrats, because the people say that the Clintons are BULLIES, as you say about Donald Trump. What happens is that we do not know that Trump's friends committed mass suicide as has happened with Clinton's friends. That they are bullies? There is no evidence. Can you file a complaint against Donald Trump and accuse him of being a bully? No, just as we, the people, cannot accuse the Clintons of the same, even if it is true. Do you see how everything is subjective? That is why your lawsuits when Donald Trump was working, you pursued them, because they were based on dirty tactics, gossip from yourselves, influenced by the resentment of Hilary Clinton for having lost the presidential elections in 2016. That was embarrassing for her, who said she was at the top of the polls, and she naively believed it from a press that during the presidential campaign worked for free for Donald Trump, discrediting him, and we supported him and won the presidency. Here I include the Clinton friends who all decided to commit suicide little by little. The list is long.

C. Victor Raiser II was Bill Clinton's national co-chairman of finance. He died in a plane crash along with his son and three others on July 30, 1992, during a fishing trip. Conspiracy theorists believe the crash was deliberately staged, but the National Transportation Safety Board ruled it an accident:

Mary Mahoney was a former White House intern who, in early summer 1997, was shot and killed during an attempted robbery inside the Starbucks in the Washington, D.C., suburb of Georgetown where Mahoney worked behind the counter. The robber entered the store and shot Mahoney after she tried to take the gun from him. He then shot two Starbucks employees and fled. However, conspiracy theorists believe Mahoney was killed on the orders of the Clintons.

Deputy White House counsel Vince Foster was found dead in Virginia's Fort Marcy Park outside Washington, D.C., on July 20, 1993. An autopsy determined he had been shot in the mouth, but no other injuries were found on his body. Five official inquiries ruled his death a suicide, but he remains the subject of conspiracy theories alleging that he was actually murdered by the Clintons for knowing too much.

The unsolved 2016 murder of Democratic National Committee staffer Seth Rich led conspiracy theorists to speculate that Hillary Clinton had arranged his death; the theory was based on a debunked, and later retracted, Fox News report that Rich had been responsible for Wikileaks' publication of Democratic National Committee emails during the 2016 US presidential campaign. Various elements of this theory have been promoted by Julian Assange and prominent rightwing figures such as Alex Jones, Newt Gingrich and Sean Hannity.

Jeffrey Epstein

Convicted sex offender Jeffrey Epstein, who was arrested on federal child sex trafficking charges, was found dead in his cell at the highsecurity Metropolitan Correctional Center in Manhattan on August 10, 2019. An official autopsy later declared the cause of death to be suicide by hanging. **Hangings that happen in prisons where coroners testify that they hanged themselves (based on damage to bones, muscles, etc.) If we go back to the MURDERS that the Ottoman Sultans ordered to kill with a rope that produced the same damage that coroners certify today. These suicides by hanging, look a lot like those of the Ottomans. What are the High Security prisons for? Were the cameras broken? Are they deceiving us? Will we ever know the truth? I bet not!**

His death gave rise to conspiracy theories that were retweeted on social media, especially related to Bill Clinton and former President Donald Trump. Hours after Epstein's death, Trump retweeted claims that Epstein's death was linked to Clinton, including the hashtag #ClintonBodyCount Political commentator Dinesh D'Souza attempted to use his time spent in a federal correctional facility to lend authority to the conspiracy theory that the Clintons were responsible for Epstein's death.

Christopher Sign

Reporter Christopher Sign broke the news of a meeting on June 27, 2016, on the tarmac at Phoenix's Sky Harbor, **between former President Bill Clinton and then-Attorney General Loretta Lynch.** The timing of the meeting came during the 2016 presidential election, when then-candidate Hilary Clinton was under scrutiny for the way she handled certain emails during her tenure as U.S. Secretary of State. **Sign was found dead in his Alabama home on June 12, 2021.** His death is being investigated as a suicide.

Several right-wing figures, including Lauren Boebert, Dan Bongino, and Charlie Kirk, as well as the pro-Trump cable news channel One America News Network, suggested that Sign had been killed by the Clintons.

Jovenel Moïse Haitian President Jovenel Moise was assassinated on July 7, 2021, when gunmen attacked his residence in Pèlerin 5, a district of Pétion-Ville. Martine Moíse, Haiti's first lady, was hospitalized for injuries sustained during the attack. Some right-wing conspiracy theorists have claimed that the Clintons were involved in Moïse's death, pointing to political controversies surrounding aid provided to Haiti by the Clinton Foundation, such as "hurricaneproof" classroom trailers that turned out to be structurally unsafe and permeated with formaldehyde. We all know from the news in Haiti that all that fundraising and foundation was a fraudulent tale by money lovers like the Clintons, but remember that: they have the immunity of being Democrats and that of vice president who has never been investigated and if they have been, it has only been simulations. 'other partners or friends of the Clintons who by chance commit suicide.

Jim McDougal, a Clinton financial partner in the real estate venture that led to the Whitewater scandal.

Edward Eugene Willey, Jr., a Clinton fundraiser whose wife, Kathleen Willey, alleged on CBS's 60 Minutes that Bill Clinton had sexually assaulted her on November 29, 1993.

Ron Brown, who served as Secretary of Commerce during President Bill Clinton's first term. He had previously been chairman of the Democratic National Committee. Brown had been investigated by an independent counsel over the Commerce Department trade mission controversy and was a material witness, who had been called to testify, in Judicial Watch's lawsuit against Clinton's Commerce Department.

Jerry Parks, Clinton's head of security during her 1992 presidential campaign, was killed on September 26, 1993, as he left a Mexican restaurant outside Little Rock, Arkansas, by a man in another car who shot him ten times with a 9mm pistol. Parks' son, Gary, claimed that his father compiled a secret file of Clinton's "sins," and that his father used the file to try to blackmail the Clinton campaign.

Jean-Luc Brunel, suspected of involvement in a global pedophile ring organised by Epstein, died by suicide in prison before going to trial on 19 February 2022. Senator Ted Cruz attempted to link Brunel's death to the Clintons by asking: "Does anyone know where Hilary was this weekend? Maybe a black-humoured binge.

Mark Middleton, an Arkansas business leader, mutual friend of Bill Clinton and Jeffrey Epstein, and former CFO of Clinton's presidential campaign and later Clinton's special assistant, was found dead hanging from a tree thirty miles from his home with a shotgun wound to the chest, with no weapon at the scene. The coroner's report ruled the death a suicide even though he was tied to a tree and no weapon was found near the body. It was disrespectful to the family of the deceased. How could he have tied himself to the tree while dead if he was hanging? This is how he was found according to the coroner "tied to a tree" Is it the coroner's fault or the journalist's fault? Who wrote this news about the murder, sorry suicide? We have to invoke the spirit of Agatha Christie to understand the situation.

What kind of detectives do we have? This has been the most disrespectful suicide that the cover-up detectives or the journalist have reported to us. With so many friends dead by suicide and all involved in the Clintons' lives, it was about time they were investigated at least to ask them why their friends commit suicide? Suicides are not common, murders are. The murderer Fidel Castro said in an interview that he had killed many, but when the first one is killed, the other faces are not memorable. Perhaps many in the USA are experiencing the same thing.

So many questions arise that will never have answers for the American people. We will continue asking to see if someone can answer them from the Departments of Justice. Should we clean up the Department of Justice or fire the forensic experts? In my personal opinion yes. When Donald Trump wins, please clean up the entire Department of Justice. They are all corrupt.

Madam Pelosi, I have not been able to find any friends of Donald Trump who have committed mass suicide like the Clintons' friends have. But I did find that Donald Trump was a friend of Jeffrey Epstein and that the two had been separated for over a decade. Why? I don't know. The journalists who have commented on this case don't say so. What I know is that Jeffrey Epstein donated money to Hilary Clinton's campaign in 2008 and was one of the largest donors and was a Democrat. They say that Jeffrey flew Bill Clinton on his private jet lined with ermine fur on at least seven trips around the world. Other friends of Epstein include Hollywood stars Dustin Hoffman, Alec Baldwin, Woody Allen, Phil Collins and journalists George Stephanopoulos, former Chief of Staff to Bill Clinton, Charlie Rose, Sarah Fergunson, Duchess of York, ex-wife of Prince Andrew, rock singer and widow of Nirvana frontman Kurt Cobain, Courtney Love and journalist Katie Couric. I believe that having been a friend of a character like this man has nothing to do with being involved if it is not officially proven. The FBI is investigating but if the majority are Democrats the case is closed. The FBI no longer has the power to dismantle the big characters involved in the "friendships of Jeffrey Epstein". There are many of them, powerful and united in misfortunes, it is assumed that they will not be very fond of unraveling the skein by adding more data to the FBI.

Mrs. Pelosi, do not say again that Donald Trump is a BULLY. They wanted to assassinate Trump and the plan was so bad that the entire population has made deductions and they all point to you in Washington D.C. Why are the Democrats losing their common sense? The Democratic people must wake up and hold you accountable electorally for involving them in their filth. Respect the Democrats who elected that political party when it was decent.

You are terrified that the Republicans will win and walk through the halls that you bought, allying themselves with traitors for money, as we all know because Soro's son has visited Biden many times and those visits are not to ask him how he feels mentally, but what will you do for the upcoming elections? We American citizens are not blind, deaf, and much less mute. Mrs. Pelosi. Naturally, Democrats do not accept the truth, and even more so if they have been appointed to their positions by Democratic presidents, or recommended by them.

As in the case of Mr. Douglas Schoen, Democrat, who described Trump's use of the MAGA phrase as "probably the most resonant campaign slogan in recent history," citing the majority of Americans who believed that the country was in decline. We did not believe it, but you do because of the immoralities of the lack of justice of the Democrats towards their people. Allow me to tell the illustrious Harvard lawyer Douglas Schoen, who should also have his bank accounts checked because he works in the hotbed of lobbying, that he was wrong when he said "that they believed that the country was in decline. Do you know why you do not see it that way? Because you must be a millionaire enriched in the Democratic corridors of Washington D.C., I may be wrong, but that is what "we the people" see and you do not want to see it.

The people are the ones who suffer the consequences, and yes, we know that the decline is imminent if you remain in power. Because you may not be a politician, but you are a "Harvard Democrat lawyer", we see the immense decline that you all have caused. Is Harvard Law School sponsored by communism by any chance? Or is it sponsored by Soros? Or is it sponsored by social shamelessness? Because many lawyers come out who scare us with their negativity, believing that all American citizens are idiots, and they are the intelligent ones. Ego is destructive for these Harvard students. They should be involved with social studies so that they learn and develop social human ideas etc. Obama also came out of there.

From there came Ted Cruz with Honors and many others who behave in accordance with the laws they must apply, and are decent people. What has happened to the Democratic lawyers from Harvard? So is it true that they are corrupt communist Democrats? If Mr. Schoen does not see it, he is unfortunately blind or does not want to recognize it, because he is not affected by the swamp. Many have wanted to destroy Donald Trump but they are destroying themselves.

THESE ARE HER WORDS Nancy Pelosi: Will you rush $15 before midnight to renew your Pelosi team membership and show that the Democrats are ready to keep Donald Trump and the MAGA extremists out of power and save our democracy, no matter the cost?

Answer: You are not saving democracy, but the mafia, using power by allying yourself with Soros and the millionaires who support him by hating Donald Trump, for not wanting to bring his big businesses here and not in China or any other country to employ the American people. If there is a very high cost and you ask us to act "REGARDLESS OF THE COST".

The cost we will have to pay if you win is not having democracy, nor constitutional rights for parents over their children, our greatest effort to unmask you, because the school districts where the Democrats operate take them away by giving them to politicians and teachers, who remain silent even though they know that what they do is wrong, deforming the minds of our children with brainwashing (which is a fact) and all of them impassive to the shamelessness of all of you. Teachers need their jobs and cannot oppose. They censor those who denounce them on the radio, they persecute individuals who are friends of Donald Trump, such as Rudy Giuliani and many others, and tomorrow they do it to the general population, as communism and its totalitarian system do. We do not accept the cost.

They have done it with the slogan of tolerance towards the gay community, but they do not teach them that there are other groups marginalized by society that need tolerance and they are the street prostitutes, because those of the mafia of the pornographic industry in our country that you govern, "do not persecute it, but rather support it, demonstrating how intolerant they are." I repeat it so that it works and you realize that: the word tolerance is infinite if its concept is not well specified.

The cost that you do not care about, Mrs. Pelosi, to win elections, the people do care about. The cost is very high, when our police are tried for killing criminals, (except when the police kill out of sadism or irresponsibility as in the case of George Floyd) and others who have died similarly. The police cannot defend themselves by preserving their lives, and the criminal is acquitted by the judges of you corrupt Democrats, who are in power allowing everything immoral.

Of course there is a cost, and it is very high, and we do not want it that way. We want Justice for all. We see police officers prosecuted for fighting crime and the violence of our criminals. For the Democratic Judges, it is better to imprison the police officer than the criminal. If the criminal is black, it is a problem, if the criminal is white, there is no problem, they imprison him. That is racism.

That is common in this era of abuse and lack of respect for citizens by those who dominate power. At least the last thing we American citizens will do is unite to save our country from so much political corruption, and this is more in its Democratic ranks than in those of the Republicans. Are we heading towards the abyss or not?

With this purpose I publish this book whether it is accepted or not, but at least it will remain as a special gift to the new generations. Even if one day at a yard sale they buy it for two cents or give it away for free to any curious young student and then they will read it with pleasure, remembering what their parents must have told them about this dirty and undemocratic time.

The Democrats do not want to recognize that they were involved in electoral fraud. Fine, they won, but what good has it done them? They have left a trail of injustices never seen before in any other administration. Our democracy collapsed in the hands of all of you, when you created the Witch Hunt. You do not tell me any more stories, because my experiences living with the communists do not allow it. Look for those who want to continue being the plucked hen of Stalin's metaphor or the flock of sheep that you command, as happened when all women had to dress in the color that you pointed out to them while entering the session. Ethics?

That was ridiculous, because history treasures conditions such as a people dressing in a color in order to protest their own government. Not the government protesting against its own government. You are here to work, negotiate, converse, and follow the rules all together for the common good, not separately as you dictate with your hammer.

The international movement "Women in Black" was born on January 9, 1988. We all know that the Women in Black were the Palestinians who protested against Israel, and always attacked them with stones, firecrackers, and the bad guy is Israel when it defends itself. And not Palestine, who are the ones who attack them. The Women in White were the Cuban activists protesting the abuses of the corrupt communists committed against their relatives in Cuba. To whom you join.

Not to protest massively in the Chamber, when they decided to dress in a certain color all the same, without knowing what that decision meant. What we do not understand is that you, Nancy, did not differentiate one passage from another. All those women in black or white were protesting the injustices they were defending, whether the Palestinians were wrong or not, but they were people of the population, not members of the government. The government is there to solve problems, and you Democrats create them.

If Nancy Pelosi with her costumes of different colors, when discussing issues that they did not like, protested by dressing like that, it means that the House of Representatives, its female members, were against their own government, and they called media attention in that way, along with the male members who, even if they did not dress in the same colors, supported them. Where was the ethics committee? Nobody follows the laws. Not the president, nor those who follow him. When Biden was giving his speech on 3/08/2024, these criticisms of Marjorie Taylor Greene happened.

The criticisms made by the Democrats and the Ethics Committee about her clothing were ridiculous and partially correct. For

Republican Marjorie Taylor Greene, there are rules, for Democrat Nancy Pelosi, there are none by the Ethics Committee itself. Hatred, discrimination, or irresponsibility, of those who use the laws to attack Republican citizens in a war without quarter, to defend not the American people, but their own monetary interests. Power. And if the people do not know it, let the politicians who receive a salary publish it to learn correctly what happens in our government.

I do not know the policy, nor the ethical rules of the Committee that prohibit wearing clothes that are related to politics while staying in those places. The clothes worn by Mrs. Marjorie Taylor Greene were considered violations and disrespect by the Democrats. She used the same right that Nancy Pelosi had when protesting Donald Trump's policy while working for the same government, and the Ethics Committee did not intervene, nor did it when she furiously tore up the president's speech in the presence of all the members of different political parties in the room, demonstrating a lack of control over her emotions, a lack of respect for a president elected by the people, hatred, divisionism, and finally, a lack of respect for herself in order to stay in power. The community of international leaders was speechless. Did Nancy Pelosi go crazy to stay in power?

The Ethics Committee did not intervene because it only follows the rules for Republicans. Democrats are exempt from them, as is the case in the courts.

In the past, Nancy Pelosi dressed in the same colors, she and her members, the women of the House of Representatives in full session as political protests against Donald Trump and his government, making plots instead of working properly. That is a betrayal of their patriotic principles. It seems to me that the Ethics Committee should be fair to everyone. According to the House Ethics Committee, it prohibits the use of official resources for campaign purposes and includes House buildings, chambers and offices as official resources. "Therefore, as a general rule, they cannot be used for campaign or political activities.

Our questions are: Why did this Committee accept that Nancy Pelosi all women wear the same colors in their clothing as a political protest in the session against Donald Trump in the places that are there to solve the problems of the people, not to make politics against the president that they must respect? Because the ethics committee is Democratic and if there are some Republicans, then they are the traitors that every group can have.

This happened several times. Hypocrisy or confusion? Politicians are there to solve problems, not to create them. Why can't we the people protest and tell them the great truths, whether written or verbal, to all of them in that same House where Alexandria Ocasio-Cortez, who is known as AOC, is a communist politician and activist, she has been serving the Democratic Party since 2019. She represents New York 14th. Ocasio came in criticizing the rich, and in a short time she wants a millionaire boyfriend who is fine, young and pretty and deserves it if he is like her, but she should not lie to us talking about the proletariat, because the proletariat and the millionaires are not related. The millions are related in democracy.

Has the FBI so honest investigated her? Can you imagine when she is three or four decades old, because of the unwary voters letting her get rich at the expense of the people and their donations? Activism is a race to wealth. They know many eminent idiots.

This means that all of them who obeyed by dressing in black or other colors but all the same, instead of looking for correct solutions for the American people, for which they are paid, regardless of our political parties, protested in full, against their own government, belonging not to a political party, but to the metaphor of Stalin or to Nancy Pelosi's flock of sheep. That is poisoning the soul of others. These are the Democratic members who do not defend the House of Representatives, they just use it. That was the clear concept of all dressing the same when they were in session against Donald Trump, except that the Ethics Committee was at the bar around the corner, celebrating the Democrats' lack of respect and ethics. Are they all the same?

Did anyone see Donald Trump take over the Capitol? Did anyone see Donald Trump with the American flag leading the demonstration or the riot at the Capitol on January 6th? No, but that is what the Democrats have declared to all of us. Donald Trump asked for the votes to be counted and for all the irregularities that those who handled the votes made to be seen and he was perfectly within his rights to request it.

The same thing that happened with Al Gore and J Bush, counting the votes properly for the sake of political democracy, but this time after the attempt to overthrow Donald Trump while he was governed by the Democratic curia and the trials where they perjured themselves by lying and receiving no legal consequences, demonstrated how deep the swamp is, and how many crocodiles live in it. January 6th was the perfect occasion to further undermine American democracy. That day the concept was born internationally and with evidence of how we are politically crumbling. That shows the international community that we are really cowards, instead of brave. In reality, our government failed by not counting the votes and they are responsible for what happened on January 6th.

It is time to clean Washington D.C., of the scourge that has infested it for many decades, because the swamp was not only made by Bill Clinton or Obama. The crocodiles were already growing in the putrid waters of Washington D.C., and they all took a good dip in it together. So many Republicans with their betrayals of the party, approving situations and programs according to their interests, not the interests of the people and their party, and all together they are responsible for the current political swamp.

It is we, the voters, who have the responsibility to save our democracy and analyze when we should act and for which candidate we should do it. The injustices perpetrated by corrupt Democratic judges who when they take the case and persecute the individual say: "I'm going for Donald Trump" that is filth and lack of morals of those types of judges who should say: "I'm going for Justice and Truth" but we have seen how the Democrats do the same as the communists. They have betrayed themselves.

They do not accept the evidence of the accused to prove innocence, and they act alone in the accusations. Enough of so much shamelessness and political injustice! All those who contributed to dirtying the waters of the swamp have never been tried, but rather "investigated" to offer the people a decoy saying that there is justice, when in truth there is corruption. The only one who has been tried in a Witch Hunt has been the one who denounced the crocodiles of the swamp, and this is Donald Trump. The thing about Biden's son is to give the signal that they are fair, but those of us who know how the left works and corruption do not believe them. You do not have to be a Trumpist, you have to love this country that protects and shelters us despite so many moral and political miseries. "Trumpism" or "Trumpist" or whatever you want to call it, is synonymous with patriotism for those of us who love Truth and Justice.

We must be fair and use our brains, which are wonderful at archiving data. Data offered by the press, whether corrupt or not, and which we must analyze in order to choose the presidential candidate. 2024 is totally crucial for us to think without emotions, and to vote for whoever wants the best for this beautiful country. When we say God Bless America, we say it with devotion. Do I want the votes for Donald Trump? Yes, not because of fanaticism or gangs as Nancy Pelosi tells us, because we saw him work for four years doing the impossible to do well and he achieved many things in four years that the Democrats did not do in 40, while the lazy people of Washington D.C., entertained themselves by presenting them with lawsuit after lawsuit.

Proverb 14-15 says: 'The naive believes everything they are told, but the prudent measures well all their steps.'

In other Bibles it says: 'Anyone who is inexperienced puts faith in every word, but the shrewd considers his steps.'

We, the voters, are the naive ones, who believe all the politicians' well-argued lies. In these cases, unfortunately, the ones who have failed are the Democrats of Washington D.C., but the prudent voters also have the right to denounce them, seeking new horizons for our country, and this is done by prudently "measuring all their steps well."

How did Chuck Schumer (Democrat) earn his money? In 1995, when this gentleman was honest, he started working in Washington D.C., with the monetary amount of $310,000.00. By the year 2000, he had the sum of $770,000.00, which was going little by little. In the year 2005, he increased his money to 3 million. In the year 2010, he had 22 million. In 2015, his income continued to increase to 57 million. He will retire from the halls that made him rich in Washington D.C., with an approximate value of 81 million increased last 2023.

Possibly before he leaves, his current fortune will increase a little more. Does he belong to the people or to the elite that Mr. Chuck Schumer shamelessly mentions? What has he given to his voters? MISERIES IN NEW YORK. A beautiful title for the current reality after so many years his voters voted out of habit without analyzing it.

His Democratic voters in New York seem not to reason properly. According to the leader of the Democratic minority on his government website he says: "American families need a better deal." "They deserve the country to work for everyone again. Not just for the elite people and interests." "Today Democrats will begin to present a better deal to the American people."

Are they sorry to retire, or do they feel sorry for how poorly they have worked? By saying that the country should go back to work for everyone, it means that they have not worked for the people for a long time, worrying about their personal coffers. "Today the Democrats will begin to present them with a better deal. Why today and not always? Naturally, we must look at the pros and cons. Here is what Mr. Chuck Schumer, leader of the Democratic minority who is part of the country's elite, said. The lies are so great on the part of the Democratic politicians, that it is impossible to remain silent any longer.

His counterpart Mitch McConnell and Chuck Schumer have amassed their fortunes by occupying a powerful position in the government. With the help of some rich real estate magnates, Schumer was able to buy many properties at the right time and at the right price. He is like Alexandria Ocacio Cortez criticizing the rich and everyone wants to go the same way. It is good for the country to have many millionaires, but not to earn their millions from Washington D.C.

That's called Government Corruption. They say the median net worth of members of the United States Congress exceeded 1.1 million dollars. The riches accumulated in the halls of Washington

D.C., which Nancy Pelosi does not want Donald Trump to step on again, must be slippery from the riches accumulated by all of them.

Schumer has 10 luxury cars, he has bought plots of land in New York that were worth a million for $49,000. He is a skilled Democrat enriching himself day by day instead of giving his voters what they always promise when elections come and do not deliver, especially with the double standard of choosing blacks and Hispanics as their guinea pigs. He lies to all of you, his voters, while in all his years in the Senate he has used his position to enrich himself, forgetting about the elderly Democrats with low salaries, their miserable insurance, high prices on medicines, who instead of buying ELIQUIS (apixaban or XARELTO (rivaroxaban have to use the cheaper product like Warfarin (Coumadin and live in laboratories having their blood measured, and he says he works for the people, while his voters live like sardines in cans, crowded together, because they cannot have efficient homes with low rents. New York voters are blind, deaf and dumb. The big criminals are not only those on the streets, but those who walk through the hallowed halls of the Democrats in the swamp. They do not want to see or hold all these corrupt people in the swamp of Washington D.C., accountable, like many other Republicans who have seized power as well, to end their old age as millionaires and we the people in misery, because our money goes by the billions abroad and even to enemies like Palestine, Iran, etc.

The leader of the Democratic minority who says he will not work for the elite of the country is right, he does not work for the elite because he is part of it. He bought two luxury yachts with a 90% discount (corruption. The leader of the Democratic minority says: "American families need better treatment."

Yes, Mr. Schumer, you should stop using your position to enrich yourself like everyone else. "You deserve for the country to work for everyone again, not just for the elite people and special interests, which are all of you in power. Democrats and others. If you consider that the country is you, then as the Mexicans say in their street slang: "WE ARE SCREWED."

Yes, Mr. Schumer, no one knows that situation better than you because you have become that elite ruling and enriching yourself using the "special interests" you refer to. Now after working to enrich yourself in the position that the voters gave you, you want to work for the people and end up retiring to enjoy your fortune and your people in misery.

You say: "Today the Democrats will begin to present a better deal to the American people." Don't you think it's too late for that? You are a despicable person. Why didn't you present the American people with that better deal from the beginning? Not only have you been disingenuous, but a traitor to your own voters who elected you to set foot in the dirty halls of Washington D.C., again and again.

If the Democrats would wake up from their false romance with all of you, America would be the country it once was. The Democratic voters are not asked to do it for the Republicans (which would be an act of responsibility and I personally would like it (subjective). They would send a clear and forceful message to the Democratic Elite that lives in Washington D.C., in this 2024. They can look for the information in Forbes magazine, in several articles on the subject and if all these reports are false, then we will have to agree with Donald Trump on how corrupt the American press is along with the government. (Except those who keep journalism in its place). Let them declare how much they started working with and how much they left with or how much they currently have.

That would be honorable. Here the IRS authorities or anyone else, investigate the poor, fining them or fixing their fraud situations and Republicans like Donald Trump want to destroy them with the same thing that everyone else does and they do not report, but no Democrat has been monitored so that they do not enrich themselves illicitly. Let them say how much they earn, how much they came in with, and With how much they will leave the halls that will have to be rubbed with the product Chlorine to disinfect them, and to be clean as when all of them set foot when they were honest, but in the end corruption enveloped them by their own decision, and the sad thing is using the job that they should respect. This is where Stalin's metaphor of the Plucked Chicken comes in. It appears on the first page of this book. This is the famous information on his government Web page. The Mission. An Article Read On His Web.

He has the nerve to say that: The mission of the Democratic Party is to build a country in which workers know that there is someone with their best interest in mind. Too many families in the United States feel that the rules of the economy are against them. Special interests and lobbyists have power over too much in Washington from the rich spending unlimited amounts of money in secret to influence our elections to our tax code that helps corporations and the rich avoid paying taxes. If you are referring to Donald Trump who does not pay taxes as you all said, then look at what the IRS did fixing the disasters and tax evasions of President Biden's son, Hunter Biden. What you say was said by Donald Trump to Hilary Clinton that they have been responsible for those good or bad regulations that should have been fixed and they did not, because you all do the same thing.

Remember that the Clintons got rich with the same thing you say, the lobbying of the Pharmacopeia and you from the real estate companies from your work trenches. Why didn't all of you Democrats fix that? The economy is a disaster, go to Los Angeles to see miles and miles of tents, garbage and people all full of filth and bugs, abandoned by the state government, the so-called homeless and among them our veterans who are addicted or severely traumatized. To Chicago where they are murdered daily and they keep quiet so as not to alert the population, where are the Democrats? Poverty is obvious. Have you seen how New York is? In misery. Now invaded by illegal immigrants that you Democrats let pass without analyzing the damage to the citizens, your voters. The resources must be divided among them, because of the hatred that you all have towards a single man, harming the American people who are not responsible for the bad feelings of the Democratic politicians, nor for the fact that the economy is a disaster in the current mandate.

The hatred towards Donald Trump who opened his mouth to tell us the truth about how corrupt the swamp is has led us to this unbridled and corrupt system. You are really not politicians working for the USA, you are immoral liars working for Russia, which is to say working for communism or for some Secret Organization to destroy our country. Yes Mr. Schumer, the economy is against all the poor in the USA because of all the inept people starting with you. The authorities should investigate it.

Schumer continues. INSTEAD OF HAVING A GOVERNMENT THAT BENEFITS SPECIAL INTERESTS AND THE RICH. Democrats believe that government should work on behalf of the middle class and those struggling to get there. For too long, government has tilted the balance of the economy toward the rich, taking the burden off of them and putting it on the backs of working people. No more. Democrats believe that government should be on the side of working people and not those at the top.

Answer. At the Top are you, Mr. Chuck Schumer, Nancy Pelosi, and those who follow you in your Machiavellian lies, your companions wanting to get rich like you are and you are forgiven, because they all want to be at the top with you. I remind you that you must work for everyone, not for the middle class and the poor, but for the rich with whom you share your trips on luxury yachts and tell them that if they want to increase the capital, they should replace you all. You are a political disgrace!

Schumer. IT DOESN'T HAVE TO BE THIS WAY; WITH THE RIGHT PRIORITIES AND THE RIGHT VISION.' The Democrats know that the United States can have unprecedented economic growth, which produces better jobs, better wages and a better future. This is the biggest contrast between Democrats and Republicans. We believe that the best way to grow the economy is to grow and strengthen the middle class, instead of using the same tactics that have failed in the past.

Answer: It seems unbelievable that you did not read what the fool who wrote this to you, on his government website, has denounced. The Democrats have failed the people and their voters. The Democrats have crucified the Americans by letting in 10 million illegals when you, who are so good, did not give citizenship to Mexicans and Central Americans as a lower class in society, who have been in the country for many decades and their children do not know any other homeland. Eight years of a Clinton government, Democrat of Obama-Biden and now Biden Kamala, left out the parents of DACA students. You are extraordinary in what is done wrong, because you do not negotiate bipartisanly, but rather you destroy.

To strengthen misery, not the economy, you let in 10 million people to whom you owe the favor of having beaten Donald Trump who has always advocated closing the borders. Biden, your president, accuses you all the time repeating that the border crisis is Donald Trump's fault. You are the best actors in the circus, your performances are terrible, and whoever wants to see the bad circus performance, let him see it. Work and let us see the truths disguised on your Web. If they knew how to get rich in Washington D.C., they should learn how to solve the problems of the citizens.

Says Chuck Schumer. TODAY THE DEMOCRATS ARE OFFERING A BETTER DEAL THAT WILL FOCUS ON THREE GOALS.

Raise wages and incomes for American workers and create millions of better paying jobs. Our plan for a better deal starts by creating millions of good paying full time jobs, investing directly in infrastructure and prioritizing small businesses and entrepreneurs instead of giving tax cuts to special interests. We will limit unfair foreign trade and fight corporations that ship American jobs overseas. We will fight to ensure a living wage for all Americans and keep our promise to millions of workers who worked for a pension, Social Security and Medicare so that seniors can retire with dignity.

Answer. Bottom line Mr. Chuck, you are jealous because that was what Donald Trump was solving and you started to persecute him by creating the Witch Hunt that he is currently in. I think you should go to the country of El Salvador and ask Mr. President Nayib Bukele on your knees to give you the formula on how to get the country back on track. How to recreate the infrastructure that American criminals destroy every time a black person is killed by a white person, but not when a white person is killed by a black person. Limit foreign trade when you have sold the US to the Chinese? Do you agree with Donald Trump in bringing companies to the US so that the people have jobs? If you don't know, US retirees have to go to third world countries to live with their social security because here we are in misery. They have never included a decent salary for retirees in the annual budget. Soon we retirees will have to ask the president of El Salvador to give us citizenship and leave here, because the Democratic elite lives in a bubble and when they show their faces, it is to lie to us and tell how many millions they made while serving us. We want reunification with the people and the decent Democratic politicians, but you will sweep them away in the next elections.

Or VOTE FOR THE REPUBLICAN PARTY, WHICH IS THE HOPE OF RECOVERING THE USA. I do not defend Donald Trump, he has his good lawyers. I admire him for his resistance to give in, for working as he did and for free, something that we should all thank you for. I say, along with the others, with justice, how badly you are working, and how well he did by raising our economy, lowering unemployment among blacks and Hispanics (separatism of groups should end if we are all American citizens). Logic has also been lost or is on endless vacations. And much more. Democrats rob Democrats, Republicans or citizens of other political parties of their hopes for a better life.

As communism says: "All equal," except the elite that you maintain. Words that our Constitution also has and are not fulfilled.

Schumer. REDUCE COSTS FOR FAMILIES

We will offer a better deal that will lower the cost of prescription drugs and the cost of college or technical school. We will fight for families who find themselves with high monthly child care, credit card and cable bills. We will crack down on monopolies and the contracting out of economic power that has resulted in higher prices for consumers, workers and small businesses and ensure that Wall Street never again endangers Main Street.

Answer. Poetic, sir! Suppressing monopolies is communist. Helping the poor by giving them money like bonuses and public aid is not good economics. Democrats instead of creating jobs, create government assistance. This is not how you get ahead, and they steal the right of citizens to live better or be looked down upon by those who work and they don't. By those who have the food card and they don't, those who have housing assistance and they don't. It is a division of social classes, instead of fixing the economy for ALL. These are the promises of Stalin's metaphor to the mistreated people. They can raise wages as much as they want, and everything will be the same, when the merchants also raise the prices of their products.

This is a domino chain. It works that way for Democrats, but not for Republicans.

Schumer. BUILDING AN ECONOMY THAT GIVES WORKERS THE TOOLS THEY NEED TO SUCCEED IN THE 21ST CENTURY.

We are committed to giving all Americans, whether they have worked their entire lives or are just starting out, the opportunity to gain the skills, tools and knowledge to find a job or advance in their careers and live a better life. We will do this by offering new tax incentives to employers to invest in workers through training and education, and by making sure the rules of the economy support businesses that focus on long-term growth, rather than short-term growth.

We will make it a national priority to bring high-speed internet to every corner of the country and offer apprenticeships to millions of new workers. We will promote innovation, invest in advanced research, and ensure that startups and small businesses can compete and thrive.

Answer. At last, you and I agree on something! Investing in advanced research would be wonderful, because then we would investigate what happened to all of you Democrats, wanting to destroy your own country in all these past decades, and what happened after the 2024 elections.

Above all, that innovation sounds fantastic, because if you were to win the presidential elections we would be waiting for an intelligence chip to be put in the brains of all of you brainless people in Washington D.C. And Hollywood would be fighting over the scriptwriters who would write the scripts for the movie "Brainless Democrats Already Have Artificial Intelligence" in this way we would open a new era, because then instead of being Stalin's Plucked Chicken Voters, we would be "The Artificial Intelligence Addicts of Our Politicians". It sounds more academic, more educated, more professional, and technological. Although we prefer the natural intelligence of candidate Donald J. Trump, former 45th President of the USA. In memory of how well he worked in his last four years in the presidency. Schumer says: American families deserve better treatment so our country can work for everyone again, not just the elites and special interests.

Answer: Oh my God! Mr. Chuck Schumer needs a psychologist to give him intensive therapy, he has a problem with the elites and special interests. I would say he feels remorse for having reached the top of the elite and their special interests using his job. He should get help quickly, so he regrets what he did. Remorse is good but they will enjoy it after we get him out of Washington D.C.

Now he says: to advance our agenda, we are going to fight to give the government back to the people.

Answer: He himself confessed it, not me. That means that if he gives us the government back, it is because it was stolen without our authorization. And he continues with the problem of the millionaires and the special interest elites and perhaps their regrets. I think he feels remorse and regret, from when he entered his political work when he was young and was honest, he has created a trauma now that he is a millionaire and a participant in the Witch Hunt against Donald Trump, all belonging to the same elite. Of course, Trump's elite is the one that worked and sweated for millions. The difference is that Donald J. Trump worked privately, and became a multimillionaire or billionaire from his work, I am not saying if he did it right or wrong, but he did not offend voters with his money, as the Democratic elites have done. And Chuck Schumer made his millions using the halls of Washington D.C., together with his friend Nancy Pelosi and all the Democrats who did it. As the Americans say, "Don't fool me." And so on, you can continue reading because they repeated the same promises that are not fulfilled and more so now, with 10 million people illegally in the country. Plus 40,000 that are allowed to enter from Nicaragua, Venezuela, Cuba and Haiti. There are no more spaces, no more promises that are kept. They benefit some and not others.

Schumer continues. AMERICAN FAMILIES DESERVE A BETTER DEAL SO OUR COUNTRY CAN WORK AGAIN FOR EVERYONE, NOT JUST THE ELITES AND SPECIAL INTERESTS.

To advance our agenda, we will fight to return government to the people, eliminating the unlimited spending of corporations and billionaires, and reducing the power and influence of special interests and lobbyists in Washington.

Answer: They have already gotten rich and are planning to retire a millionaire, and now they don't want those who come next to do what they did. Remember when Trump won the first thing he did was shut down lobbying?

Chuck Schumer continues. From small towns to big cities, Democrats will fight for a better deal, resulting in higher wages, lower costs, and an economy that works for everyone.

Answers: They have been governing for several decades. The Appalachians have great poverty, in Los Angeles the filth is marginalizing the city with homeless people on the streets and for miles in an inhuman deterioration. That stigma persists and they have not been able to organize them in new houses, new lands etc., why don't they work for the people, but for their personal affairs? The Democratic governments are corrupt and do not solve problems, the gasoline is very expensive, the food is exorbitantly priced, the rents of the houses are high. The young people are not even Democrats who can become independent. The same promises of several past decades. The elderly with miserable salaries etc.

Schumer continues. In the days and weeks to come, we will propose bolder ideas to achieve our goal of reducing daily costs, filling and creating millions of new full-time and well-paid jobs with a diverse and trained workforce that has the tools they need to succeed in the 21st century.

Answer. Bravo, for such beautiful words, but all full of lies. Your tools rusted from having them lying around in the halls of Washington D.C. Obama had eight years and American life was like Julio Iglesias' song. "Everything stays the same." He left Washington D.C., a millionaire. Trump, who is the bad guy in the movie, but who you all envy internally, demonstrated, without being a politician, more things in four years than you have been promising for decades.

Schumer continues. Connecting America to high-speed internet.

Answer. With the low-speed internet, we have seen everything that you from Washington D.C., have done to kill Democracy and something more valuable than Democracy and we have just experienced it. When we elected Donald Trump to make changes, you attacked him with all your strength, simply because he told you the truth. Something that cannot be said in democratic times.

Schumer says. Cracking Down on foreign countries that manipulate our trade laws. Answer. You said it. Foreign countries manipulate our laws. Why don't you speak clearly? Why don't you say: we have manipulated our laws in every way? You are the ones who have to put high taxes on foreign products and you spend your time selling to China everything that they ask to buy and what they send us. What taxes did you put on them?

Schumer continues to make the same promises that are no longer believed, seeing that for more than several decades they have not fulfilled them. Are they going to fulfill them now in 2024 by seeking re-election or retiring to enjoy the money they made while serving the people?

Connecting America to high-speed Internet.

Cracking Down on foreign countries that manipulate our trade laws.

Keeping our promise of pensions and a secure retirement. (In 40 years they have not done so.)

Giving workers the freedom to negotiate

And much more. Analyze whether the vote for these wealthy elite in Washington D.C. Can they be believed? We all wonder why they did not do what they are promising now to win the 2024 elections? We have been waiting for all that for several decades and they were broken promises. These are the politicians who govern us.

"The vote is stronger than the bullet." - Abraham Lincoln.

ADAM SCHIFF

Mrs. Nancy Pelosi chose Adam Schiff instead of Jerry Nadler, Chairman of the Judiciary Committee, to lead the impeachment process against Trump. It was not impeachment, it was a COUP D'ETAT disguised with our own laws.

Pelosi said: Schiff is "logical, linear, measured but forceful. Now we know after having lost the trials against Donald Trump, that Nancy Pelosi was wrong on everything. Adam Schiff was not logical, he was foolish to allow himself to be entangled in your fabricated lies. He was not measured because by saying that Donald Trump was a mobster or a corrupt politician, he showed that he was not a measured or ethical person. He was not forceful, because to be so he must work with Truth and Justice and he worked with gossip, from all of you basing your accusations on murmurs within the halls of Washington D.C., where the first persecution of Donald Trump was carried out along with the other Democrats and Republican traitors. Nancy Pelosi is an expert at making mistakes with the people. Who do they want to fool?

Donald Trump came out free of all the stains you smeared on him. Only a desperate man trying to win a trial demonstrated his inefficiency in his career and if we go beyond the conspiracy against Donald Trump, the Universities that graduate lawyers like Adam Schiff should withdraw his license until he takes classes on work ethics, where justice is involved. This bad behavior by Adam Schiff discredits his University and his classmates who graduated with him. His classmates will be less famous than him, but more honorable. Bad practice in any career should be addressed by an ethics committee and evaluate the consequences that this brings to the profession and the country in these cases.

Adam Schiff, desperate because he knew he would not win the case, said: "Americans will hear directly from dedicated and patriotic public officials how they realized that the foreign policy of the United States had been subverted to benefit the personal political interests of the president." Adam Schiff, the Democratic head of the investigation against the president of the United States, Donald Trump, should have stayed as an actor in Hollywood, since that was his dream, repeating the scripts of the Hollywood smart guys because the script that led to the media trial against Trump demoralized him as a lawyer, prosecutor, and actor by creating an incoherent script based on evil and not on justice.

This means that he only serves to muddy the Senate as well. (His new political aspiration) so that he lies every day to the skimmed chickens that follow him without investigating how he behaves. The vote is sacred and through it we can solve the problems by wisely and emotionlessly choosing those who will represent us in Washington D.C., regardless of color, race and religious beliefs, but if they all converge in honesty, so that all this never happens again.

They are not the only ones to blame, it is us who, in moments of hate, rage, or ignorance, become those famous "plucked chickens" – men and women – that all politicians are fascinated by. If the Senate gets there, the members will have to speak to Adam Schiff clearly and seriously, that at the first attempt at lies and dirt they will send him to the ethics college that many of them, including Bob Menendez, a lawyer, who studied at Rutgers University, need so much. Coincidentally, are they all Democrats? Senators who wish the best for the country and its people must begin to be scrutinized, and with this we give Jesus Christ a hand while he is still waiting. It seems that God is closer than we think, because Bob Menendez has already fallen. That is called "purge" in communism. They clean up what they can to create the image of good and just. Don't fool yourselves! As chairman of the Intelligence Committee, Mr. Schiff demonstrated in his failed plot against Donald Trump, by losing the trials in which everyone was involved, that they were not trustworthy to Democracy. What kind of Intelligence Committee we have in power!

They could not prove that Trump violated his oath of office and the law by seeking help from Ukraine for his 2020 re-election campaign. Trump's request for a "favor" in July to Ukrainian President Volodymyr Zelensky reflects "a typical scam by a mafia guy to a foreign leader," said Schiff. If Schiff calls the president to whom he owed respect a "mafia guy," what can citizens expect? Although citizens have reacted to all the chaos caused by the Democrats defending Democracy, Truth and Justice that they all want to destroy, we already feel exhausted. Adam Schiff is nothing more than a very weak lawyer or prosecutor. What could be said to him? If the Ethics Committee did not see this, it is because they are all accomplices from Washington D.C.

This is how a mob boss speaks: "What have you done for us? Now tell us Mr. Schiff, what have you done for us? If not enrich yourselves, defraud American justice, lie, conjure up plots like witches, to stop him and they could not achieve it." They proved that the plot was genuine, but without evidence, because they could not accuse President Donald Trump and failed in their dirty attempts.

All the conspirators in those trials demonstrated the political ineptitudes involved in the plot and unfortunately they are the ones who lead and govern us. Trump responded that Schiff fabricated his words, and now he does not miss the opportunity to label him, without any evidence, as a "corrupt politician." The defenders of the Swamp describe Trump as labeling him as corrupt, it is not a label, it is a Truth. Do those who defend political corruption want to change the name of truth into a label? In a tweet, Trump said that "Schiff must testify why he fabricated a statement of mine." He also said that "corrupt politician Schiff should be investigated for fraud!" Mr. ex-President, you are not the only one who thinks that this forceful failed jurist should be investigated. We as a people are crying out to the Department of Justice to investigate, but since everyone is involved in one way or another, they would only remain investigations and not consummated trials.

Democratic politicians are investigated to silence the people, but none have been prosecuted, much less punished. President Biden and his son are an example, Hillary Clinton, Obama now buying mansions in the Real Estate industry competing with Donald Trump. And the list is long. The Department of Justice believes in them and they will not be investigated. This shows that the swamp is much bigger than reported. The relatives who have had members investigated or sentenced by Adam Schiff, should ask for a review of the cases, because the way he acted with the former president, what would this forceful failed jurist not do for fame? At the end of the 1980s, when he had not long left Harvard Law School, he prosecuted the first FBI agent imprisoned for spying for Moscow. Perhaps he is innocently celebrating his birthday.

That is why Nancy Pelosi affiliated him with her plot, because she knew he had no ethics whatsoever. A jurist without professional ethics is a bomb ready to explode against the accused. These are the Senators nominated in these primaries in California, which has always shown that they do not elect their representatives for their agendas, but for their corruption and hatred to achieve the power that Nancy Pelosi has desperately wanted to destroy Donald Trump. Not because of the envy of millions, because Nancy made them in the corridors with the information obtained in Washington D.C., Wall Street, etc. The pharmacopoeia and much more and they all know it. They are not slander, they are realities. They are famous and their profits appear in the magazines where they are published and the people find out and make objective comparisons.

Just as the Democrats also know that Donald Trump is a great danger to them, or just as the Witch Hunt was to Christianity in the past. However, when Schiff described the call that Trump made to Zelensky, making it clear that he was outlining "the essence of the president's communication" not his exact words. How poetic the blunt failed jurist came out! "The essence of the president's communication, not his exact words." The slanderer's sense of smell, or mind, is wrong, not distinguishing the essence of honesty and justice, but confusing it with his own corruptions, is a sign that he should go to elementary school or offer him treatment in the first mental hospital that Nikki Haley wants and so do we.

Poor Adam Schiff, with his past traumas, because he could not be a movie actor, has made a script in his own way, inspired by the scum or the Democratic leadership behind that show, which they showed to the American people with the title THE PLOT AGAINST DONALD TRUMP DID NOT WORK in its first part, because in the second, the title is THE WITCH HUNT ACCUSING DONALD TRUMP, of how many ideas have occurred to them to leave the path of corruption free and to be able to bathe quietly in the swamp of Washington D.C. Please find a professional Screenwriter!

With all due respect to Harvard, I don't know if Harvard teaches lawyers to be like Adam Schiff to win cases. Why didn't Mr. Schiff investigate the FBI agent who blatantly lied throughout the process of bringing down Donald Trump with a "rebellion or insurrection of all of you against him? Why didn't you judge yourself in the hoax invented by Naci Pelosi Schumer Chuck and many others? Do you know why?

Because your background took you to the House Intelligence Committee, for having investigated in recent years how the Russians helped the 2016 election campaign and by stirring up the waters wanting to blame Trump, the dirt on all of you came out. The saddest thing is that the people saw what you did wrong. If he were as good as a lawyer, he should have investigated how all of you are enriched by the pharmaceutical companies, the corporations and the millionaires who donate to you to achieve your objectives, which the American citizens know and among them you. The international community saw the same thing we saw, how the Democrats invent dramas to sustain themselves in power. What kind of lawyer are you who lost the case to remove Donald Trump from the presidency? Nancy Pelosi's epithets about you led you to legal failure.

Congratulations to the University that turned you into a lawyer to defend Justice and you have not done so. Can we believe that the FBI agent you investigated and who was sentenced did not fabricate the same tricks that they used against Donald Trump? When laws are broken, anything happens. The family of that agent sanctioned and investigated by you should reopen the case, because whoever did what you did in Washington D.C., was a political complicity, not a process of Justice.

It is a shame that there are lawyers with mentalities like yours practicing the profession. The desire inherent to all corrupt people is to stand out and be famous at the expense of deviations from Justice. This is how we live in our country with Presidents, judges, lawyers, politicians, and all kinds of situations, where the truth is covered up so that the people do not know it and they do not comply with their lies and deceptions.

Did you forget that we have every right to express ourselves and not hide the negative things about others to look good and that is called freedom of expression? The same that you use to destroy and defame people! But the people do not defame, they denounce what you do wrong before our eyes. You are a political disgrace, but you are in the right place to run, because California is a source of the Washington D.C., swamp. Even if voters continue to go to the polls for the image of the candidate, and have not read the political agenda in which injustices have been involved, we will continue on the path to not drain the swamp.

Poor Mrs. Katie Porter would have to do magic to achieve what decent politicians want in Washington D.C. But until the Democrats get together and analyze the damage caused first to their Political Party and to the people in general and apologize and stop the persecutions and the 91 trials of Donald Trump, they will have to bear the bad image left in the history of the United States as the demolition of democracy. Californian Democratic voters have distinguished themselves by their great political mistakes. Not knowing how to choose their candidates by decency, but by their bad actions and wellsponsored propaganda to impress them. This is how communism works. But be sure that: EVIL WILL NOT ESCAPE JUSTICE.

Oscar Levant was an American concert pianist, composer, conductor, author, radio talk show host, television talk show host, comedian, and actor. "The only difference between Democrats and Republicans is that Democrats also allow poor people to be corrupt."

TERRORISM

When moral, political, religious, and social values are forgotten, we fall into government corruption, dragging along its people in any part of the globe, and we have already hit rock bottom in the U.S. Education and religion could stop these omissions, if they were discussed in all the schools of the country and changes were recommended by teachers, sociologists, psychologists, pedagogues in charge of restructuring society again without allowing politicians to interfere in it. We have seen that politics in schools by the orientations or demands of conflictive governors, does not work because they fall into discrimination and violations of the rights of citizens, whether adults or children. De Santis demonstrated this in Florida.

We believe that what they call the separation of powers of the Church and the State should be analyzed. Or analyze that if the Bible is not present in elementary school, the homosexual philosophy disguised with the word Tolerance, which many governors want to introduce to children in the nation, should not be present. A fair balance is what will end the doubt of our governmental institutions or continue with the right to let children enjoy their childhood.

The laws misinterpreted in the States of the Nation, most of them violate the constitution. When the FBI so respected in times past was becoming vulnerable, due to plots exposed in lawsuits where they defamed and lied. And the CIA is nowhere to be seen anymore. Who defends us? Others have asked themselves in this political tangle, Where is the CIA? Where is the Pentagon? The hopes of the American people were to know that these institutions honorably defended the people, without questioning, whether all of them acted in their decent jobs or not, to achieve the objective which was to Serve their country.

Today we have to speak in the past, because the present is severely contaminated and compromised. In this era, Cuban spies roam around Florida and many states of this nation, Chinese spies, spies from all over the world, who are not monitored, investigated upon entry, and persecuted as in times past. Today they work openly defending their foreign countries in the Middle East for the sake of democracy and freedom of expression on American soil. The Cubans who abused their power by extorting the people and attacking them, denouncing them, imprisoning them, today thanks to Obama and the Biden administration, many are in the USA without being persecuted, we are victims and victimizers enjoying capitalism. If Obama interfered with the FBI to not arrest the Iranian spies and get them off the plane to investigate them, what can we expect from the climbing mission between Cuba and the USA on the spies?

Please, let us wake up from the historical lethargy! We all want the USA back. We do not want to see foreign students defending Hamas in the streets. That is not defending the country that is making you a professional, with a lot of benefits from cultural exchanges, scholarships or other types of aid or payments received by relatives.

Those students who defend terrorism are the ones who will do what Osama Bin Mohammed Laden did, who was an Islamic militant leader born in Saudi Arabia. Osama was the founder and first general emir of al-Qaeda from 1988 until his death in 2011, leaving as an intellectual legacy learned in this same country, the destruction of the TWIN TOWERS, where more than 3,000 people died, destabilizations in all orders. They changed us to the peaceful life that we had in comparison to other countries. And that President Obama, out of "ethics," did not show us his corpse.

It wasn't morbid to see him, it was to check if it was true or not that he was dead, because we no longer believed the Democrats at that time. But we did see the bodies that killed us in those attacks. Hypocrites, Accomplices or Cowards? When we talk about cowardice, we have to include former President Obama, who closed all his public information to command the country. That's why I didn't vote for him (I don't like cowards of any race), even though I wished he was elected because he was black, showing that the

American people were not racist at this time, but all the rebellious and ill-educated blacks in their Marxist philosophies, using that word to benefit themselves as a social banner receiving donations that they later misuse. The same thing happened when Hamas attacked the concert in Israel, and the number of deaths caused by the terrorists is not important, but rather the pretensions of subduing and demoralizing Israeli society, as well as ours, which students here and abroad defend in these demonstrations in the name of freedom of expression, always trampling on the rights of others.

These are the enemies of the USA. We must identify them and demand that the government authorities, especially the CIA and the FBI, investigate them, and then return them to their countries and exercise their right to protest in their terrorist towns, defending their ideals (which will not be allowed by those same terrorists they defend in the USA). The USA does not accept terrorism!

Alan Lee Keyes is an American politician and perennial candidate who served as Assistant Secretary of State for International Organization Affairs from 1985 to 1987. He graduated from Harvard. "The act of voting is an opportunity for us to remember that our entire way of life is based on the ability of ordinary people to judge carefully and accurately."

EDUCATION

"Being cultured is the only way to be free." (José J. Martí) When institutions like HILLSDALE COLLEGE provide us with their newsletters in all areas, the information begins to exert on readers the idea of a better world. Through culture the world changes. The articles of this private institution provide information analyzed and offered by experts in their fields, they educate us, and that means that education is within reach of all those who wish to take advantage of it.

Although there are many Americans who do not believe in the work they do (social networks), we must all give our best for the sake of young people and children, to whom the future belongs, since parents have been leaving aside their parental responsibilities without even helping them with their daily schoolwork. They offer wonderful electronic courses, from different branches in education, simply for free, they only receive large or small donations according to the income of the donors and if they want to cooperate. It is not mandatory to donate money, but donations are deserved for what they give back to society. Adults and children benefit culturally.

The American people want the best for everyone. It is when parents should urge their children to enter those courses that will give them enlightenment through education, to know more every day, and to understand others by covering all branches of knowledge and they take them too, since everyone can participate because in most of all states subjects like these are not taught. When you have the right information, it gives you peace. We all know that many young people have faced academic difficulties about the knowledge offered in our poorly programmed schools.

Others have done well. The sad thing is to see how our laws are in the public debate, our institutions, agencies like the FBI and the

CIA, that we all ask ourselves today Where is the CIA? Fortunately, HILLSDALE COLLEGE has a newsletter entitled "Why the CIA no longer works and how to fix it." By Charles S. Faddis Request it! They are the experts who explain these matters.

A large percentage of the population does not know when or why the institutions that are there to defend them in their own country were created, much less the children of poor immigrants in recent times, who speaking the Spanish language and poorly learning the English language and their true history have had a hard time getting ahead, while others have succeeded.

We cannot generalize. Biden Kamala continues to support bilingualism in Spanish and English and leaving out the other languages of children from different continents who live in the US and are the immigrants he says he defends. Does he discriminate against them freely or ignorantly?

It should be noted that Asians learned the English language better and faster than Hispanic children. I believe without fear of being wrong, that I was the only mother who protested to the school authorities and did not allow bilingual classes to be given to my young daughter as such in the City of La Puente, California. I was shocked when the principal told me that the school received money for this program, and I told her that this program was holding back my daughter's and other Hispanic children's English skills and that I would not allow it. But I got on the bad side of the PTA for telling the truth. I told them that my daughter was not to bring home any Spanish material again, but English, because we supervised the school materials and reviewed homework together. The answer was that she would continue to be paid for this student in the bilingual program, and that the girl would be taught in the same classrooms where the Asians learned, according to my request. It was a deal. And they kept it. We took care of the Spanish language in our home, and they all speak both languages, but English correctly. Parents are fundamental in society, we defend them as much as we pass on to them our miseries, our ignorance, the "racism" without distinctions of class, race or skin color and even our frustrations.

Learning different languages is wonderful, but separated from the school curriculum that everyone must learn the same thing, and in the English language, which although it is not official in the country, is where development is. The institutions that are there to protect Hispanics are made up of backwardness and corruption, and that is the same way we have lived in California.

It is worth mentioning that many Hispanic children and children from other groups have been passed to the next grade without basic knowledge, because the progress of teachers is measured by the learning of children, and no teacher wants to lose their job and they pass children to grades that do not correspond to them, with the little knowledge they have. In addition to the lack of knowledge of the English language that was denied to them.

Hispanic children are as intelligent as any other child, and they should not be segregated by those who criticize segregation, and in these modern times, they practice it in schools in different ways. Bilingual learning and passing them to grades without knowledge. Where are the parents? That is an absolute scandal and unacceptable! In California, little by little, the governor or previous governors did not really care about the education of the citizens. They gave them money, they gave them part of the lottery profits (another corrupt entity that steals almost half of the money that the players earn), they gave them media propaganda, but they did not supervise where the bad was and it is because their children went to private schools, where they are taught even the Chinese language, as a separate language from the English language, something that they do not do in poor elementary schools, although some schools already have it in areas with greater purchasing power in California, making the school curriculum much better and they even teach another language but the basic subjects in the English language. They have improved somewhat.

Black families complained about the low educational level for their children when segregation. Segregation continues in California elementary schools with bilingual education, under our laws and the legacy of Martin Luther King almost forgotten. The same violent black groups, those who destroy the country's infrastructure, moral values, political values, etc., those who protest violently in street demonstrations, are those who have betrayed their great leader and do not read black literature that is inspiring to everyone. They have forgotten the one who promoted pacifism, respect, education, equality of values for whites and blacks in schools, restaurants, cinemas and bars, etc. We cannot blame only the governors and members of the school district boards, the greatest responsibility is that of the parents, who must demand a correct education so that their children can reach their goals in the future and that they are not indoctrinated, to then defend terrorists and attack countries like Israel without even knowing what they are doing.

If Jesse Watters were to ask university students why they defend Hamas, they wouldn't even answer him, because they themselves don't know anything about the conflict. They follow the terrorists' directions like a flock of sheep. Many journalists ask, almost out of fear, why terrorism and the defense they make of it, and future professionals don't know how to answer. And this happens not only with terrorism. If you ask any of the democrats of the voters, why do they hate Donald Trump? The answer is not understandable. They end up seeing that he is rude because of his way of speaking, but it is more self-defense than rudeness. No one has put themselves in Donald Trump's shoes to know how they would have acted if they were persecuted as they have been. Those who have suffered persecution understand it.

The same thing happens with Israel. They would only tell him that Israel committed genocide and that Hamas and its terrorists are angels fallen from heaven. And those will be the professionals of tomorrow with brainwashed or empty brains. In California, I sued Nogales High School for violating the constitutional rights of my daughter and us, her parents, because she was a minor to make false comments in the yearbook. No lawyer wanted to take the case, because they would pay almost nothing. Finally I contacted the lawyer Mr. Cueto, Cuban, he accepted it, although he did not defend that branch and knowing that he would not be paid well simply out of solidarity.

He did it for the fair concepts of the case. He won it and it is true that the Judge did not understand why we sued. The lawyer explained our "legal-cultural" points of view and he accepted it. I consider that education is the basis of society and must always be defended. My daughter felt satisfied. Problems in schools must be worked on in teams, parents-teachers with education, and respect, but when they do not agree to communicate, there are the laws. "Not the groups that defend Hispanics, blacks, etc." We all know where the law firms are in our cities. We don't need more.

We admire men like Martin Luther King who used peace to leave us the act that defends us all from Washington D.C., but we must cooperate and protest when politicians deify themselves and make laws in their states that are harmful to the population, with good manners, not stealing, killing and destroying the history of the country, which has nothing to do with social problems, but with hatred, anger, and bad manners intimidating the people.

When we begin to love and respect the national symbols, starting with the Flag, the Country, its National Anthem and what it means despite not being able to pronounce it correctly or remember its lyrics, when we begin to interact with our neighbors, despite poor linguistic communication, that is when we know that we are American citizens and we nobly compose a poem for the new homeland, which is already old in our hearts.

When an American neighbor knocks on our door to tell us that it is raining and that we should remove the flag that we have in front of us due to ignorance about it. (But when we almost faint while searching for information because very few things come true), we learn to deal with small situations, because we live in a capitalist country and even with the flag big business is done, but when we see it proudly floating in the air, or on the sarcophagus of one of our heroes, that is when the heart beats faster for love of our country and tears flow like springs and we do not pay attention if it is in the men's underwear or in the women's bikinis. We are in spiritual communion with the country and God and with gratitude to our neighbors as a Spanish saying goes: Who is your brother? Your closest neighbor.

When we see clean, green and quiet areas, we feel happy to be in this beautiful country. (Sadly, many immigrants continue to disfigure the landscape with garbage and loud music, disturbing others), because it is part of their idiosyncrasies in their countries of origin and they do not understand that there is a saying that says: "in the land you go, do as you see."

This means, out of education, to adapt and respect the laws and customs of the country in which one is, while advising not to stand out by going beyond the established ways and customs in each place, avoiding conflicts between neighbors.

Hispanic music is heard throughout the block, whether it is Cuban, Mexican, Colombian, etc. This causes rejection, because no one wants to listen to other people's music. If the Americans played their music loud, the Hispanics on the block would say that they are discriminating against them and forcing them to listen to music they do not like. And the Americans think that they are being disrespectful and lacking consideration for the neighbors by calling the police to put things in order. When the police arrive, resentments come out, hating the gringos who reported them. And protesting that the police force was inconsiderate, because they sent police officers who do not know the Spanish language, and some guest had to serve as interpreters.

When blacks or Hispanics drive by in cars that shake at the highest volume, the decibels penetrate the ears of others, bothering them, and they put themselves in the same place as others, and then they complain that they are discriminated against, when they do not comply with the harmony of good neighborliness.

It is not discrimination, it is a lack of respect for others. Respect is earned by respecting. This saying "do as the Romans do" was first pronounced in the 4th century by Ambrose of Milan, one of the fathers of the current Catholic Church, but with a different meaning. He was referring to the faithful who had to follow the mandates of the Roman Church, instead of Arianism, a philosophy that denied the divinity of Christ.

For all immigrants, wherever they come from, reason that the American government, with some exceptions, did not invite us to come to this wonderful land. We decided to do so in search of what was denied to us in our countries: opportunities of all kinds, freedoms and democracy. Others decided to do so because of a lack of jobs, education, political persecution, religious persecution, etc. We must be grateful and RESPECTFUL, not perfect, because only God is perfect, in order to integrate into this American society. In all jobs, one must respect one another. In all places there are rules and disciplines.

Large companies offering us work without knowing the language, is when we strengthen the bonds of love and we already have the ability to comment, analyze, or point out what is wrong or right in our country. Criticism seeking to educate, even if the words are not academic, or often not appropriate, is a strong bastion for reflecting on what is right or wrong in our lives, or societies.

The Bible says: "Biblical criticism is helpful, loving, and based on truth. Correction should be gentle. It comes from love, not from a spiteful attitude." Galatians. In the Bible it sounds beautiful, but in our days, our Democratic politicians do not understand gentle language, much less loving or polite.

An example of this is: The death of the mother of our First Lady Melania Trump, who at that time needed her husband by her side, and he asked the judge for more time (from the orchestrated trials) and was denied it and although they let him be at the ceremony, the media comment was enough to evaluate the moral values of the persecutors who are questioning their prestige. We Democrats could say that they are committing hara-kiri.

Finally, the graduation of his son and the press reporting that Judge Juan Merchant denied him the right to go and share that moment with his son. It left a lot to say about the concept of family and education that the judge has. We all have Pandora's Box at some point, no matter what academic level we have. I think the wife told the Judge: that's not fair, you wouldn't like that to happen to you (the golden rule), but being Hispanic and in Hispanic culture, supporting the achievements of children is as fundamental as in any culture.

All cultures, so to speak, are equal when it comes to defending the family and prosecutor Juan Merchant took the reins knowing that he was crossing the line by granting the minutes to his son Baron's ceremony, but he didn't take it back to withdraw from the case with dignity because of a conflict of interest in the Trump trial. Why doesn't this happen? Because they are Democrats and the laws they use seem to be unconstitutional. They want us to see that there is only one criminal in the USA and that is Donald Trump. Because of hatred, racism, envy, and fear that Trump will return to the presidency, these judges try to destroy the emotional environment of citizens, not Donald Trump. They attack their own people based on Justice, which is very good but exercised by corrupt people.

The behavior of the Democrats is the same as that of the communists. They act without mercy. Family values do not exist for them, education, because the educated do not follow them, they analyze them and that is why our young people are lost in this society because it is the first thing they disintegrate in society to achieve their objectives. They are violent and approve of lies and lack of education. Criticism is when we tell the truth, without much preamble.

Truths that the people know, and many remain silent, for fear of being pointed out, and that fear is what we had in Cuba and now they trample on the population and cannot defend themselves. The Constitution must be reviewed, analyzed, and studied again as well as implementing new amendments, to see if it can be applied correctly in this era. We are terrified to hear and read the news every day about what the Democrats do based on our laws and applaud them, without reading if what the Constitution says by which they act incorrectly is true. The communists, liberals, black or white supremacist rebels, among them Hispanic groups would like to eliminate it, and live without laws that protect us. The Democrats with their socialist tendencies do not allow opponents on the ballot to compete with them and from all this comes the bad education that helps the destruction of democracy.

DEMOCRACY. A system of government in which sovereignty resides in the people, who exercise it directly or through their representatives elected by vote. 2. f. A country whose form of government is a democracy.3. f. A form of society that recognizes and respects the freedom and equality of all citizens before the law as essential values. 4. f. Participation of all members of a group or association in decision-making. This community of neighbors is a democracy. (Violated today with the democrats in power by taking away the moral force from parents in schools, imposing almost pornographic books and theories of "tolerance towards homosexuals" being totally INTOLERANT towards theories such as prostitutes are persecuted even though they make laws in different states. The two groups are taken out of dictionaries as immoral and taken out of psychiatric books as mentally ill. So today everyone should have the same rights. Prostitutes are denied even to adopt children that homosexuals can do, many of them being mothers. TOLERANCE According to the Royal Spanish Academy (RAE) defines the term tolerance as "respect for the thoughts and actions of third parties when they are opposite or different from one's own." Democracy and its definition say it very clearly. CITIZENS in this word is the key to everything. The religious, the homosexuals, the prostitutes, the drunk, etc., are citizens, no matter what lifestyle they have. We must tolerate everyone, and include BIBLES in schools again, so that everyone knows that there are different concepts, or else, if there are no Bibles because of the separation of powers, there will be no politicking that goes against biblical concepts. The Trump era has made us think, whether our opinions are liked or not, based on the reality of what is happening, that we are heading straight to the abyss if we do not take correct measures in the presidential elections. We were living off the glories, and forgetting the memories. This is how Democracy is destroyed. We hear the country asking for divine mercy! What has happened in all the countries where communism laid its foundations. "They do not accept competition or democracy." Know it! Love for your country based on the elastic that is the Constitution, which each group stretches and shrinks or interprets in its own way, is the most direct way to destroy it, so we hear the voice of the country metaphorically telling them: DEMOCRATS PLEASE DO NOT HURT ME ANYMORE. It was a shame for the Democrats to have put former President Donald Trump in the Fulton County Jail on August 24 for hatred and conspiracies. Nancy Pelosi, Adam Schiff, Chuck Schumer, Hilary Clinton, Obama and Joe Biden should have been there for all the bad actions they have committed. And if we hurry, the Department of Justice, the FBI, the CIA, the Senate, the Congress, and the House of Representatives in full, for not constitutionally stopping corruption knowing it, but they have all participated in one way or another. They are all dirty! Who is working? I won't mention the Supreme Court for now because someone has to invade their tables with the people's complaints, so that they legislate constitutionally, not based on gossip or political entanglements, as they did in the trials of Donald Trump. But with Judge Sonia Soto Mayor, what we saw on CNN in Spanish is enough. Speechless!

It is time to take the judicial reins and stop the destruction that they see from us internationally of what happens in our home. Let us wash our dirty laundry together and within the territory.

They cross themselves or visit different churches on Sundays, and they are offending God, as well as the people, because by making so many trials against Donald Trump while he was in office and not proving anything, and continuing to harass him with 91 more trials, apart from those that each Attorney General has filed against him in their States, (Becerra, the former Attorney General of California filed 100 cases), it is more than enough to recognize the great Witch Hunt of a president who did not steal, did not make millions in the halls of Washington D.C., while fulfilling his duty to his people. What the Bible says is very true. "By their fruits you shall know them" and by the way, by defaming Donald Trump they violated not only political and religious ethics, but also the morality that each individual carries within.

If you go to any church, the first pillar is to cultivate love and forgiveness. By hating, parishioners are breaking the laws of God. It must be repeated. Ignorance is the mother of all evils. Gratitude is also in extinction. The philosophy of the people says: "they eat saints and defecate the devil." To criticize, denounce, ask or clarify is to seek that the bad be eliminated and the good come, based on truth and moral justice, not only constitutional. When we leave the memories of our childhood and youth in the homeland we abandoned, and the one we adopted at a given moment became the true homeland, we feel totally free.

And as José Martí said, "He who tells the truth serves the homeland better." Although unfortunately in this era, it is very difficult to assimilate the truth, and because of the truth, the social and political conflicts that we have all witnessed have occurred. It is wise to recognize where we come from, and where we are with respect and love. That is called integration. There are no bad countries, there are bad leaders, there are bad people, but fortunately there are millions of good people, wanting to return to the peace that the democrats have stolen from us with their bad political behavior in this era.

We must all fraternize and respect the laws together, but they must respect us all.

The United States of America par excellence, was always considered a world leader. In all continents, citizens frustrated by the bad policies of their countries thought of emigrating to this land. No one thought of emigrating to third world countries, only if they were dangerous criminals, or had a lot of money.

Progress existed in the USA before the migratory avalanches. This was the promised land that God gave us one day. Today, little by little, the Chinese are buying everything and we do not know if it is progress or negligence in our country.

We will have another language to learn, even if it is from the enemy, and the most beautiful thing is, not because of the immigrants, but because of the democracy of the founding fathers who did not make the English language official.

The medicines that we elderly people take are made in India, China, etc., and on the day of a conflict between those countries, we all die or they start to manufacture them here as they did with the masks and equipment for the Covid 19 pandemic, thanks to Donald Trump who mobilized companies to manufacture them because former President Obama had not realized that the country should be prepared for any pandemic. The country that should have the leadership in the manufacture of our medicines is the USA. If there are international conflicts, we elderly people are the first to die and not from bullets, but from the lack of our medicines.

In foreign countries the "Made in USA" seal was synonymous with quality. We have given up rights to foreign countries because of true labor exploitation, and to continue obtaining more monetary profits for businessmen, taking away the opportunity for their compatriots to work in it and for us to enjoy security. We are not saying that business should not expand abroad, that is economics, but the essential thing is to think about your country first and to have good jobs for citizens as the lady asked at the Trump rally in the Bronx shouting loudly, "we do not want welfare, we want good jobs" and that is the concept, to abandon public aid for young people who have it.

We buy cheap from the Chinese, but they do not deliver the manuals, online, or physical, and the quality is disastrous, even if the product looks the same. Those are the ones who defend the swamp. Money is power and they have it, and they know how to buy consciences in the halls of Washington D.C., in the famous lobbying of the puppets that we have.

The pharmacopoeia or owners of the medicines that prescribe us pay a pittance abroad for manufacturing, and the price to pay is devastating for poor patients. Medicines that even if they have recovered what is called "research" are still so expensive that they are not within the reach of the most needy, the poor. Everything is made in China. Food, the textile industry, technology, and they own large corporations, and even land near military bases, etc., according to those who know the news, they spy on us anyway and instead of protesting, the current politicians shake their hands. And by the way, they send them the oil from our reserve for not wanting to drill and being independent to go against Donald Trump. Do you know how we workers in the USA would be if all that was manufactured here? In heaven! Like in times past. The politicians in Washington D.C., are the accomplices of our social ills, not our defenders as they claim. The American people need to wake up and see what is best for the country, whether to leave the factories abroad or bring them back for the benefit of the workers. Because of this issue, even the Democratic voters and some Republicans who were brainwashed discredited Donald Trump, without understanding that those who are not prepared efficiently or technologically need the poor's workforce, to work on the machines and bring bread to their families.

Although it is better to live with many millionaires solving problems, even if their capital comes from China or not, than with the poor asking for public aid in the country. It would be very good if they invested in the USA. The people would be very grateful. A society that does not respect money is a weak society. This is what California does, so many companies have had to leave the state due to so many regulations and so many taxes.

Why do you think they hate Donald Trump? For asking them to return industries to their country to provide jobs and take many off public aid. The Bronx rally represented Martin Luther King's dream, whites, blacks, Hispanics, like brothers, supporting the country, not a man. Paradoxically, that man is the right one to be President of the USA, although the Democrats are already awakening from the lethargy in which they had been subjected for years. Trump saying what the people want to be, all Americans, regardless of color or race. That is how we will move forward. That day of the rally in the Bronx, not only went down in history for the support of everyone united, but it also fulfilled the dream of that great leader Martin Luther King, forgotten by the Marxist rebels of his groups.

Little by little, with third-world customs, immigrants were changing the history of the United States of America, due to the political apathy of many of its citizens, and their generosity. You can be magnanimous, but do not exaggerate. The patriotic activism of going out to vote is the effective one, not the one that walks through the streets with the flag shouting. Generosity at the expense of one's own rights leads to the marginalization of those who grant them. There are philosophies that teach us to have a balance in all aspects of life, and that we should not give to others at the expense of our needs.

This means that: when rights are granted to others, above others, we are facing political delinquency and divisionism bringing violent social consequences sooner or later. Not before magnanimous politicians. They operate these actions in search of ratifying their positions acquired mostly by vote, and on the eve of state or presidential elections, they take these aids to extremes, marginalizing the people who provide them and in this way the states function by denying some, and benefiting others, planning the votes of the future.

The immigration of large exoduses that enter due to non-compliance with the country's laws, especially now due to the irresponsible maneuver of President Joe Biden Kamala, letting in even spies and putting national security in danger and Biden's followers silent. They have marked the high rates of political deterioration in our country and the large deficit faced by these states that embezzle the money of Americans in unjustifiable causes, for not complying with existing laws. As has been the flow of illegal immigration in California, Texas, Florida, New York and many other states.

During Biden's presidency, what he promised in his campaign to contradict Donald Trump, who wanted controlled immigration, was fulfilled. In California, the money destined for the homeless is lost.

California Democrats are frustrated with Governor Gavin Newsom's Council for the Homeless. The irresponsibility in the waste is great, when they have not been able to trace billions of dollars spent to address the homeless crisis in the last five years. Who and on what did they squander that money that they can't find it now? Democratic Assemblyman Phil Ting expressed his concern about the lack of accountability and transparency regarding the funds allocated for homeless programs. Have they found them? Officials with the California Interagency Council on the Homeless (CICH) have acknowledged that they have faced major challenges with "data quality" making it difficult for them to provide metrics (data and figures on the impact of $20 billion spent since the Council was established.

These are not expenses, they are waste and misuse of money that was not for the Council, it was for veterans and other homeless to help them in their needs. If they don't know where the $20 billion is, the same goes for the electoral votes in California. They make them disappear. The transparency of the money with the Democrats is the same as the electoral votes that they don't know or have the metrics to know where they put or counted them. Corruption, and that is how Gavin Newsom wants to be the President of this country one day.

When he gets to the Treasury Department, even the printing presses will be lost.

The American people, regardless of what political party they belong to, must recognize that we are all affected. The resources are for illegalities in almost all Democratic states, and not for their decent and law-abiding citizens, bringing great resentment and with obvious reasons. Many have already been fired from their jobs in order to employ others who entered illegally. That is happening. Counties have had to cut the budgets of public gardens in cities to be able to use that money to help illegal citizens who entered due to Democratic violations.

What extraordinary power has immigration had that has impacted all continents? The United States, due to its generosity, was digging its own grave without knowing or imagining it, and with Biden Kamala the funeral arrived. Ordinary Americans far removed from politics, or registered in the different parties such as the Democrats or the Republicans, the Independent Party, etc., little by little relegated their rights as citizens, without realizing the reality. Many did not vote. The politicians who were, or are there to defend them, live in the imaginary bubble that everything is fine, when it is not true. While the immigrant mobs were developing new plans for the country, and the violent blacks in their communist, Marxist, Leninist organizations, African Americans wrongly called that because if you are American you must be without putting the prefix "Afro" in front, which only serves to remind them that they are not completely American, (that is why these black organizations hate their true country USA, blaming the white man for what they did to their ancestors in slavery). It is time to turn the page and heal the wounds.

If they felt American, they would not hate the white man of today, who is not guilty of their bad feelings, nor of the hatred or stories made by their parents. As parents we have the unavoidable duty to smooth things over and not pass on our human miseries to our children. Children should not pay for the frustrations of their parents. This sows hatred and resentment in them, because they suffer what their parents and grandparents suffered. Results: Racial hatred and intolerance towards others, and this happens in white families where children defend the white race out of ignorance, because if they have their DNA tested they will have to urgently separate themselves from their racist communist affiliations in these times. It is time to make social changes individually.

Hispanic families are the same. When children are constantly told about the miseries, they absorb them and will become the future criminals of society. Parents who are drunk or drug addicts, negligent parents, who do not teach their children education, raise them like animals in the jungle. Parents who do not give their children a hug or a kiss, telling them that they love them, that they are the best thing in their lives so that they feel loved, cuddled and safe. Love begets love. What can come out of all this? Delinquency from whites, blacks, Hispanics, Asians, and from any group that does not pay attention to what they transmit to their children.

The highest percentage of social miseries come from homes, except for mental illnesses. Many parents know that their children have these illnesses that can be controlled by medication and refuse to take them to doctors for help. We must break the taboo that mental illness incapacitates anyone, if there are medications, therapies of all kinds, and we can function perfectly in society. Society must face these social problems head on because it can happen to all of us.

When talking to children, we must not tell them what they will not be able to handle due to their immaturity. Let them learn the stories in schools, in libraries, and on Google. Let them compare, because we learn from everything. Parents are there to support them, not make them mentally ill. There are no different statuses. We must be responsible. We have enough with corrupt Democratic politicians to bring more misery to our homes.

Those who adopt communist philosophies because of the poor education provided in the country regarding civic-patriotic values in schools, and the resentment towards whites for past segregation and discrimination, which still persists in their minds, must distance themselves from all that. The racism of whites in these times coming from their homes, makes us never finish discussing these topics so necessary to live correctly in society. We are tired of repeating the same thing all the time, and when we say it, they crucify us because we do not filter the truths. Creating corrupt societies.

That is why we must all cooperate and clarify to the people in general, that the communist, Marxist ideologies, and those that are added to the list without being communist, are those that IDIOTIZE weak minds, to subject people to their purposes of destruction, Russia, Cuba, Venezuela and many more, know how these destructive ideologies work, which the ignorant do not know. Among them, the communist ideologies, Woke and all the others that pull the international strings. The worst philosophy is the one that comes out of the mouths of the politicians in Washington D.C., that the police abuse criminals and especially blacks. That is the philosophy of the power of the Democrats in Washington D.C., united with communism.

The truth hurts, but it does not offend, as the saying goes. Without fear of saying the proven truths today in the USA. It is time that if they change words, situations, based on their deceptions, we have the same right to refute those ideologies, say what they say, and whoever falls. "They were willing to go out no matter what" is the synonym for "at any cost" that Nancy Pelosi speaks of in her emails. Have they reached the criminal cost? Many think so with the attempted assassination of Donald J. Trump. Young students must be alert to these types of indoctrination that come from our educational system in different types of ideologies. I do not know what Social Studies teachers are doing, if they are promoting destruction, or clarifying how these ideological organizations work to destroy us or are the promoters of these philosophies or educating them so that they are not deceived.

The Jews were a group mistreated by society in many countries and in the USA, and the Holocaust was aimed at exterminating them in concentration camps, gas chambers, entire families, persecuted and murdered, by white men against white men. The children died as well as their parents, and there were few survivors. The Jews took on the task of rebuilding their country and forgiving their aggressors by becoming morally strong, and not sitting in the chairs of pain and the past. We know about the past and we do not forget, but the future and present is what will make you strong. We cannot destroy the federalist flag because the rebellious blacks associate it with racist white groups, we cannot destroy the memory of the KU KLUX KLAN because it went down in history dirty, just as we cannot forget the attacks by racist blacks on the destruction of statues, beatings and deaths. No one can throw the first stone.

They do not go to Germany to destroy and insult those who are now not guilty of those actions. We must learn from that example. Remember that what happened to the Jews was more terrible than what the Ku Klux Klan did to the blacks in the USA. But everyone measures their pain in a different way, and respect is always given when it is in order.

That example should be taken by the American blacks who forgot their great leader Martin Luther King. Bad actions demoralize their group and themselves. Correct citizens who do not want to see themselves reflected in the crimes of others will never support them. With education, respect, and humility, more is gained than with violence. Proverbs 9:9. Give instruction to a wise man, and he will become wiser. Teach a righteous man, and he will increase his learning.

All those who have committed these errors up to now have time to correct them and behave properly before society, but if they want to be politicians, not to represent only the blacks, but to represent all of us. Men like Martin Luther King have no skin color. Their human sensitivity was stronger than their color and justified resentment in that era. He defended the oppressed and the poor, whether white or black, he knew that the fight was not easy, and he did not give up, showing extraordinary resilience. That is why he earned worldwide admiration, something that his groups with their violence have not been able to overcome in this era, receiving the absolute contempt that they have earned for their bad behavior, not for their ideals. Ideals are respected, crimes are not. We all condemn the crimes of white supremacists and we would also like to see them learning where their ancestors came from and turning their energies into working for the country. White supremacists have the same opportunities as you to redeem themselves by respecting and respecting themselves. And to demand rights without trampling on the rights of others.

Martin Luther King did not stand out only for his pleasant physical presence, which illuminated itself with his elegance, good dress, with his beautiful attributes such as education, respect, humility, intelligence, love for one's neighbor, and courage. He showed that violence breeds the same, and that love disarms the aggressors. Gandhi was his inspiration and he was his great student. We all want to know the places where our parents and grandparents were born and raised, to know their culture, to know where we come from, even if we were born in other countries, even to wear the clothes of their culture from time to time, but they must never forget that they are BLACK AND WHITE AMERICANS UNITED BY THEIR COUNTRY, because that was Martin Luther King's dream and as long as racism persists in their hearts and homes, they will never be free men, just like whites and their children, as long as they are not honest, there will always be a Ku Klux Klan, a Holocaust, a Religious, Social or Political Persecution, in their hearts staining their actions within their homes. The Democrats of Washington D.C., should analyze and change everything negative for Justice and Truth, because they are harming the people and their hatred, they pour it into social injustices.

In Cuba, Haiti and many others, slavery existed, but when they were freed, they all closed their accounts. The bad is not forgotten, but the good we have in the present should not be annulled and Trump will return to the presidency.

Biden, President of the best nation in the world, had to withdraw so that Kamala could take his place without removing Biden with the 25th Amendment as they wanted to do with Donald Trump. They never supported Kamala Harris, she had to withdraw with more or less 13% of the votes. It is a sign that the Democrats will not win the presidential elections, because any Democrat they put in is an accomplice of the clique that I have continually mentioned to you and not only that, analyze that the Democratic voters to whom they gave their money was Biden, not Kamala, and they must return it to him, not give it to her. That is betraying the same Democratic voters or manipulating them like puppets if they let themselves. We will see how in Africa. He wants to pay black families because they suffered the slavery of their relatives, but he has not said anything about paying all the white men, whose relatives died defending that slavery. He is reviving racism, terrorism. If he pays black descendants, he will have to pay the descendants of white people for the same reason.

When I say that President Biden is racist, and inconsiderate, it is because of his own actions, not because of those of the people who criticize him. These are not personal opinions, they are realities. Black people in any country where they were slaves should not hate the country in which they have always lived with negative stories or without them, but rather analyze that they were different stages, and that not only they suffered in slavery because they were black, the slaves where they were white against white also suffered and it had nothing to do with the color of their skin.

If they want to hate something, let them hate their African compatriots, who hunted them like animals to sell them to white smugglers in England, and other countries. It would also be unfair for them to pay for what they did to their ancestors a hundred years ago. They were engaged in this inhuman business, and since we live in a world of lies and misinformation, they do not mention this dark part of African history. The bad guys are the whites of today. Have they lost their minds?

In Cuba, to give a Caribbean example, slavery was abolished in 1886. Cuba practiced slavery (slave trade) not as abusively as any other country that had it, but they abused it. The slave trade on the Island was to obtain cheap labor to work on sugar plantations from the 16th century onwards. But abuses to a greater or lesser degree were inherent to slavery. Cuba officially stopped participating in the slave trade in 1867 but the institution of slavery was not abolished until 1886.

Black Cubans never identified with Africa, even though they know that their ancestors are from that area. They are proudly black Cubans, and we can all use the word black without fear or worry, because we have lived in brotherhood. This does not mean that when

I was a child there was class division, as in any country that existed. That is a division of social classes where we are all involved.

Blacks with their dance clubs and parties and whites with theirs, but in hospitals, parks and schools, we all had the same rights. Even if a black went to the white club, he was treated as a friend, and the same in their clubs. Each country handled that situation in its own way, but finally racial integration came by making a single club, which is the right thing to do.

Everything was happening until today thanks to Martin Luther King who had the guts to face that situation peacefully. What happens to violent blacks in the USA who retain slavery as a motive for their social misdeeds? Does the same happen to white supremacists who feel superior when their wrong actions define them just like black supremacists, equally fraternal social delinquencies? Why don't they become brothers as a society?

Today we can all be together. The class division still exists, because where a millionaire black man goes, a poor white man does not. Where a white millionaire goes, a poor black man does not go. That is society, and it must be understood, because groups come together for money in the upper social class, for common business interests, or intellectual affinities and so on. And there is no need to have resentments. Each group joins its counterparts. What would we do at a neurosurgery medical symposium? Look for Dr. Carson, not for anyone off the street. He can come in, but we can't.

That is not discrimination, that is a reality that each person joins his group. The earth is still not a paradise. We leave that to Jehovah and his promises. Every society has its rules.

Cuban blacks do not have the emotional traumas that many American blacks have, seeking to separate themselves and not integrate into society. The conditions in Cuba were not the same as in the USA either. Blacks who integrate body and soul into their society make a difference, as did Martin Luther King, Dr. Carson, Condoleezza Rice, Secretary of State under George Bush, Colin Powell, black artists in different fields, decent athletes who love the country, humble families, our Navy, our Army, where white and black men offer their valuable lives, from the intellectuals to the humblest uneducated worker, all those who are decent have a place. Enough of the lies of these white supremacist groups intimidating society, there is no time for that anymore. It is time to work for the country. It is possible that they carry the memories of their ancestors when slavery was in their hearts, or when the whites came to become the new Americans, but they should not involve others in their resentments and ignorance.

That is knowing where they come from and where they belong, but they did not sit down to cry and pity us, but they have shown who they are with their intelligence, talents and civic decency. Just like Hispanics or any other group in this blessed land including its people called white Americans. That is social, cultural, and intellectual integration, and it serves as an example to all those young, violent rioters of any race in the USA who want to conquer the country that is already conquered. A clumsy and vain struggle. Both Kennedy and Martin Luther King were assassinated by whites. Will we condemn all whites for the bad attitudes and actions of those white murderers? No!

That great man left us all his great legacy of peace and love. If there is a Nobel Prize justly awarded by the Academy, it is that of Martin Luther King. If there are unjust prizes awarded by the same academy, they are those of former President Obama and Al Gore. A white man and a black man unduly awarded. Nobody went to Oslo, Norway to attack and destroy the academy, although other prizes are awarded in Stockholm, Sweden and nobody is going to destroy them either, because they do not agree with the prizes awarded. Education is vital in society. The Academy received protest letters from many, including mine, and that is democracy. It just happened. In the case of Martin Luther King, the student was awarded and the teacher was forgotten. That is why I considered that the award given by former President Obama with two wars inherited from Bush. It was totally unfair to award him the Nobel Peace Prize, leaving the true promoter Mohamed Gandhi behind. Martin Luther King left us his legacy in the Civil Rights Act, black and white children in schools, the black vote, among many things that he achieved to improve American society. Influenced by Mohamed Gandhi, we ask ourselves: What is the difference between black abusers and white abusers? The same!

Abusers! It does not matter what cause they have in mind. Those who integrate are those who do not need to remember that they are African, but American, and fight for their country as we saw at this time at Donald Trump's Rally in the Bronx. There, the dream of this great leader was fulfilled.

Many of us, when we begin to read the Bible, realize that those who follow the word of God are also called slaves. In many verses, slavery is mentioned, but when we ask, we are told that it is in a figurative sense, because a person is a slave to his own destiny, to a philosophy to follow, to a job to do, etc. Each person chooses the best version.

According to some information, "In Jesus' time, servants were the property of their masters, more like a slave than an employee, and they were obliged by law to do everything their master needed, such as planting the fields, caring for the cattle, or preparing and serving meals." In return, the master took care of his servants. (Philippians 1:1). Paul and Timothy, servants of Jesus Christ, to all the saints in Christ Jesus who are in Philippi, with the bishops and deacons: Grace to you and peace from God our Father and the Lord."

Since Biblical times, humanity has been confronted with social miseries on all continents. Young blacks have not learned the lesson, and the elderly must stop these exacerbated waves of resentment by injecting their emotional miseries into their meeting circles, without any malice, but harmful, in their own homes, in politics, and every opportunity they have to bring out their emotional pains, not yet healed, by the abuses perpetrated by the "American whites" with all their reasons are their pains, but we must necessarily heal the wounds for the sake of our children. In that era, if you look a little further into history, they were not Americans either, but descendants of the great invasion of immigrants who came to the USA from different countries on different continents, as uneducated or intelligent as many of today.

Africans were also immigrants enslaved by force. To give an example, we see how wrong they were in wanting to defend a cause at the cost of violating the rights of others, using violence that Martin Luther King did not support. Open your eyes, the time of slavery has passed, and we need mixed schools, mixed activities, not separate, mixed Chambers of Commerce, not separate, mixed Colleges and Universities, not separate, mixed Television programs, not separate, mixed Churches, not separate. Mixed marriages for love, not separate. What reasons are there in this era for separation?

Segregation is in every person who has not known, or has not wanted, to get rid of it by keeping hatred in their hearts instead of racial equality, forgiveness and love. They have not followed the examples of their great leader betrayed by all those who embrace violence. We must act with logic, not with emotions. I have a dream! Martin Luther King today and always will be remembered as one of the greatest AMERICANS of the 20th century. When I said 20th century, I thought of looking for information, and we have conflicts even in pointing out this date. As we are led by politicians who have not served the people for many years, brewing difficulties between white and black racial groups, along with these the Hispanics, and unfortunately because the laws of the country are not complied with. Forming the beginning of the swamp in Washington D.C., for many decades ago. These violent groups proliferated having obvious reasons to form, both blacks, as well as white racist supremacists, but it does not give any group the right to destroy history, nor does it give them the right to kill each other as happens, as a good example, the crimes in Chicago, Los Angeles and New York in poor neighborhoods.

Obama has been in power for eight years, and he has not been able to do anything for his race, opening spaces for education and healing. He did not want to, coming from that same corrupt state of Chicago, because that senseless division of the people helps the friends of the socialists to be rioting in the streets and Obama is not only a friend of them, but of the terrorists, interfering many times with the FBI so as not to arrest them, when they decided to pursue the Iranians who were working to destroy our country and no one accused him of being a traitor to the country or any kind of persecution.

No former President of the United States of any of the political parties with which they held their positions, has appeared on the TELEVISION CHANNELS to say Enough! With what is happening to Donald Trump, in bipartisan solidarity before justice. No one better than them, to know that if they investigate them all, we will run out of spaces in the State Courts and the Supreme Court of the Country. And that is why they do not defend justice, because at certain times, whether to defend the country or for other matters, they violated it. The only one who pays is Donald Trump. That is the Witch Hunt accepted by those who are only interested in their personal affairs, not humanity, or they have all been cowards being the heads of our army in our country. Cowards to confront social injustices. Good God, these former presidents are the ones who have governed us and we are their plucked chickens. The henhouse is already getting upset and using one of their rights, FREEDOM OF EXPRESSION, to denounce the facts!

The misinformed people create young people without patriotic, civic, moral or religious education. Instructing young people is everyone's task. What can they ask of the people, if those who lead us or led us betray us? Violent groups emerge that marginalize others in order to achieve their goals, and whether it is white, Hispanic, black, Asian, or other groups, they are on the wrong path and the people do not want to be singled out, to peacefully protest by telling the truth.

By not complying correctly and officially with the laws, it generates animosity in the American people, both in blacks, as in supremacist banks, and other ethnicities and white supremacists shout at the top of their lungs that they will not "replace us." This happens because they see their government acting incorrectly, and they become violent, just like violent blacks, who still feel threatened by whites, but both groups are the example of ignorance due to the non-compliance with the laws that are there to prevent this from happening.

With fear, history is not taught, with fear, Jesus Christ or Jehovah is not spoken of, with fear, one should not defend one group and marginalize others, because then we are facing a fearful, hypocritical, and lying society, and we do not want that to be so.

We can tell these groups that they are wrong, that they are ignorant, that they are violent, but we cannot change their minds until each one decides to abandon the nefarious theories that support them and begin to read, to study, to see the past as history and work futuristically to maintain a society at least balanced, since we will never live in Eden until Christ arrives, but in the meantime we must unite and give him a hand to live in harmony. Stop belonging to violent groups, their members must know that none is better than the other, regardless of the color of the skin, that they are all doing the same thing, and have been captured by other minds, and not by the individual mind of each one who has the right not to follow erroneous crowds.

This is done individually, not by existing laws, which are also not enforced. Compliance with the laws begins in the American Government with the President, the Senate, Congress and the House of Representatives, the Pentagon, the Department of Justice together with the CIA and the FBI and even the IRS. Today we have seen the collapse of democracy coming from these institutions. The Government must focus on its people and solve internal problems first, rather than external ones. To Mexico for the problem currently created by Biden, illegal immigration and their passage through that country, which is where they should ask for asylum first and they do not do so, nor do they grant it, they let in nine to ten million illegals.

It is time for the government to reflect and ask themselves for whom they work, whether for the American people, or for foreign countries and their interests full of social misery. The directors of the country's universities do the same as the government, in a different way. They sustain monetary funds, and it is logical in a capitalist society. What is happening in schools and universities throughout the country? The famous freedom of expression in the Constitution was murdered just as democracy is being murdered, because if in this century, with so many scientific and technological advances, men cannot converse, debate, and dialogue with their teachers about religions, racism, and social problems, all with education, respect, and tolerance, in an open forum of ideas and concepts, we are becoming accomplices of what cannot be fixed. (Only politicians now use the word "tolerance" in schools, but they do not use "moral and civic" to educate them regarding the political, patriotic, and social issues of their own country.)

Education is not in the hands of pedagogues, it is in the hands of left-wing politicians who want to silence the people. They have had to organize a fund to defend students in different universities and schools for not following or reading what is in the constitution. Shameful!

The Free Speech organization constantly fights to ensure that students are not indoctrinated and can freely express themselves on school and university campuses. With totalitarianism infiltrating many principals and many teachers, they cannot speak out in favor of free speech because they even lose their jobs, violating constitutional amendments. Students and teachers who protest to put corrupt institutions in order lose their jobs.

WHITE OR BLACK SUPREMACY GROUPS IN THE USA

We all know what is happening in our American society, but it is not fair to criticize, accuse, and prosecute white supremacists and ignore what black supremacists are doing in the era of Joe Biden. All of them have operated for decades in the name of democracy and free expression as excuses for their social miseries. Truth and Justice go hand in hand. Most groups affiliated with organizations focus on defending their European or black races (It takes the intervention of anthropologists for many to recognize their mistakes or DNA tests). And blacks who criticize white supremacists, instead of doing what Martin Luther King did, joining together, create exalted groups to discredit both groups by involving their relatives and friends in their miseries. None is better than the other, they are all the worst that can happen to a society and they should know that decent people do not accept them. These are demographics all in the twenties and thirties, and blacks and whites try to recruit more young people into their ignorant philosophies by getting them into colleges and universities, social media, and any other means they can.

Groups like Identity, AWD, and Patriot Front operate and distribute their propaganda on college campuses, and groups like the National Socialist Movement and the League of the South have created youth groups and even student memberships. All ignorant of even their ancestry. Most of them are still serving life sentences or on death row today.

These social outcasts suffered sexual, physical, and emotional abuse from their own parents. What can society expect?

Parents must play the role of parents. Make it clear to children when they enter universities and community colleges that they should not be afraid to say "No" to destructive philosophies that lead to nothing good. Nancy Reagan projected herself by inciting young people to say "no" to drugs. While drugs invaded the USA, so many black and white supremacists, along with many churches with the same topics, undermined society with unacceptable doctrines and the government either stood aside or did not see the damage that was being perpetrated on the country. By accepting the monster in the house, when they approved the American Communist Party, all the evils came together in the worst way. In the way that we can keep this legally official party in a low profile, but its activities are not monitored, they are destroying Democracy.

Uniting is the only way for us, the people, to overthrow them, by not offering them one of the freedoms that we have and that is the Electoral Vote. Communism is affecting capitalism and Democracy is dying.

The end of everything that we are living in this era of the Democrats, cannot be predicted even by those who say that God speaks to them. The American people have already woken up and between now and November 2024, much can happen and that will be the red, blue, and white tsunami recovering the country from so many constitutional violations against the people or the blue vote destroying what little is left. The ideal would be for us to march united in voting, punishing the communist democratic government. I say communist, because they obey the criminals and that is how communism is taking shape, although many do not believe it, or do not understand it.

Destroy democracy with liberal, socialist, Marxist ideas without foundation, because if they had any, they would not form groups, they would follow the course in society like all of us who are here and do not belong to any. If they come with these stories to the house, they must be explained in detail, that their teachers are wrong, that their classmates who want to recruit them are wrong, and that they should look for the information that everything is on Google for better or worse. Neither parents nor teachers want to engage, and we say that: "Ignorance is the mother of all crimes." *The Counter Extremism Project (CEP) has identified multiple virulent white supremacist groups, which mainly advocate white ethnonationalism and/or national socialism (neo-Nazi). Neo-Nazi groups, such as the National Socialist Movement (NSM), generally do nothing fruitful. The Counter Extremism Project (CEP) has identified multiple white supremacist groups espousing primarily white ethnonationalism and/or National Socialism (neo-Nazi). Neo-Nazi groups, such as the National Socialist Movement (NSM), generally make no effort to hide their belief that the white race is superior to others. Criticizing one and hiding the other is lying. Truth must always prevail and criticizing all who cause harm to society. As God says, "if they repent, their sins will be forgiven." They have won the battle to be right again if everyone joins hands and works together for the good of the country that belongs to "us" all. In the articles I read, they consider that only white supremacists are destructive, when we see violent blacks who do the same, and demonstrate violently, killing to defend their rights, violating the fundamental rights of citizens, they do not call them "black supremacists"; in addition to that, gangs and criminals who work on their own without being affiliated with any philosophy. All violent groups are equal, regardless of their race or skin color. All those who separate themselves under racism or communist ideologies, we are not concerned about who they are, but what they do. In the end, when the "murderous" police officers as they proclaim, arrest them and go to trial, both blacks and whites, they say the same thing "we are innocent" and want to be pardoned under the VIII Amendment. Excessive bail will not be required, nor will excessive fines or cruel and unusual punishments be imposed. And the crimes of blacks and whites are benign? It is true that the judicial system has made mistakes and imprisoned innocent people, but it is also true that it has made more good trials than bad ones. None of these groups wants to redeem themselves and they end up in the electric chair, where these practices exist. We must be clear and tell the truth, not gloss over it as the ACLU wants.

This violence has been brewing for several decades and continues to this day. They have not achieved what they demand through violence, it is intelligent to change tactics and return to pacifism, which is not the same as not denouncing what is politically wrong.

These tactics of all these violent black or white groups must analyze that the enemy is defeated through dialogue.

The Black Panthers, who were also like all those white supremacist groups wanting to have Africa within the USA, by not identifying themselves as Americans, demonstrated violently and continue to do so to this day, for example. Black Lives Matter. Historians must have recorded this. We cannot condemn these totally wrong groups of blacks and whites defending the indefensible, when they all converge on the same thing: racial fanaticism and communist philosophies and in this era, including terrorism. Enough is enough!

On August 11 and 12, 2017, white nationalists carrying Confederate flags, tiki torches, and shields gathered in Charlottesville, Virginia, for the United the Right rally. Protesters marched through the streets of Charlottesville chanting "You will not replace us" and "Jews will not replace us." The chants allude to the Great Replacement Theory, which posits that black and brown immigrants are reverse-colonizing the dominant European. If everyone decided to live like civilized people, leaving good examples for future generations, these social misfortunes would end.

What people are tired of is the hidden lies, which do not generate followers, because when the lie appears, the truth exposes it. The lie appears because of journalists who do not see both sides of the coin, and if they do, they keep quiet, out of fear, and that is cowardice. Articles should be written with the truth, not lies or slander intended to hurt.

When they report what white supremacists do, they all remain silent about what black supremacists do. Both groups behave the same way. Aggression, violence, and murder. This does not come from the people, it comes from the governors of each state and their peculiar laws or covert cowardice. President Trump addressed the violence in televised remarks from New Jersey, condemning an "appalling display of hatred, bigotry, and violence on many sides" and calling for the "swift restoration of law and order." His critic, Senator Ron Wyden of Oregon, said: "What happened in Charlottesville is domestic terrorism," Wyden tweeted. "The President's words only serve to cover up heinous acts."

I tell Senator Wyden of Oregon, a Democrat affiliated with the Democratic Party, that his words also cover up atrocious acts by black supremacists, which you are afraid to mention. Have you not heard that what you call "domestic terrorism" has been occurring in our country for many decades with the same behavior by both groups? The Black Lives Matter took the streets hostage. (Which are also ours.) Killing a policeman, killing each other, intimidating the people, stealing from private businesses, and destroying the history of the country, because they are bothered by the stories, considering them racist, destroying the statues, which are those that represent the historical events of our nation, whether good or bad. Therefore, the statues belong to all of us. You are right when you said that white supremacists foment domestic terrorism, but you forgot to add that black supremacists act in the same way with domestic terrorism. Why don't you, Mr. Democratic Senator, have the courage to face the negative truths in our society? What kind of Senator are you? We have to be honest. What can we expect from many Democratic senators who only see part of the truth? Where is the Department of Justice? Do you belong to the Ocasio Squad?

Almost the same thing happened when Martin Luther King was assassinated. Black people took to the streets killing police officers and civilians, social disorders turned to racial aspects that persist to this day. Violence exists and will continue to exist until we all individually try to be better citizens. Every group of white supremacists, as well as black supremacists, have made these serious mistakes. Who do we criticize or judge first? History is recorded even if it hurts. We cannot continue with the story of racial discrimination, if the law is not complied with in the CIVIL RIGHTS ACT, which seems to have been made so that they know that there is a law, but it is not complied with and violated by the current American president Joe Biden. Both blacks and whites discriminate against each other, and the existing laws that are not complied with must be applied to them. Decent people, white and black, distance ourselves from those crimes called today Internal Terrorism, which many of us call Urban Terrorism.

All seen by the same television cameras that saw the Charlottesville. Do you know why these barbaric acts happen?

Because the laws are not complied with and the authorities are afraid of both groups, because if they act then the Democratic judges put the police in jail and they set all of them free, white and black criminals. The same thing happened with the Maras Salva Truchas in the country of El Salvador and if Nayib Bukele, the president, could put them all in jail, why don't they do it here with more resources? The Woke? The truths should be equal! We are tired of information separatism by a totally corrupt press, or by government officials full of hate. Journalists who do not inform us of the truth, but rather what the owners come up with to discredit their own country. (I am not generalizing about the press, there are good ones and in these modern times, bloggers are more graduated in journalism than the same professionals who are cowards when exposing information).

That is not being good journalists. That is being complicit with the radical left, which in the end, if they triumph (which we will not allow them to do), the first to fall are the media, since communism hides everything that it does not want to be known. Senator Wyden of Oregon, affiliated with the Democratic Party, open your eyes and ears. We Americans can still dialogue using the weapon of truth.

Tired of hearing "they discriminate against us," I wanted to bring up this article on the Black Panthers, to see how communism, the radical left, socialism or poorly focused liberalism wreak havoc on our society. From past to present, these dissatisfied groups with hearts full of hatred towards their country, (towards the imaginary white, because the whites of today were not responsible for slavery). All due to ignorance, or listening to ignorant professors in the Universities and Colleges of the Country, promoting divisionism and hatred etc., for their own dogmas, that precisely the religious ones were better to be able to live in peace and in the process we have to pay them salaries and benefits so that they destroy our freedoms focused on changing the mentality of young people. A social disaster that we will have to analyze and change.

Both black racists and white supremacists have a common denominator in their actions and this is Communism and its philosophies together with violence destroying everything.

What was the Black Panther movement? According to the Internet, they were and still are part of a larger group, the so-called Black Power, which defended black pride and unity for the rights of racial minorities. Can blacks defend their pride and white supremacists cannot? That black pride is the same as that of white supremacists and homosexuals. We should not judge them but educate them. However, Newton Seal and others did not conform to the ideology of that organization and based themselves on Marxism.

When they say based on Marxism, they include the White Supremacists, the Black Panthers, the Antifa, the Black Lives Matter, to name a few of these organizations, but the Gay organizations let themselves be influenced by the communists and their beliefs. All with concepts that are incongruent with each other. If the White Supremacists are racist and they are not, why do they all have the same philosophy as a base? The truth? It is not only the communist philosophy that moves them, it is the hatred and resentment for the days of the slaves and the sufferings passed in the era of unhealed slavery, but the truth is that in all countries slavery existed with the same situations and they overcame it. And the white supremacists, for their hatred perpetrated, not only against blacks, but against many whites, Jews, Hispanics, Asians, etc., showing that none of them are of any use, because so much hatred towards different races that have done nothing to them, is that they are mentally ill and do not defend their race, they defend their ignorance. All of them have a large percentage of their race mixed. The same thing happens to blacks against whites.

We have not seen demonstrations of Mormons burning businesses, stealing from stores, blaming half the world for what happened, we have seen them practicing their gospel and forgiving. That is what we expect from blacks and Hispanics protesting discrimination or past slavery and from white supremacists. That they apologize and start a new life full of love for their neighbors. As long as we do not tell them the truth publicly, we will be living off the lies of politicians, mostly Democrats, and corrupt or fearful journalists. It is not time to be afraid and raise our voices. All of these situations are spiraling out of control, affecting us all.

In 1862, Congress passed the Morrill Anti-Bigamy Act, which authorized the federal government to "punish and prevent the practice of polygamy in the Territories." Mormons, although they felt that their religious rights were being affected, understood that without destroying anything. Criticism has expanded to include claims of historical revisionism, homophobia, racism, and sexist policies in their literature. No one is exempt from criticism, but we can be exempt from thieves, criminals, murderers, and supremacists of any race. What politicians should never do is fix situations like Senator Wyden of Oregon, who was affiliated with the Democratic Party, did out of fear of his voters, if he was telling the truth, or out of collateral hatred of Donald Trump. (Injustices are not good, no matter who they come from.)

Mormons are based on their Bible and the Book of Mormons. Like any Bible-based church, they have the same concepts as the Catholic Church, Jehovah's Witnesses, and other Christian denominations regarding homosexuality. They are not homophobic, as those who do not accept opinions different from them want to call them. Religious people fulfill what Jehovah said and it is written biblically in different Bibles with different words, but all with the same concept. The only one who does not accept or detest homosexuality is Jehovah. The non-religious can think and accept and do what they want, but the religious cannot. In the Bible of the Americas Corinthians 6:9-10 NBLA and in many others it says the same thing with different words.

"Or do you not know that the unrighteous will not inherit the kingdom of God? Do not be deceived: neither the immoral, nor the idolaters, nor the adulterers, nor the effeminate, nor the homosexuals, nor the thieves, nor the greedy, nor the drunkards, nor the slanderers, nor the swindlers will inherit the kingdom of God. (There I am playing the lottery) the fraud of modern times and we do not learn."

So you cannot call homophobic those who believe in God and follow his laws, and those who do not like to accept these practices cannot be called homophobic either, because they have the right to accept or not. This means that they do not accept homosexuality as a philosophy of life, but they accept the friend or relative who is, with respect and love, because no mortal should or can convert homosexuality into heterosexuality. That is a matter for each person who practices it and for God alone.

Respect must be mutual and we must accept each other as human beings, not for our preferences, political parties or religions or philosophies. It is time to stop these senseless attacks in this millennium, no matter who they come from. Let us not be afraid to express our opinions based on truth, not lies, slander, much less defamation, and when the truth comes, the lie falls silent.

But all the groups mentioned should not drag their sexual, political or religious situations to others, they should reason and fix it for themselves. They are not registered as political or social parties and until they are adults and support themselves, they must respect their parents and disciplines, then they can leave. Neither are doors closed nor opened to them. They must do it for themselves and take responsibility so that they grow strong. Society is not responsible for their preferences, that is something personal.

Families of different races were responsible for sowing good feelings and paradoxically, bad memories in their children, which encourage hatred towards whites, which made them suffer by awakening racism for past slavery. And sadly, almost all groups tend to do the same with their children through the sad stories they have lived. I could say that 98% of black families passed on to their children their bad experiences from the stories of their ancestors, during slavery. The same happens with all groups or almost all of them. Whites or blacks or Hispanics. The cultural level of the black population was minimal in those times, and not all of them could see the light at the end of the tunnel.

Their parents, instead of supporting them and telling them you are as beautiful as them, and be proud of your race, sowed their pain in the hearts of their children without any malice, but out of resentment and poor intellectual education, or because they felt better by telling their stories.

All human beings have a story to tell. Some good and some bad, etc. Decent and educated black families, even if others cleaned floors, sent their children to school telling them: "do what your parents couldn't do" and that was to have an assured education. And that has happened throughout the globe in all cultures, whether poor or rich. All black families are from that school, regardless of their socioeconomic status, who do not approve of theft, violence, the constant epithets that the police are bad and murderous. When these groups of violent blacks do the same thing by killing black or white police officers, everyone remains silent for fear of reprisals, and if they complied with the laws and codes that each state has to combat crime, that would have already happened.

The police, judges and governors in this Biden administration have imprisoned the police who protect us and enforce order, and have left out black criminals for fear that if they are sentenced they will be called racists. Justice has no racial preferences and we have taken many steps backwards in a sham government. Wanting to turn a blind eye has been very risky for the Democrats who are determined from Washington D.C., to destroy our legal values.

Abraham Lincoln was not black (as far as we know). And he was the one who wanted to give them a free life without slavery. Whites fought for blacks, and there were many interracial marriages in those times too, when the civil war happened. White families should stop their insinuations and criticisms towards their children's friends or boyfriends/girlfriends when they meet or fall in love with blacks. Just like black families, who often do not accept white daughters or sons-in-law. Both groups, without intending to, and for the same reasons, behave in racist ways. This is how racism is maintained in both groups. What can be asked of the children affected by these bad feelings?

The result was: Slavery abolished, Beginning of the reconstruction era. Dissolution of the Confederate States, U.S. Territorial integrity preserved, Approval and ratification of the 13th, 14th and 15th amendments to the United States Constitution. All descendants of slaves, whether black or white, should be eternally grateful for the blood shed by their relatives and the white men and women who also gave their lives to end social abuses.

What always happens and is highlighted during the times of primary or presidential elections is that: everyone uses Hispanics, blacks, homosexuals, etc. as a banner to capture the votes of these groups, creating division. Resentment is not good, it is corrosive, and it harms the children and grandchildren who are and will be the current and future generations. We should not, out of hatred, destroy the history of the country that welcomed us who are naturalized immigrants, and much less those who were born under this flag, whether black, white, or of other ethnicities. When looking for information about the BLACK PANTHERS, I read the ten points of the Party or organization, which ran after their own chimeras in the name of Marxism, to end racial discrimination, something that everyone fell into, just like white racists, becoming criminals for their bad actions.

Transforming everything to their own way is not tolerated because we all have the same rights and duties. Both black racists and white supremacists, even many homosexuals join communist philosophies believing that they support them in their personal problems, and that is the closest thing to stupidity that we can observe. Almost all have a common denominator in their actions and this is Communism and its philosophy that are already obsolete. Who do they want to fool?

THE BLACK PANTHERS

The Ten Point Program of the Black Panther Party in the Past. **WHAT THEY SAY. 1.** "We want freedom. We want the power to determine the destiny of our black and oppressed communities. We believe that black and oppressed people are not going to be free until we can determine our destinies in our own communities, ourselves, by completely controlling all the institutions that exist in our communities."

Answer. They were wrong no group should prevail over another or control the institutions because that is what communism does, "control" and they were based on that ideology, which is totally abominable separatist and historically proven that wherever they have developed, they end up being corrupt and discriminating against the people.

2. "We want jobs for all our people. We believe that the federal government is responsible and obligated to give every person a job or guaranteed income. We believe that if the American businessman will not give us all jobs, then the technology and the means of production should be taken from the businessman and given to the community, so that the people of the community can organize and employ all their people and give them a high standard of living."

Answer. That is how communists think, that the businessmen should distribute their assets to them. That the government should give them a salary without working (guaranteed income). That theory does not work in practice. Many black women and men in the era of great racism, were businessmen and respected because they did not sit and wait for them to give them, but rather they fought for their principles and rights by giving to their own communities. History has recorded this.

3. "We want an end to the plundering of our black and oppressed communities by the capitalists. We believe that this racist government has stolen from us and now we are demanding the back debt of 40 acres and two mules. We were promised 40 acres and two mules 100 years ago as restitution for slave labor and the mass killing of black people. We will accept payment in cash, which will be distributed in our communities. The American racist has participated in the massacre of more than 50 million black people. So we feel that the demand we make is modest."

Answer. Another mistake by the communists. That same demand should have been included by the Black Panthers for the whites and their descendants who died in masse for defending the abolition of slavery, but when they only think about themselves, out of hatred they become racist and a sign of arrogance and ingratitude towards the charitable works of others. Then we should give the 100 acres and the two mules to all the whites and their descendants who died in masse for defending slaves and abolishing the mistreatment of slavery. Regarding the thefts from the nation's capitalists that they consider racist, we have references in the archives of the TV channels that from the Black Panthers to the present day, the negative black groups, violent communists and racists, say one thing and do another. They take advantage of any street disturbance, encourage it and end up stealing the capitalist's merchandise from his businesses, and the decent black community of before, and now, does not identify with this armed crime and condemns it.

4. "We want decent housing and adequate housing for the shelter of human beings. We believe that if the landowners do not give decent housing to our black and oppressed communities, then the housing and the land should be converted into cooperatives, so that the people in our communities, with the help of the government, can build and have decent housing for the people.

Answer: Communism is the worst snake that exists. That is their method of operations, that the lands are converted into cooperatives, but they do not talk about working them, but with the help of the government. This happened from Russia to any naive Latin American country and when communism creates cooperatives, the leaders get richer, and the people are more miserable every day. Cuba, Venezuela, Nicaragua, are great examples of the misery that their people live, but not their leaders. Unfortunately, communism has infiltrated our universities and groups are emerging that want to destroy the empire (This is what communists think when they read and believe these perverse doctrines, but they have not lived through this situation and do not know it.)

5. We want decent education for our people that exposes the true nature of this decadent American society. We want education that teaches us our true history and role in today's society. We believe in an educational system that gives our people a knowledge of themselves. If you do not have knowledge of yourself and your position in society and in the world, then you will have little chance of learning more.

Answer. Education begins with integration. Unfortunately, the weapon used by communist and ignorant teachers, because they do not know what it is to live under that yoke, but they are communists in a capitalist country and so is anyone. They teach social classes encouraging the left. (Not all) If we separate ourselves into groups we do not advance.

Progress is to overcome and change the bad for the good, but all integrated as American citizens, not as Hispanics, not as Afro blacks, not as Indians, not divided by political parties, but with a vision of social integrity seeking that the country advance by giving to them, not waiting for them to give to us. It is not in school where we learn to know ourselves, it is in the homes where we learn to respect, to love our neighbors, not to hate each other.

6. We want completely free medical service for all black and oppressed people. We believe that the government has to provide free and for all people, medical service facilities, which not only treat our illnesses, most of which exist because of our oppression, but also develop preventive medical programs to guarantee our future survival to give all black and oppressed people access to advanced scientific and medical information, so that we can provide ourselves with adequate medical care.

Answer. That is how communists think, give me, give me, give me, without making the effort to do, do, do. We all want free medical services, I agree with that, because with the money that our nation gives to countries and even to enemies, it could be achieved. In Cuba there were private medical consultations and clinics, and the people received the same for free in government hospitals through taxpayers' money, before the Castro Revolution, which claimed that merit. But private companies or businesses were never eliminated until the arrival of corrupt communism. I totally agree that these services should be free, but for everyone, not only as a privilege for black and oppressed families. Those who are not black or oppressed, if they are American citizens, should be given the same services.

7. We want an immediate stop to police brutality and the killing of black people, other people of color, and all oppressed people within the United States. We believe that the racist and fascist government of the United States uses its domestic security agencies to carry out its program of oppression against black people, other people of color, and poor people within the United States. Therefore, we believe that it is our right to defend ourselves against such armed forces and that all black and oppressed people should be armed for the self-defense of our homes and communities against these fascist police forces."

Answer. The police are there to preserve order, not to offer social services. If criminals obeyed police orders, there would be no chases or crossfire. If blacks suffered repression, they were not the only ones in the world. If they did not know how to defend themselves against the Ku Klux Klan aggressors, it is not the fault of this generation. The best way to progress was the concepts of Martin Luther King fighting for peace, and with education, something that these misguided groups did not learn. When negative blacks think that they are living in a racist and fascist country they should leave it and go live where they like, or continue to defend themselves passively as Luther King wanted, not attacking and killing policemen, because then they are equal to them (whom the leftists call murderers) and that is called having common sense. I agree with being armed, I defend this amendment to the Constitution, because also whites, Hispanics, Asians, Europeans etc., as American citizens, have the same right to carry weapons to defend ourselves from crime, and the saddest thing, from our ethnic groups more than from whites. You seem to have not read the Constitution of your own country when asking to be armed. If the police are wrong, we are not going to kill them, we are going to report them, but we have to have the responsibility of stopping and obeying when a police officer stops us, and that is what neither blacks, nor Hispanics, nor white criminals do. They create problems with their civil disobedience and then say that they are discriminated against and murdered. We are not yet as "forgetful" as President Joe Biden, as the prosecutor sentenced him for having documents without authorization, so that we do not realize all the constant repetitions that the police murder. Blacks, whites and Hispanics murder too, and they do not even repeat it themselves, therefore, they are slanders and lies necessary to sustain fear and division in the country. Enough of the lies!

8. "We want an immediate end to all wars of aggression. We believe that the various conflicts that exist in the world come directly from the aggressive desire of the elites and the United States government to impose their domination over the oppressed people of the world. We believe that if the United States or its lackeys do not cease these aggressive wars, the people will have the right to defend themselves by all necessary means against their aggressors."

Answer. The United States government is blamed for everything, along with the millionaire politicians who form the elite to which the Panthers refer. And I have to accept that there is a lot of reason in all that, but it is not a reason to demand rights by trampling on others' rights. The sad thing is that black soldiers who formed battalions in the racial era, served their country with love. Nobody denies racism, because it exists among blacks themselves. Among whites etc. Is it racist to call them black? Is it racist to call them Chinese? Is it racist to call them fat, skinny etc.? No, when in our homes among ourselves these words are everyday. We are all the aggressors, not the government that makes laws for the benefit of citizens even if many do not comply with them. We should not arm ourselves to attack the government, but rather fight to correct, through the Constitution and the electoral vote, whatever is wrong. Of course, in the last presidential elections of 2020, there were embarrassing situations that only existed in underdeveloped countries, such as not wanting to count the electoral votes to show that everything was correct. The

Democrats crossed the line of decency, honesty, and that is why these groups are growing.

9. We want freedom for all black and oppressed people currently detained in federal, state, local, and military prisons and jails in the United States. For all persons accused of alleged crimes under the laws of this country, we want trials by a jury of people of their color. We believe that many black and poor and oppressed people currently detained in American prisons and jails have not received fair and impartial trials under a racist and fascist judicial system and should be free from incarceration. We believe in the ultimate elimination of all wretched and inhuman penal institutions, because the masses of men and women incarcerated within the United States or by the U.S. military are the victims of oppressive conditions, which are the real cause of their incarceration. We believe that when people are tried, the United States should guarantee juries of their colleagues of color, lawyers of their choice, and freedom from incarceration while awaiting trial."

Answer. There is nothing more racist than thinking that in order to defend a person, the judge must be the same color as the person or that in order to cure a person, the doctor must be the same color as the person. Justice, nor any other identity, should be represented by colors, but by evidence and knowledge. With racism, we always think about the color of the skin and that has been a big business in this country. There have always been abuses in the world, from judges to presidents. That is not why we are going to kill each other, but rather denounce them. Hate breeds hate, and so does racism. In this paragraph we see how negative black groups before and now, look for reasons to become racist and discriminatory, by asking judges of their own color to defend them and then criticizing white supremacists.

In this era of 2024, we must recognize that black and white judges have joined forces to dismantle the fortune of former President Donald Trump, judges evaluating the properties of the accused, white and black judges fiercely attacking him with excessive fines of up to four hundred million and more. Despite everything that has happened and been experienced by the American people, it does not give us the right to attack each other and shoot ourselves in the chest. It gives us the right to denounce these abuses publicly and internationally.

Let everyone know about the filth that has happened to both whites and blacks. And do not think that because you are black or white you are not racist, envious or vile. You can also be fair, correct and good, regardless of race and skin color. Pandora's Box belongs to all of us. Today the members of the Black Panthers are seeing that they are not the only ones being persecuted. They must be happy, right?

10. "We want land, bread, housing, education, clothing, justice, peace and community control by the people of modern technology. When, in the Course of human events, it becomes necessary for one people to dissolve the political bands which have connected them with another, and to assume, among the powers of the earth, the separate and equal station to which the laws of nature and nature's God entitle them, a decent respect to the opinions of mankind requires that they should declare the causes which impel them to the separation. We hold these truths to be self-evident, that all men are created equal; that they are endowed by their Creator with certain unalienable Rights; that among these are Life, Liberty and the pursuit of Happiness. That to secure these rights, Governments are instituted among Men, deriving their just powers from the consent of the governed; That whenever any Form of Government becomes destructive of these ends, it is the Right of the People to alter or to abolish it, and to institute new Government, fashioning their way on such principles, and organizing their powers in such form, as to them shall seem most likely to effect their Safety and Happiness. Prudence, indeed, will dictate, that a government of long duration should not be changed for light and transitory causes; and consequently experience hath shewn, that men are more disposed to suffer, whilst evils are endurable, than to abolish the forms to which they are accustomed. But, when a long train of abuses and usurpations, pursuing invariably the same object, evinces an intention to reduce them under an absolute despotism, it will be their right, it will be their duty, to throw off such government, and to provide new guards for their future security.

Answer: The Black Panthers acted more out of racial hatred toward whites than for compelling reasons of equality. Hating whites because they were enslaved would mean hating African blacks who sold them and hunted them like animals for the slave trade. The slave trade of blacks and whites existed and still exists, although covertly, but in another concept and covertly until the authorities discover them or the citizens denounce them if they know about the matter. Communism or its theory infiltrates the minds of workers, university professors, and students, considering that the left will free them from all social ills, when in reality it destroys them. There is not a single communist or socialist who fights for just causes who is not bourgeois or thieves. The Black Panthers asked for PEACE, something that they took away from the American people.

COINTELPRO

What is COINTELPRO? It was a series of covert and illegal projects carried out by the FBI of the United States between 1956 and 1971 with the objective of monitoring, infiltrating, discrediting and disrupting American national political organizations, according to what was found on Wikipedia. I am not going to defend one or the other, but with the experience of having lived in corrupt communism in Cuba, I can clearly say that this writing was published by communist organizations altering the truths of what could have been that nucleus called COINTELPRO. Why do I doubt it? Because all the organizations affiliated with the communists, their common platform is lies, deceit, misinformation, defamation, injustices, violations of the laws and their law enforcement agents, so what they write, I will never be able to assimilate as a truth and no Cuban Democrat or Republican will doubt what I say, because we have all lived through it and we are spread across the globe for these reasons.

Beginning in 1969, Black Panther Party leaders across the country were targeted by COINTELPRO and were "neutralized" by being killed, imprisoned, publicly humiliated, or falsely accused of crimes. The usual tactics used by COINTELPRO were perjury, witness harassment, witness intimidation, and withholding evidence. If that happened, both the communist organizations and the FBI were on the same level of murder, violations of laws, extortion, etc. The same when I say that Black Lives Matter and White Supremacists are on equal terms.

If you notice, the FBI agents were criminals. The Black Panthers were angels fallen from heaven and they humiliated them. That is the same policy they have with the police, saying that they are murderers and the people already believe it. This is how communism works, systematically, and slowly it undermines the minds of the people who, in the end, end up believing what the communist system has in its objectives, demoralizing the national protection agencies of the country they want to govern. We already have two bodies in the country that are murderers and criminals. The FBI and the Police, and we could not miss the accused without guilt, Donald Trump. Sadly, this is spread by people like Nancy Pelosi, Chuck Schumer, Alexandria Ocasio Cortez and their friends in Congress.

If this was happening with the FBI, who cleaned up the mess? Have we been living in it for many decades? Or the writing on Wikipedia was written by the Communist Party, which knows a lot about editing documents (those who edited the prosecutor's report to Biden for the ill-gotten documents) or stored them. Compare the information on Wikipedia with others before making the reports, because you will find everything and sadly mixed up. Who contaminates the truth? The communists and the Democrats of Washington D.C.

Bush inherited the dirtiest part of the swamp, attacking it with the terrorism that we also had and still have within. Is it hysteria? Who contaminated the evidence of Donald Trump's documents in Mar a lago? The FBI is lying again, confessing its political miseries. If this is not communist infiltration, with all its reasons, because the American people made the Communist Party official, we can only denounce them, because they are within their rights to be officially communists, but the people have the duty to deny them the vote, defending the country from the destroyers of capitalism who are precisely the Democrats linked to rot.

They all are, and they are going to "defend communism, not the country." There is not a single socialist, social democrat, leftist or communist, Leninist, Marxist, social progressive (another form of communism) who defends his country. They destroy it defending their own interests and discredit all the bodies that are there to defend the country, to turn them into weaklings.

It is on Wikipedia and university students who momentarily look for information find that the FBI in their country is the worst in the world, worse than the Gestapo.

So what are we complaining about in the USA? They made the Communist Party official, which today is united with Hamas, the Democrats and other terrorists. We, the DEMOCRATIC and REPUBLICAN voters, will actually be those who are going to save the country by refusing to let its corrupt politicians go, if they love their country. They speak ill of the Police and the FBI, and I'm not saying they haven't made their mistakes, but of the two bad ones, I'll stick with the best. I'd rather we be governed and run by them than by our communist criminals. This is the true mission of the FBI. Investigate before acting.

Our mission (taken from the pages of their website).

The FBI is a national security organization that responds to threats and is governed by the collection and interpretation of information. Its mission is to protect and defend the United States against terrorist and foreign intelligence threats, to defend and enforce the laws of the United States criminal code, and to provide leadership and criminal justice services to federal, state, municipal and international agencies, as well as other partners.

Does it look like the information on Wikipedia? (although this platform gives the opportunity to amend the texts) but those who should make the difference do not, which are the university graduates in social studies or the FBI agents.

The bombardment of disinformation is extraordinary and toxic. These groups unite in these destructive communist philosophies to achieve their ends. But unfortunately we saw an FBI lie in a trial against Donald J. Trump.

We saw an FBI intercept documents in the home of former President Donald Trump and with an extraordinary media show, something that they did not do to Pence, to Biden, either at home or at the trial, but they did to him. We saw that they lied and contaminated the evidence on purpose. What are we waiting for? Please let us open our eyes without hysteria, with logical conclusions and these are to remove from Washington D.C., the weeds or the rotten apple, which are all of them, worse than Biden and this causes that: the Democratic Party is not allowed to work honestly and those responsible, I say it again clearly, are: Nancy Pelosi, Chuck Schumer, Adam Schiff, Obama, and the Clinton family, along with the toxic Bidens, who are not declared communists but work very closely together. Those disguised as Democrats will be swept away with our votes. The power is ours, not theirs. With our electoral votes on November 5, 2024, we will begin the cleaning of the Swamp. Together we will go down in history by saying no to communists. Our country is not a land of misery, but of progress. We do not want communists in the government in collusion with the Democrats, we want Progress, Freedom, compliance with the laws of our Constitution, etc. Is the sacrifice too much to ask for?

Congress is like the voters, they do not want problems. They will never gather two-thirds of any chamber to solve the violations of Washington D.C. This has been happening for years.

What a huge mistake our country made in making the Communist Party official! Undermining the Government with all of them, the affiliates, and those who work without being affiliated, but the swamp suits them and fight for power.

In the Biden Kamala era, the FBI, the CIA, the Department of Justice and the Secret Service are highly discredited. Are we undermined by communism-terrorism? Of course we are!

BLACK LIVE MATTER MARXIST ORGANIZATION

In 2013, the Black Live Matter movement began as a result of the death of Trayvon Martin in Florida. When the Black Live Matter started the riots because of the death by strangulation of George Floyd by a policeman, they were joined by all kinds of white and Hispanic criminals and together they committed crimes. In crime, everyone finds their favorite place and everyone joins hands in the task of equal conditions. The television news is in the archives, although many were edited by the corrupt press that we have.

We saw statues destroyed throughout the country, we saw clothes and electrical appliances stolen from stores, we saw this group take hostage the streets that belong to all of us, and we saw the hatred of blacks rise to very high numbers defending their rights to discrimination and equality and in many cases in the supremacy of blacks over whites in a fierce attack of hatred trampling on the rights of others. What Black Lives Matter considers racism is not the same as what the population sees, since we all think differently.

We saw them on TV, their leaders saying that they are guided by Marxism (but none of them are guided by the concepts of Martin Luther King, whom they betrayed), nor have we seen them in demonstrations defending when one of them kills a policeman, whether white or black, or one of themselves. If we are going to speak, or criticize, we must say everything. If we are going to act, we must do it correctly, so that they believe us, and if we are going to hide, we will have to hide everything. Citizens who are complicit in social delinquency is the new social trend.

The Press like CNN see them as the saviors of racism, because they do not want to say what is really happening. When a black person kills a policeman, or does not obey him, and there are confrontations, no black institution holds a meeting with the press condemning the bad behavior of that black person, or a street demonstration in solidarity with the family of the dead person.

No group demonstrates to end that. Nowadays, with social media, it is easy to lie to the people, and they believe the lies. Now it turns out that the Black Lives Matter do not threaten, do not destroy, they are very fine people, but what we saw during the assault on the streets defending George Floyd was something else.

They are looking for seats in the government and the image must be cleaned up, and if you raise your voice they accuse you of being RACIST. They claim that they did nothing, and the press helps them lie, and by the way, most Americans are blind, deaf and mute. Taking to the streets of the nation in any neighborhood is URBAN TERRORISM. Threatening is terrorizing citizens whether they are white or black, and that happened before our eyes, through the country's television channels. That they have repented of all their bad actions is something else, and they want to pretend that they are correct citizens is what we do not believe until we see the good actions.

It doesn't matter that the newspapers want to say that they are angels fallen from heaven, but the public saw them and observed that no Democrat came forward to even criticize that situation. We are not blind yet, and much less have we lost our minds, even if they want to pretend otherwise, they will not be believed until they apologize to their compatriots at a press conference. There is no justice or decency in our country if we remain silent out of fear, and before the Constitution it is our duty to denounce the bad peacefully so that better results come because if we do not we will be accomplices.

The communist or Leninist or Marxist behavior as the leaders of Black Lives Matter said on television, shows that the plague of communism makes all these manifestations of hatred seeking separation, not discrimination, because the urban terrorism demonstrated in those days by George Floyd, made it very clear to us the behavior of this group that now wants to cleanse itself and hopefully they get it, everyone has the right to repentance if it is genuine.

Nothing that is related to Marxism in street organizations is good. They have the right to close the streets, take them over, and make their headquarters for surveillance and attacks, so the people have every right to criticize their bad actions and their well-planned lies, even if the corrupt press hides the reality and to denounce them publicly, since the Department of Justice has its doors closed to the people due to its own corruption in the Democratic Biden-Kamala government.

Let the black organizations go out to the streets, to the press, to denounce the bad actions of blacks who kill, steal, intimidate like any Hispanic, Asian, white American or European group. If so, then there is justice, but if blacks do not criticize their black communities that commit all these types of crimes, drug addictions and robberies, accepting their miseries, then we are talking about a false and complicit defense. Decent, family-oriented, educated blacks, whether professional or not, suffer these shames from their groups, and do not want to be involved in these vandalisms, just like any ethnic group that does not tolerate bad things in their communities. And I will always repeat it, whether you like it or not, until you are tired, and you can understand how badly you have behaved.

It does not matter the reason why these groups are formed until they get out of the philosophies of Marxism that they themselves do not know.

No one can believe their good intentions. No one can deny racism and how it happened on a global level. Blacks can call themselves "black" among themselves, but another group cannot say it because it is racism.

Racism? Equality? More than anything, it is MANIPULATION. When each group feels proud of who they are, and of their ancestors, racial manipulation ends. In the past, many of them, for being black, suffered investigations and trials to prove that the fortune they had earned was right and theirs. From that time to this, society has not changed much, the same for blacks as for whites.

If all the liars, who use the corrupt computer media, to sow the seed of discrimination in the country, then they will be able to see how their black and white judges persecute Donald Trump as their ancestors in Africa were persecuted for black slavery, showing them that there are violations of the laws by the Democrats of Washington D.C., there is hatred and envy, there is government shamelessness, etc. Just as in communist countries they have persecuted those who think differently. In this government, the Democrats are the ones who cover up the bad behavior of all these groups, wanting to put forward their great ideas and marginalizing other citizens. Lack of respect for their Democratic voters who are not idiots. These examples of black men and women who were able to overcome adversity in the worst time of racism show us that if they succeeded in that fateful time, why do black people who are resentful of the past still continue to obtain benefits for the sake of discrimination that often begins in their own homes? There is much to think about and work on in our country.

Black Lives Matter declared themselves Marxists-Leninists, etc. All those with communist philosophies end their groups by stealing from each other. According to the press, the members of this organization have seized the funds they collect for their supposedly "just causes." Did they have an audit? Have they killed police officers and kidnapped the streets that belong to everyone to make their own war headquarters, destroying the cultural works of their own country, and justice and investigations went on vacation? Were they imprisoned for being criminals? Those who accuse the federalists and all those racist organizations should do the same with the radical black racist groups, so that others see that they are all the same, some with black skin and others with white skin and discolored brains, but every human being has the ability to reform their attitudes and return to the path of good. That is called Repentance.

Leaders in favor of the proletariat end up being rich, because they want those who have fortunes to give them to their causes, but they do not use their own money to end poverty. That is proven. If the black student organizations had integrated correctly or had followed the concepts of their great leader whom they defrauded, there would not be "the discrimination to which they allude and which many black separatists use for their own ends and monetary collections, but which people are afraid to tell the truth so that they are not branded as racists. The real racists in American society are those who do not step forward to expose the corrupt press and those who live off discrimination."

The whites do not hate you. Nor do they discriminate against you, as they want to make you believe. With your low self-esteem you still feel enslaved, and that is a psychological problem that many will have to resolve. Change your manners, your attitudes, get rid of Marxist philosophies, work honestly for your country, break the chains that bind you to slavery and integrate. You speak the same language as the whites, the same guts, the same blood color and the same intellectual formation.

Look at what unites you and not what separates you. (Words of John F. Kennedy.)

We are tired of so many lies disguised as truths or vice versa. If there were a school for whites only, they would use it to say that they are racist, while educated blacks take the right to have one for blacks, and that is an abuse of intellectual power, converted into racism, even if they accept some of them. According to the census, "White Americans" are the largest racial group quantified in the 2000 census, accounting for 77.1% of the population and those electoral votes (those who voted) were for Obama. Demonstrating that this famous racism is in question. Racism today is supported by both groups, remembering the past of their ancestors and becoming racist, because after July 2, 1964 when Lyndon B. Johnson signed the Civil Rights Act ending racial segregation (Civil Rights Act of 1964). In the United States no one can discriminate against another if proven, Therefore, blacks must abide by that law and not open any institution for blacks. The word is INTEGRATION where all black whites and other ethnic groups work together regardless of who they are, but just the name "Colleges for blacks" is a broad example of racial segregation and not by whites.

Today racial conflicts continue both from blacks to whites or vice versa, but not from the decent population in general, in our neighborhoods and streets, but from conflicting groups of blacks and whites mentioned above. We all know that slavery occurred in the 18th and 19th centuries and was the consequence of the Civil War of

1861 when this bad practice of human submission was abolished. Blacks and whites who defended them died, those to whom the 100 acres and two mules belong, as much as any black that the Black Panthers defended with their bad social behavior and still continue trying to divide the population, the rest of the disintegrated members and President Biden wanting to gratify the blacks and leaving behind the whites who died fighting for the abolition of slavery violating the Civil Rights Act if he succeeds. Rebellious, resentful blacks never talk about giving thanks and gratitude to the whites who defended them and died for the abolitionist cause. White supremacists also do not thank the squads of blacks who fought to defend the country for them. They do not see that because of their bitter resentments. This reminds us when we talk about Hiroshima, and not Pearl Harbor. That's how we humans are! We blame everyone without distinction for our deficiencies. After the Civil Rights Act of 1964, there is no reason for "schools for blacks" unless they receive federal funding and this is a dirty double move by the US government, which should be investigated but who bells the cat? We will have to change the politicians, presidents, judges etc. who for so many decades in office (due to the negligence of the voters), do not care about the people, but about their jobs. It is time for us all to wake up from the eternal sleep and go to the polls in 2024. Abraham Lincoln said. "America will never be destroyed from without. If we fail and lose our liberties, it will be because we destroy ourselves."

You may think it is hysteria when communism is accused of social evils, but those of us who lived through these situations before in communist countries know that we are led by the radical left from Washington D.C. Joseph McCarthur, historians criticized him for being a liar, with Anti-Communist Hysteria to achieve his goals, and many said he was homosexual. Cubans who fought the communist enemy in 1980 and other past, present and future decades, are told the same thing, that we suffer from Anti-Communist Hysteria. And in Cuba we were even called homosexuals without being so, because of the safe-conduct passes of the police of the city of Camagüey for not accepting the system. Like me, hundreds of Cubans were classified as anti-communist hysterics and homosexuals.

We were all called Marielitos. Communism has no mercy and uses lies to deceive. We read the Bible and do not apply its concepts, we read the Constitution and especially the corrupt judges and lawyers in the Biden-Kamala era, it is not convenient for them to apply what it says, so they interpret it according to their meager criteria. We write and speak, and we do not read the dictionary. This is how we are living. We must all analyze and break the chains that bind us mentally, in order to be free from the political Democrats of Washington D.C., until those who remain decide to change course towards patriotism and bipartisanship in 2028 by holding decent presidential elections. They have to analyze how their political party, the toxic ones from Washington D.C., have demoralized them nationally and internationally.

Separatism and racism, even in this millennium, continue in the media as important news, regardless of the country's Constitution, regardless of the Civil Rights Act. The blacks who are comfortable with this situation, remain retrograde, their emotions damaged since childhood. Racism and separatism play on the same field with whites, defending the race. For both groups it is a business that generates money for their organizations (federal or state funds or donations) and public attention. The decent black groups, professionals, simple workers, do not approve the violence of their groups, they integrate with the whites who were not responsible for slavery since its abolition nor did the blacks succeed their relatives.

White women marry black men, blacks marry white women, both poor and millionaires, artists, writers, judges, magistrates, doctors. Can you tell me where racism is? It is in the minds of those who remain slaves because of hatred and resentment. And I confirm: it is in blacks, whites, Hispanics, etc. It is in all the rioters, who start like this, and end up being common criminals, sowing Urban Terrorism in our communities, and these are the ones who want to govern us, change the course of society for the worse, defended by those who should apply the laws, defended by the democratic politicians and we will not allow it, whether they are street criminals, or government criminals, of which there are many and we have to denounce them. They will not silence us.

Love, understanding, tolerance and acceptance of each other in society is fundamental to keep us united, respected and loved. It is the key to living in harmony in society, not separating each group. Integration is what will promote the future of our youth, but those of us who are classified by groups will continue with psychological disintegration. (Unconstitutionally) because the Constitution says it clearly: XIV (1868) Section 1. Every person born or naturalized in the United States and subject to its jurisdiction, shall be a citizen of the United States and of the state in which he resides.

It must be repeated so that in the future we will all be American citizens and leave segregation behind. We are tired of group divisions in schools and universities, we are tired of the same issue of discrimination and segregation, we are tired of lies disguised as truths. We are tired of laws that are gathering dust on the shelves, and they are not used correctly to stop those lies, those deceptions in society. It is time to think and analyze, to stop following the ignorant who govern us. Judges who persecute men, and not truth and justice, must be unmasked by an impartial press and by the laws of our country, and they are all gathered in Washington D.C. And nobody acts.

Foreign university students, if they do not correctly comply with the student statutes, should be deported and never received again, and they should study in their universities and not undermine ours with their radical and terrorist hatred.

We have to apply the dusty laws that we have to the American citizen students and withdraw their scholarships and money loans if they support terrorists. That is not FREEDOM OF EXPRESSION, that is COMPLICITY with terrorism. Let them pay out of their own pockets. We are tired of our authorities not complying with our laws! Remember that the Twin Towers destroyed by terrorism, more than 3000 American dead, we owe it to Bin Laden, a former student of our universities. The people must never forget it.

Samuel Taylor Coleridge was an English poet, literary critic, philosopher and theologian, founder of the Romantic Movement in England and member of the Lake Poets along with his friend William Wordsworth.

"In politics, what begins with fear often ends in failure."

MONEY AND GOVERNMENTAL POWER

Acts 20:25) "In everything I have shown you that by working hard in this way we ought to help the weak and remember the words of the Lord Jesus, how he himself said, 'It is more blessed to give than to receive.'"

Money and government power taken from the hands of corrupt people destroy us all, while in the hands of the righteous it is generous and solves problems. Bad behavior is not approved by any citizen, no matter if the American government separates us into groups to support racial, social, political divisions, for its governmental purposes, or by the authorities who count us (Census) so that we all receive governmental or state donations etc. The communists consider that the rich should give to the poor and that is where social misery begins. The government should not give money to the poor either, it should give them the tools so that each one can work for it. Only the communists are those who think that the money of the rich should be in the hands of the poor to equalize wealth. That is, the rich are trying hard and the poor are sitting watching TV enjoying the equal riches.

The only president in several decades who thought the right thing to do was to say "American First" was Donald J. Trump. He did not specify with those words, whether they were for one group or another. Those words are sacred, because they represent all of us as the American people, and that we owe that respect before the world to his efforts to negotiate with foreign countries and put everyone in their place. He cut funds to corrupt groups and organizations. Our money was used properly and may it serve to help, negotiate with foreigners and their needs, but cover ours first. Biden is a dollar-minting machine, and the Treasury Department will have to implement new sophisticated equipment to continue printing them, and he gives them away and his blind voters. Destroying our American economy.

The economy is the efficient and reasonable administration of assets. It can be defined as the science that deals with the way in which scarce resources are managed, with the aim of producing goods and services and distributing them for consumption among the members of a society. Economics studies the use of resources that are scarce, but how to reproduce them is what many do not know, and in the Biden administration everything changed radically. He had the nerve to speak at the press conference that was scheduled for him so that the people could see how well things were going. That the economy was strong, but we all know that is not true.

The poor do not understand figures and concepts about what the economy means, but they do know what measures it. When they cannot support their household expenses, buy what they need, celebrate an event, put gas in the car, pay the high costs of rent, buy expensive medicines, etc. That is the economy that the poor know exists because they are living it.

The American people, due to the large masses of immigrants entering the country, have been gradually losing their rights. When the people see that more money is going abroad than to their citizens, they must begin to change their plans.

And it is very careful to select who to vote for. Shameless are all those who receive it, manipulating the most inept president the US has ever had, Joe Biden. The countries that will receive that money are the first immoral ones in the Corrupt Sociological Chain, who do not give their people even the basic basket to live on, and the United States (the owner of the dollars) has to pay them or bribe them, so that they do not send their illegal citizens to the country. The president of the United States, Joe Biden, asked Congress to invest 861 million dollars in Central America, to stop irregular immigration, in addition to 10,000 million to help refugees and displaced people around the world. Mr. Biden, this is not called irregular immigration. It is called illegal immigration allowed by you violating our laws and your entire cabinet as accomplices.

You must be senile, a president who wants to give our money to the displaced or refugees of the world. And what about us? Let him not lie and not say "stop illegal immigration", it is not irregular, it is regular, because he planned it, he shouted it in his electoral campaign saying that he wanted Open Borders to go against Donald Trump, and there they are, now they are afraid of his serious mistakes and illegalities, because all countries want to come to live in the USA and their violations of immigration laws are paid for by us, the people.

Mexico $1.4 billion is the "first step" to fulfill Biden's plan to invest millions of dollars in the region within a period of four years. He promised it during his electoral campaign, the White House explained in an official document. All this is to stop illegal immigration caused in these times by Biden. Donald Trump's proposal was 20 million and he was accused of wanting to separate children from their parents. Biden wants to solve the same thing with more money, but no one accuses him of separating children from their parents. That is the corrupt press that is silent when it suits the Democrats. Corrupt politics has a lot to learn, and that is that the people are not as stupid as they seem. We are going to unite the American people so that our money stays here, and everyone's problems are solved. Cooperation is one thing, and Biden Kamala's wastefulness is another. A very simple exercise will show you that the Democrats have done nothing but breed hatred among us. From one to ten, name how you have benefited, for four decades in your own country. I am talking about non-monetary social conditions.

Go back to the pages of what Donald Trump did for four years and compare the years and the solutions.

34 million dollars to "confidential" non-profit agencies for UN Agencies to help Hamas terrorists. The terrorists in this government have more power than we the people.

$120 million to help Palestinians in Gaza, as well as in Judea and Samaria. Less for Israel. Biden asks for $1.4 billion to reduce migration from Latin America, which he is responsible for, but since he does not care about the people because he has millions in his personal checkbook, he gives the money away and distributes it as he pleases and everyone in Washington D.C., the two major parties have never put in the budget the miserable salary that they give us retired seniors through Social Security, not the SSI which compensates for the misery granted by the government. The people should not protest, foreign countries and even enemies enjoy our dollars and if they do not, they will never be heard. Absolute corruption!

And so on, from NATO, the UN, Africa, Cuba, Central America, the enemies of the USA, Europe and many more receive our kind dollars. We are almost like in Africa. The saddest thing is that the President and the Senate and everyone else together are sending money to the enemies of the country, something that is prohibited by the Constitution under the 14th Amendment, which they only want to apply to Donald Trump, and all of them dirty their hands and dry them with the pages of the American Constitution. It's too much!

If there is something that everyone who has not known how to make money (millionaires) should admire, it is to admire them. Money is only bad for communists, who then all end up being communists, but with the difference that the communist appropriates what belongs to others and the millionaire works for it and must enjoy what he made to the fullest, without feeling guilty for being one. Donald Trump and many others are examples of this. The Trump family has known how to do it, manage it, and enjoy it. God blesses that money that souls degraded by envy consider evil, while the masses follow the erroneous multitudes defending dirty politicians, who deform society with ill-gotten money, involved in transactions as dirty as they are, accepting as many destructive philosophies as they are presented and paid and these are those in Washington D.C., along with the socalled: "good professors" in the Universities, Colleges and academies all infested with the virus of so-called communism disguised with many philosophical names, brainwashing them for not having taken the necessary measures and putting the "Big House" in order, our government. From within Washington D.C., are those who destroy our society.

No matter how much you read about the different philosophies explaining finance, we do not find the concrete parameters. Society defines it philosophically in this way: "Never expect luck or money or fortune, work child if you want, to be the owner of a fortune."

ABORTIONS JUSTIFIED OR NOT

In Cuba, having an abortion was like drinking a glass of water. Parents took their young daughters to terminate the pregnancy because these mothers had already had several with complicit doctors, midwives, or by themselves with natural herbs or medicines. That was the established culture, some because of poverty, others because they did not want to have them, others because they did not care about having an abortion annually until they decided to have one after having interrupted the previous pregnancies and nobody thought that they were killing the child, because there were no studies or policies in favor of fetuses. Ignorance towards this topic was very normal in Cuban society, (I don't know in these times).

In the USA there is enough information to begin to spread the pros and cons. There is another side of the coin, the psychological suffering that rape or premature sex bring to young minors. If the date of pregnancy is considered to have an abortion, they are killing a baby no matter how many months old it is. Although I agree with the movement that defends fetuses and I support it, I consider that when laws and religion come into play together, in my opinion, it is not advisable, because both will never agree, they have different concepts to defend.

The sensible thing would be to make campaigns that help women understand that the fetus has life. As Dr. Carson is doing. Television is a medium but it costs money. If it is not for some extreme medically proven issue of the danger that it represents for the mother or the disease that the fetus carries, abortions should not be performed. When a country does not give prophylactic information about abortions, they will continue to be done with or without laws. Nothing more feasible than to create awareness of this situation, especially starting from the seventh grade in schools.

Religions speak of abstinence and educate their parishioners, both men and women, to make decisions based on the Bible. Nonbelievers cannot be influenced by these verses, because they do not believe in God or if they do believe it is incorrectly and they all end up in great disagreements. If there are therapies for people who suffer a mastectomy, there should be therapies where several women meet and freely talk about these issues, which most end up with emotional trauma and never recover, because they have aborted them. They have not considered the option of putting them up for adoption, which will also be a trauma at the end of their days. Giving up a child is not mentally healthy. Children are not born to give them away, nor to kill them before they are born. These issues are up to each person's conscience. And to each belief of the mothers.

Coming from a communist country where the rights of individuals are violated, I feel a certain aversion to taking away the right of couples to make their own decisions. Gynecologists who perform abortions in clinics and hospitals should be involved in this. When individuals are deprived of their right to make decisions under communism, it is like being naked before misfortune. That is why I advocate laws such as not giving health insurance to these women but giving it to those who want to mutilate their penis, then the solution would have to be to deny it to everyone or to give it to both groups.

In 1969 my family and I (personal story) were about to present our documents to travel to Spain. The way out was through that route at that time. After five years of marriage, when I had a medical checkup, the doctor asked me if I had not had children and why I did not undergo treatment? I told him. Because I want to leave the country and that would be a problem and we are going to leave it for when we are in Spain.

In my mind, instead of a blessing, it was a problem, because it is not the same to live in Capitalism than in Communism where there is nothing to buy for the new family member and that would imply a delay in our trip by making documents for the new member of the household, which was not easy either. Selfishly, I proceeded until that moment.

At that time, Cuba was attacked by the Dengue virus, and like Covid 19, the protection campaign began, which consisted of not going to hospitals and not visiting houses where any of its members had the virus, and that was it. I got the disease and got over it, our neighbor died. Several months went by and again the news that dengue was still present.

One day when I was going down the stairs of my house I almost fell to the ground, I felt terrible dizziness, nausea, my mother helped me and told me: if this doesn't go away, we'll go to the hospital. We ended up in the hospital telling the doctor, "I think I'm infected with dengue again." He did several tests and after several hours, he came to my room and told me. It's not dengue, she has two little arms and two little feet. At that moment I felt a feeling of euphoria, which vanished when I thought that the trip would be delayed for another year, because in Cuba after three months of pregnancy they didn't let you get on the plane.

I said that I would have an abortion because I came from a family and culture where abortion was normal. My husband told me it's your decision, not mine, and I thought I would have to get a divorce because I was so upset. My mother, who had had several abortions in her life, refused to let me have one because she was on the verge of death during her last curettage. My cousin, a nurse at the Maternity and Children's Hospital, refused to put me in touch with the doctors at the hospital who performed abortions. My sister-in-law, a pediatric nurse, refused to help me. All doors were closed. I kept insisting and was two months pregnant when, finally, through a school friend who had attended high school together, they told me that he was a doctor and that he performed abortions.

I went to see him, and he asked me if I was sure of what I wanted. I said yes. He attended to me immediately. When he put me on the table to perform the examination, he looked at me and said two words that have marked me for the rest of my life to this day. "It's big." Referring to the fetus.

I began to sob compulsively, the words did not come out and I stammered: let me have the girl. He had to hold me and to calm me down he said: How do you know it is a girl? I answered: I have a feeling. He helped me get down and dry my tears. At that time ultrasound had not been introduced in Cuba.

I traveled 92 km to return to the rural area where we lived. When my husband and my mother saw me, I began to cry and my mother, thinking the worst, said: "It is not time to cry, you have already done it and now you have to move on," hugging me and comforting me. Crying, I told them: "I could not have the abortion." We all cried together and my happy husband said to me hugging me: that was your best decision and he was not wrong, it was the decision that marked my life by letting her live and enjoying my first pregnancy. Everyone was happy and there was no problem anymore, and I said, well, when the girl is born we will make her a passport to leave here.

In the first three weeks of my return, I was half asleep in the morning, feeling my mother in the kitchen making coffee. We both worked at the hair salon from home and the clients arrived early. I felt lethargic and fell asleep and saw a very white little hand slowly come out of my belly, up to her elbow, and turning her little hand she greeted me moving her little fingers and when I tried to take her little hand, the vision that I swore was real disappeared. I ran to the kitchen and told my mother. The little girl is white as mother-of-pearl and she thanked me with her little fingers. She is like my mother-in-law. My mother-in-law was another mother to me and I was her daughter.

My mother looked at me and said: sit down. What are you talking about? I told her: about your granddaughter. Mommy thought that the trauma suffered by wanting to have an abortion and regretting it had driven me crazy. She asked me: did you dream it? And I told her: no, I just saw it. I was almost taken to the psychiatrist that same day. My mother said to me quietly: "Don't tell anyone what you saw." Because that was a dream or a nightmare, because of the tension you had about whether to have the abortion or not. If the neighbors find out, they will talk saying that you are not well.

Everyone who came to my house told me the story that I was pregnant and what had happened to me with the vision of the little hand thanking me. For me it was an act of grace. Friends who wanted to have an abortion told each other, look what happened to Alila, that the girl thanked her and so it was, believe it or not, that several did not have the abortion. After the girl was born, we laughed because she was as white as mother-of-pearl and looked just like my motherin-law. One day we decided to start with the passport because she was already about six months old and that day my father turned on the TV and we heard Fidel Castro shouting in his speech that no one would leave the Island and that the people who had arranged the documents to leave through Spain retroactively were annulled until further notice, the communist who led us moving his hands like windmills thinking how to disgrace Cuba.

I could have killed my daughter, and in any case I would not have been able to get out of that hell. Today I would regret that bad action like many who did. No one could leave the country. Eight years passed and the second girl came. We left through the Port of Mariel towards the United States, Key West in 1980. The oldest was eight and a half years old and the second was one year and three months old.

Abortion is a matter of conscience and education, involving the morals and ethics of the doctors who perform them and creating awareness that from the first day of gestation the fetus is already alive in pregnant women. We see Dr. Carson explaining that it is true and creating awareness so that abortion does not happen. Having them and giving them up for adoption is almost a perennial death for those who regret it and for children raised outside of maternal contact. Creating awareness in women from an early age, because parents pass traumas on to their children for generations without wanting to, and often with our own actions. Countries like Cuba that have always been like this, with this culture of abortion, it is very difficult to eradicate it with laws or with medicines, because they will always look for those who can help them and will be exposed to death due to the ignorance of those who help them. (They are not doctors or midwives). Not everything is good and not everything is bad, as the wise man says. Our country has the tools to raise awareness through good school programs, organizing and directing it to Social Studies, preventing abortions. No matter how many laws politicians and religious people create, abortion will continue to occur illegally, with abortive herbs known since creation and health insurance, if they approve the mutilation of penises of those who suffer from their traumas, by whatever methods, in justice, they will have to include abortions as well and that is what those outside the government think, "the people." They should be wise in providing aid and education preventing abortion.

In the 1970s, activists promoted the Hyde Amendment (which successfully prohibited federal funding of abortions through Medicaid) and unsuccessfully pushed for a constitutional amendment that prohibited abortion. They prohibit federal funding of abortion, because it kills the fetus, and do not prohibit the abusive practices of atrophying the member of a child who has decided to be a woman or vice versa using federal funding. Not everyone has the same opportunities to have breast implant surgery, because it is considered cosmetic and insurance does not cover it. They cannot remove wrinkles because it is also cosmetic, without seeing that these conditions of sagging breasts and wrinkles affect a woman's selfesteem, just as it affects homosexuals who want to make changes, and today they are covered in California. They patch up on one side, tear on the other, and they do not end up doing things right.

When the laws are so interpretive, they end up affecting the people. The majority begin to see the laws as their enemies, especially if they are linked to religion. What is written is relaxed, leading to harmful interpretations, and that is where all the communist philosophies that are not in the communist party come in. They have the purpose of disorienting multitudes and they succeed while the governments from Washington D.C., entertain themselves by delaying their work in their endless discussions. Imagine, the judges with the same attitude problems. Interpreting what your neurons send you to elucidate what is right from what is wrong. Ecclesiastes 3-14.

What society are we forging? If the Constitution must be modified or amendments added, it must be legally as it is written in it. Let us work bipartisanly with organizations against and in favor of abortion looking for true solutions to benefit the fetus that already has life since it is in its mother's womb. I have always thanked God that He enlightened me and that I did not kill the most precious thing I have, my two daughters.

Hegemony is the dominance or supremacy that a group exercises, in such a way as to dictate the terms and parameters of social action in all senses and to keep opposition outside the law or legitimacy, that is why it is so difficult for politics and religion to converge in a great agreement resolving these abortion issues. If one party is benefited or not the other.

In the Bible, abortion is not directly mentioned, but it is implicitly.

All religions go towards the same objective, not to kill the fetus by blessing it from the first moment of its conception.

Education is key to solving problems, conscience, understanding and love do more than hundreds of laws in the constitutions of any country. Couples must resolve these cases together. An abortion is very traumatic, but giving the child up for adoption is as traumatic as abortion or more. In abortion, the child dies; in life, the child is longing to be with the mother even if there are substitute parents or one of the parents and it is almost like dying in life. The human being is also complex. Family members should always work well for the child, not for their personal emotions. We are told that the child, even before being born, has formed a close relationship with the mother in the womb (uterus). From the moment of birth until the age of ten, the child receives from the mother the moral values that will shape them forever. We know from experience that there are mothers who have to have their children taken away from them. If it were not so, there would be no Department of Child Care or parents recovering them in the Courts. Do not risk your lives or kill your children with abortions. Parents will never be the owners of the children, we are the guides. Children are not merchandise that should be kept under the protective wing of one of the parents, they are the fruit of love, of the agreement that they had before bringing them into the world and they will always be independent whether the parents like it or not and for the emotional well-being of the children, parents, even if divorced, must work together to protect and love them. Couples divorce but never their children. The more love they have from both parents, the more stable their emotions will be.

Psalm 127:3. "Children are a heritage from the Lord, the fruit of the womb is a reward."

FAMILIES

For psychology, the "group of people united by a common goal or by feelings of affection and affiliation" means the family. We are living in times of fear when it comes to expressing ourselves publicly, because everything offends liberals, but they offend us with their senseless demands and we have to tolerate it, because if not, we will be judged. Do liberals have more rights than conservatives? No.

Should we fear those who openly express their points of view and do not accept those of others? No, we all have the same rights and duties. All according to the Interpretative Constitution. (Now the democrats considered it that way), we have the same rights before the laws, but when working judicially, the Judge or Magistrate, seeing the intentions of the accused individuals, make their unjust sentences. The Judges do not see or do not want to see the accomplished facts and interpret them. The sentences that ordinary citizens find unfair and unconstitutional when reading the Constitution, they interpret them according to what their negative neurons sent them, to discern when an intention occurs and when it does not. We are lost in our American society if we do not act well.

Full of fear of the governors, of the district chiefs, who do not work for free, and all are there to serve the community, not to change the threads of society without consulting the citizens. This is how communism works by imposing laws and decrees, destroying everyone equally. (Those who speak and denounce these issues, historians call them Hysterical Anticommunists), but those who destroy our values call them "Saviors of Human Rights."

Families are the ones who must take back control of their children while they are minors, speaking the truth, so that they know who is leading them until they are of age and do what they want when they leave home. Children are the continuation of their parents and there is wonderful advice in the Bible, but it is not considered. "Train up a child in the way he should go, and he will not turn away even when he is old."

They consider what the Bible says about excessive liberalism, and we all go like sheep to the slaughter. The rights given to children in the USA violate the rights of parents who are the ones who support them, love them and do not wish evil for them. Psalm 127:3. "Children are an inheritance from the Lord, the fruits of the womb are a reward." No parent is the owner of their children to go to such an extreme of atrophying their sex, whether by hormones or surgery or any other method used in these matters and the unconscious authorities authorize it in defense of children's rights trampling on the rights of parents.

If a child decides that he wants to be a pirate and asks to have his arm or leg cut off and his eye gouged out, should he be indulged or taken to a psychologist or psychiatrist? I heard this anecdote about the pirate in a video by a Christian pastor and he was quite right. It should be repeated to psychologists and all those involved in wanting to cut off children's genitals or sexual impulses. The government should make laws prohibiting these mutilations until they are of age and decide for themselves. They should not involve parents or minors in wanting to inhibit the sexual development of the minor. If they have suicidal tendencies, they should be taken to therapy and given love and understanding at home, not complaints or insults that are more painful than the disorder they suffer from.

Children should be spoken to clearly by establishing limits. The fact that a child feels trapped in someone else's body does not give them the right to have parents decide for them either. This is discussed from the beginning and is supported by several factors. If they want to dress as a woman, they should be allowed to do so, but no parent should go that far to stunt part of their body and development while they are minors. If they participate, they will always feel overwhelmed if they do not receive family therapy or therapy in agreement with the character of each parent.

Parents are there to educate and guide their children, not to stunt them from the tender age of childhood, because when the sexually mutilated child decides to change his thoughts, they will always blame and hate them for having marginalized them and violated their rights to do with their body what they decide after becoming adults, but not in childhood. It is very difficult to confront these situations in the family. But if love intervenes and not shouting and reproaches, everything is resolved. Each individual has a brain, and it is not precisely a copy of that of their parents. We support the activists who do not want African girls to have their clitoris mutilated according to their customs and tribes, and here, we mutilate their genitals approved by senseless laws, indolent parents, liberal societies confusing their brains. In the USA we are scandalized by these practices and in Africa, where they carry them out, there is a movement in favor of young women and girls who mutilate their clitoris, to end these savage practices even though in Africa it is normal in these tribes.

Our country is ashamed, with the laws they have made in recent times and sadly the Constitution kept in a vault or in the cemetery and they have not informed us when the death and funeral occurred.

Every human being has the right to choose their sexual preference regardless of age, but the treatments paid for by medical insurance must wait until the child is of adult age and they must pay for them with their money, not with the money of the people who oppose these practices. Many parents have collaborated with their children's sexual preferences and it is good that they support them, but there are rules and disciplines in everything in life and in homes as well.

It is not fair that many medical insurance companies cover operations and hormonal plans for minors, which involve excessive expenses and physical modifications, totally dangerous and extremely expensive medications with the people's money. Do we need to repeat it? Yes, to see if anyone listens.

Should everyone who wants to change their sex reach adulthood and do it out of their own pocket? Do we have the same laws under the Constitution or under state laws? Simply No!

Remember the Obama era when they paid for surgeries for men to turn them into women (who will never be) in the military? Biologically they will never be happy, emotionally they will be happy. Did they perform cosmetic surgeries on female soldiers for the same health insurance? They did not tell the people. When everyone joins together to destroy ethical values in society we are destroying the most important thing which is the freedom to express ourselves, to defend ourselves, being complicit in the social catastrophe.

Now in California Governor Newsom wants to take away the right of homeowners to raise or lower rents with a proposition for the new elections forgetting that the majority of families who rent do not take care of the properties, and when they are forced to leave the property, it must be rebuilt, and those expenses go to the owners, and not to those who destroyed other people's property. He doesn't make any plans to end these situations and yet the California people re-elected him despite his destructive policies taking away the rights of parents over their children, disastrous teachings in schools promoting laws in favor of homosexuality.

A new state law that prohibits schools from requiring transgender children to show themselves to their parents. That is totally crazy. Both Bonta and Gavin Newsom feel like Roman emperors in California and the plucked chickens will be as affected as those who oppose. Unless the Democratic parents want to continue allowing them to abuse them all.

In protest of what is happening in California I continue sending letters. Throw them in the trash, it is not my problem, but they will never silence me. I will always tell you the truth even if you don't listen. The Democrats are destructive, unconstitutional laws, communist Democrats.

I don't plan on moving from California, my last years will end here, but I have the dream of seeing many of those unconstitutional laws fall, bringing back a beautiful and healthy California and keeping its name of the Golden State and not that of the State of Marijuana and Sanctuary Cities.

February 22, 2024

Capitol Office

State Capitol P.O.

Box 942849

Sacramento, CA 94249-0011

LORI D. WILSON

Assemblywoman, District 11, Ms. Lori D Wilson. I was reading your proposal on the Internet about your Assembly Bill 957. And although I do not belong to your district, I live in California and we share the same Governor, the same gender, the same status as mothers and we belong to minority groups, uniting us in many aspects. I liked that Governor Newsom did not sign that proposal because of many difficult aspects that it entails although he is a hypocrite who discriminates against some above others, as happens with homosexuals and prostitutes. I would like to share my humble opinion with you. I read your political career and I say congratulations!

Having a trans child does not mean that you have to take children away from parents who do not support them. There are ways in California to take them to a psychologist or psychiatrist, or offer them family therapy before taking a child away from the parents. Parents who in your time and mine, (I don't know where we are now with social shamelessness), parents protected us from any situation that could affect us, and until we were of age, we did not "govern ourselves", they governed us. Taking a child away from a parent is in extreme cases where the child is in danger due to physical abuse, drugs, alcoholism, etc. It is another matter.

Today politicians have freely introduced marijuana to us as the panacea of modern times,(so that the money it generates stays with them, and not with the drug cartels) something that "I do not agree" with that because our young people are using it and "it is a drug" affecting their brain. Because of the politicking that uses that money to solve problems that federal funds do not provide, but should we obey whether we like it or not? We obey traffic laws, moral laws and social laws. My question is why do trans youth not obey their parents? According to your approach to Law 957, parents must obey the wishes of their minor children on this issue and keep them away from them if they do not listen to them. There are many issues that are not about homosexuality, but about mental disorders.

You are failing as a mother, woman and politician. The personal problems of each family are not those of others and based on that, requests like yours must be deeply analyzed.

If a young person wants to be a pirate and his parents do not tolerate it, then should they have an arm, a leg and an eye removed? If they want to be lesbians, should they be allowed to have sex even if they are minors? If they want to be gang members, do parents have to obey them and allow them to affect their family and neighbors in the community? If they want to be thieves, do their parents have to allow them to do so by fulfilling their wishes? If they want to be prostitutes, do their parents have to allow them to do so because they want to? Or that the social workers you propose come and take them away from their parents because they did not support them. Why are parents obliged to obey their children and children not their parents? That is the problem that we all have to unite and work on in our society and first of all in our homes. When they are adults they will be able to do what they want, even leave their parents' homes if that is their wish, not that we are the parents manipulated by our children. In every home there are rules and if they are not followed they must accept them as we accept the rules of the DMV. Do you see, Mrs. Wilson, how we all have a different perspective than what others propose in all aspects of politics? Homosexuals must respect their parents, their relatives, and their friends, because their condition is their problem, not that of society in general. What nobody wants to say is that they need mental health professionals and acceptance and love in their homes. These young people are looking for more love than gender reassignment. They want tolerance and they do not tolerate even the family they have. This is a product of communist tendencies that precisely take advantage of these situations to twist the destiny of people. This is due to bad psychologists, teachers and doctors involved in all these social miseries, forgetting about moral values. The letter was long and I left it until that topic because I am as fed up as many are with these out-of-control issues.

California is the slope of the swamp, but soon it will be the complete swamp. God is separated from the schools and Satan comes to do his thing.

California voters, if you do not want to continue living in social misery, in the lack of respect for the parents of the children, vote for Donald Trump as if he were the bitter medicine we need to clean up this current misery. Many parents have faced family debates when their children go to university. It is a focus of social misery that must begin to take shape from what was a society that always had everything, but each one in its place. Which is equivalent in street slang to "Together but not mixed up." De Santis in Florida marked the line to follow, but the national swamp is so deep that it is very difficult to attack it, but not impossible, if all families analyze that the harmed ones are the children and the young people would pay more attention to what is happening. Whoever uses their influence in the government to enrich themselves is a political hypocrite and it is our civic responsibility to deny them the electoral vote and in the process publicly unmask them. This can only be achieved by reading the information that is sent to us at the time of the elections to know who or who to give the vote to. In California the swamp is deep, very deep! So deep that the Democratic voters themselves are deceived by their own politicians and do not open their eyes.

The case of the primary elections with Katie Porter trying to clean up the swamp of Washington D.C., and Adams Schiff wanting to destroy his own country by engendering hatred among citizens, is an example of following crowds without being informed. This is our current society and it is worth making changes to counteract the devastating impact of the so-called communists, Marxists and the rest of the philosophical spectrum that surrounds social misery. We remove God from our lives and Satan is doing his job. You do not need to be religious to try to have family harmony. Children should never be lied to and parents should never discuss their marital problems in front of them, much less make them take part in the problem. Many complain that religions brainwash young people and children, but if we analyze which brainwashing is the best and gives the best results, the decisions are obvious. God first and crush the head of communism like a snake.

When you are told about communism, you will say that it is obsessed with it, but those who have experienced it, see what others ignore. International communism is doing its work to such an extent that in London they removed a statue that according to them, was racist and replaced it with one of the Black Lives Matter. In Paris, the Opening Ceremony of the Olympic Games featured a range of artists who mocked God. They cross the line of communist social vulgarity and continue their paths infesting society and that is what the corrupt take advantage of and we already know where corruption comes from. These groups ask for tolerance and do not apply it to other groups, offending religious people with these presentations. That is part of Global Communism. Psalm 74:22 Arise, O God, plead Your cause; Remember how the fool reviles You all day long.

THE TOWER OF BABEL AND MUCH MORE

The Constitution should not be fixed to someone's wishes, but to delve deeper and analyze that what was written at that time, as an official document to educate and guide us, is not feasible today to comply with. The worst thing is not whether certain laws are interpreted or not, the tragic thing is that Congress, the Electoral College, the House of Representatives do not come to the rescue of the laws regarding the 2020 elections, and this has affected the morale of the citizens.

The Englishman only promoted, his detractors or opponents who are in everything, except in constitutionally defending the abuse towards Donald Trump, all protected by the same constitution, make the country an internal hell.

In 1907, US President Theodore Roosevelt wrote, "We have room for only one language in this country, and that is the English language, as we intend to see that the melting pot brings out our people as Americans, of American nationality AND NOT AS INHABITANTS IN A POLYGLOT BOARDING OUT. He told the Truth.

In 1923, a bill drafted by Congressman Washington J. McCormick became the first proposed US national language legislation that would have made the national language "American" to differentiate the language of the United States from that of England. This bill failed to pass Congress despite significant support, especially from Irish immigrants who resented British influence. (Two-thirds of the chambers apparently did not want to meet to make that bill happen.) Just as they did not want to meet to count the votes from the stolen 2020 election. Who tied their hands so they would not count the votes?

How many traitors to our democracy are there in all of Washington D.C.? We will have to invoke Sherlock Holmes for his proficiency in observation, deduction, forensic science, and logical reasoning to help us interpret our laws that the inept, and of which there are plenty, do not know how to interpret and the little they know they cannot apply because the target is Donald Trump. Or that the spirit of Agatha Christie enlightens them and gives them legal guidance because they are lost in the forest of judicial ignorance and unfortunately, they are the judges who dismiss charges of racism. We would ask these beautiful and admired literary characters to give us a hand as well. These problems are about to cause a civil war due to the noncompliance with the laws that exist and are violated by the Democrats from Washington D.C. Not the Republicans as they make the masses believe. In the late 1880s, Wisconsin and Illinois passed English-only instruction laws for public and parochial schools. In 1896, under the government of the Republic of Hawaii, English became the primary medium of public education for Hawaiian children. And after the Spanish-American War, English was declared "the official language of the schoolroom" in Puerto Rico. (Puerto Rico followed with the Spanish language.) Similarly, English was declared the official language in the Philippines, after the Philippine-American War.

An 1847 law authorized Anglo-French instruction in public schools in Louisiana. French language rights were abolished after the American Civil War. In 1849, the California Constitution recognized Spanish language rights. (California has had every Governor except Ronald Reagan.) The California Constitution was rewritten to state that a law of the laws of the State of California, and all official writings, and executive, legislative, and judicial proceedings shall be made, preserved, and not published in any other than the English language. Does California comply?

In good language means: "backwards." Although California had only recognized Spanish language rights in its state Constitution, it was too much to write all the laws in both Spanish and English and they opted for the unofficial and unrecognized English language, which is the one we all communicate in. Why didn't they write the documents in the recognized language "Spanish" and wrote them in the unofficial and unrecognized one "the English language"? Where is the ACLU?

In 1868, the Indian Peace Commission recommended English-only schooling for Native Americans. In 1878–79, .With this linguistic Tower of Babel, one cannot even think of the English-only 28th Amendment proposal that many of us want to push through because as long as we have a Congress that does not work, earns its salary by looking for people to lobby with, it will take more than 21 years to achieve it and by then if the Americans, being benefactors of everything, do not open their eyes in this era, we will have to speak the Chinese language officially.

All countries, or most of them globally, have their official languages. In the United States, politicians and since the founding fathers wrote the country's Constitution and each state writes its own without consulting the official one, all have put their grain of sand in national ignorance.

History and Social Studies teachers are not exempt from criticism or suggestions because they are not working either. No offense, it is not correct, but if we were to take what California did when it recognized the Spanish language in 1849 and wrote everything in the English language that was not recognized, we see that California has always stood out in wanting to be on good terms with God and the Devil. And if we were to take it to the street slang of any Californian neighborhood, we could call them "dunghills."

Political corruption is not born in a single presidential term. It is a dormant virus that attacks all presidential terms and throughout time and history, today we have rampant corruption in our country because a Donald Trump did not arrive in time to move those rotten waters, creating the current swamp.

I say Mr. Trump, because since I have been in this country he has been the only president capable of declaring corruption in the government to the people, which is our great home, and in doing so, the crocodiles came out ready to destroy him in the worst possible way wanting to lock him up in jail. Can you imagine when past presidents can come to see Donald Trump in prison, to tell him "THANK YOU, FRIEND, YOU ARE PAYING FOR ALL OF US." And the Secret

Service that accompanies them, (because I don't think the Woke plot would dare to take them all away) rolling out a green carpet for them to play a round of golf in the corridors of the prison among all of them. Obama telling him "I hate you but I suggest you go to the prison that I had made for me, just in case what is happening to you happens to me." A good short film!

These crocodiles are part of the American system and unfortunately in recent times we saw how the Republican Party harbored traitors to the cause, not only President Trump. McCain would be the hero for many, but for pilots when the plane is shot down and the enemy surprises you, you go to jail and there is no heroism, there is captivity.

Then, with the influence of his family members with a long military history in wanting to free him alone, McCain demonstrated his nobility, which has nothing to do with being a hero (according to history), because then all those who were imprisoned with him should have the same title of heroes. By telling them that they had to free everyone, it was a great act of generosity, not heroism, but this is how we have been confusing the dictionary terminologies for many decades, although these two terms converge.

John Sidney McCain III was born on August 29, 1936 and died on August 25, 2018. An American and officer in the United States Navy, he served as a United States Senator for Arizona from 1987 until his death in 2018. Many said that his father-in-law was the one who made his political career, but that would have to be asked to the family.

John McCain ran for president twice without success, the American people seem to have not esteemed him enough to make him the President of this great Nation. His presidential campaigns were named after John McCain in 2000. John McCain's presidential campaign 2008. Heroism is when that aviator defends his companion or any person affected or not by the circumstances in the face of danger.

According to the dictionary Hero. It is: a feminine or masculine word. Person who performs a very selfless action for the benefit of a noble cause. Illustrious person famous for his exploits or virtues.

Nobility: feminine noun. Quality of noble. Similar. Honesty, sincerity, loyalty, kindness, generosity, selflessness, magnanimity, altruism, lordship, majesty.

Group or body of the nobles of a State or a region. We could say that J. McCain was a noble person, and the others similar. McCain's family had a glorious path in American history and we all understand that as parents anyone would intervene with the authorities in Vietnam to save him, but granting him a title of hero is another matter and the 45th President of the Nation at one point told the truth that hurt McCain, by publicly denying that he was a hero. When talking about pilots in wars, THEY ARE ALL HEROES, even if they are not officially awarded that title. And if they declared McCain a hero, they should have declared all his companions who had fewer privileges than him in captivity heroes. Vietnam. A war that marked American history where men fought to the point of offering their lives, and those who returned were shamefully received in many states by those who did not have the guts to go fight, but did judge them negatively, when the people knew that this war was directed by politicians sitting at their desks in Washington D.C., but not in the face of hand-to-hand battle. It was all a dirty political business of bureaucratic leaders, without allowing experts and generals to openly deal with their strategies and knowledge. Power blinds, and politicians mostly feel more powerful than God. That is why the Swamp exists.

This senator stood out by turning his back on the Obama Care vote like a Roman leader in that era, where slaves were thrown into the lions' den, betraying the Republican Party because of grudges against what President Trump said or did. As a voter in recent years we can do the math and ask ourselves: Which president tried to give the best to the people? Which president tried to end government corruption by making it public? Which president thought of boosting the economy and bringing back all the millionaires who went to China to bring millions of dollars to their bank accounts? Who among the politicians in Washington D.C., including former Presidents, have big deals with China, and the American people are losing their jobs? These politicians are the ones who entered office moderately wealthy at the beginning of their political careers, and have come out extremely wealthy, after having plundered all the opportunities in their offices, which are supposed to serve the people, and not their monetary coffers.

A clear example is Mrs. Ocacio who came in speaking badly about the rich and in a short time (they say she is already an online businesswoman selling pullovers), with good profits and if it is a lie, Donald Trump is also right in saying that the press is deceitful and corrupt, affecting us all in society, and that is a short period of time, serving the people. Imagine when she has been like the Democrats and Republicans for four decades, enriched by using the information that everyone handles about the economies and their functions, and the Democratic fanatics continue to give them the continuous vote, without thinking that they are accomplices of the swamp for believing that their political party was the one of many years ago, respectful, and responsible with its voters when it is no longer true.

Trump's rally in the Bronx demonstrated Martin Luther King's dream. Everyone united and that we have the right to vote for whoever we want without being attacked as happened in 2016. Ocasio said on television the night before Donald Trump's rally in the Bronx that the Bronx would not support him. This was wrong, said a Hispanic woman like her and like me and like the rest of us who are in the USA. Margarita Rosario is her name, a sixty-nine-year-old lady who has lived in that district for more than 60 years, almost all her life. Upon hearing the predictions of Alexandria Ocasio Cortes of New York on television the night before the rally suggesting that the Bronx would not support him, the lady, upset with what Ocasio was saying, decided to show up, holding a Trump flag and a sign with the slogan "Make America Great Again" (MAGA).

Telling the press: "How dare you speak on behalf of everyone that the Bronx will not be represented? Hispanic, black, gay and other groups have a personalized brain. They do not need any Democrat or Republican to lead them and today, with the economy in the ground where families can barely live, the option is totally for the people through Donald J. Trump. If Trump changes political party we all change with him, because we are not favoring Trump, nor the Political Party even if we should, we are favoring the Economic Growth of Our Country."

Trump will return home as a billionaire as when he entered the presidency, even if the Democrats die of envy. We do not follow a successful billionaire, who has provoked the envy of the inefficient Democratic politicians. We are positively sure that America will return from where the Democrats of Washington D.C., the woke, the communists and all the neuron-less, those of the Senate, Congress and the House of Representatives have it and we all know where it is. In the basket of the ship! And we will rescue it.

Donald Trump showed us in his last administration how the country is headed, but you did not let him work, all entangled in false lawsuits. We already know the facts, and that is why we follow him. The poor are not thinking of living on welfare, or receiving bonuses, to buy votes as the Democrats do, they are thinking of development for all as a woman said at the Bronx rally. The people are tired of lies and political dirt and false promises. Schumer came into New York poor and will leave a millionaire and his state in rampant misery. Ocacio talking about poverty and looking for a millionaire boyfriend. With real facts, the Mexicans without parole for their entire lives in this country and those who entered last almost American citizens. They have not fulfilled anything. The Bronx has opened its eyes as American citizens, not as racial groups. Martin Luther King must be applauding from his rest.

When Trump told us many times that there was government corruption, he was called crazy, rude, just like Cubans are called for denouncing the violations of their human rights in Cuba, but the "prestigious or corrupt UN" that has its definition in Wikipedia says: The UN is financed by voluntary contributions from member states. Its main objectives are to guarantee compliance with international law, the maintenance of international peace, the promotion and protection of human rights, achieving sustainable development of nations and international cooperation in economic, social, cultural and humanitarian matters. With such nice words we can only applaud frantically.

Now we have to ask ourselves: What human rights? Those that are in their false documents? Or what true human rights mean as such?

This is what the UN says about human rights taken from the same page in Wiki asked:

Human rights, abbreviated as DD. HH.

1- They are those "instruments based on human dignity, which allow people to achieve their full authorization." Consequently, it subsumes those freedoms, faculties, institutions or claims related to primary or basic goods that include every person, by the simple fact of their human condition, to guarantee a dignified life and the satisfaction of their needs without any distinction of race, color, sex, language, religion, political or any other opinion, national or social origin, economic position or any other condition."

Analyze whether the UN is corrupt or not. They talk about human dignity, authorization, freedoms, faculties, needs, race, color, sex, language, religion, political opinion, (thousands of Cubans imprisoned for having a different opinion from the government), national origin, economic position. From all this we can appreciate how corrupt the members of the UN Assembly are, because in Cuba for decades all that verbiage that the famous Human Rights documents have has been violated. If the UN does not know this, all the rights of citizens are violated in Cuba, there is no human dignity when the people peacefully demonstrate and even minors are imprisoned. Selfrealization does not exist in Cuba when the people cannot even have a representative of the dissidence to choose between the corrupt rulers and whoever represents them politically on the basis of democracy. There are no institutions in Cuba that are not directed and plundered by the Cuban leaders. When they are allowed to open a restaurant or other business they are constantly being watched. The Cuban people do not have a dignified life, but a miserable one, and the UN knows this, allows it and applauds it.

The leaders of the Cuban government are miserable with their discrimination between the dollar, euros and Cuban money. Whoever does not have a relative exiled in any country in the world does not eat, does not dress, does not have medicine, not even an aspirin, the most common thing in the world to relieve pain. What do the corrupt members of the UN understand about the needs of a people when that condition does not exist in Cuba? The entire Cuban people are in great need while their leaders have stolen Cuban capital and distributed it among all of them. Are these the communists that young people worldwide want to follow?

The Cuban leaders and the Puppet Diaz Canel know this perfectly, along with the Castro clique that continues to govern in Cuba and fight for positions as if Cuba were a dynasty, when in reality it is the Corruption of the Communists.

The irrational thing is that baseball player Victor Mesa is here and the FBI, the CIA and the Immigration Department have not classified him as a spy. He is immoral. He comes to the United States to do dirty business with the communist regime, but not from exile, but because of the shamelessness of the American government and Cuba, both accomplices of these dealings. They do not investigate him because he has business with his house 32 in Vedado, Havana, Cuba. A house that was surely stolen from the owners when they left Cuba without compensation.

Now it is a hotel for Americans who are fans of the baseball game. The lack of compliance with American laws has no limits. We are living among communists infiltrated only for Cubans, because the authorities allow them these businesses under democracy. The Etecsa company, of telecommunications in Cuba should be investigated by the FBI and this is my public complaint. This company is questioned for the connection cuts they make at the slightest sign of popular protests on the Island.

Everyone working from the USA And now let the historians tell me if communism is a reality embedded in all the sources of the USA order working together. It is not an Anti-Communist Hysteria, it is the reality. Now after many decades the Cuban leaders who are not leaders per se, because they do not lead, persecute the people, they opened spaces to religions, but many were imprisoned for defending their religion specifically "Jehovah's Witnesses" in the past. Catholic priests and many more. What do the members of the corrupt UN say about the immigration of Cubans in the world? Did we emigrate because we did not like Cuba? No, because of the abuses of our human rights, blatantly violated, which are in their corrupt documents only, and in the bad conscience of its members representing their countries and destroying others like Cuba with their terrible lies.

To the point that the UN does not see how Russia and the Island of Cuba transfer and recruit young men to fight in the war between Russia and Ukraine, paying them a pittance and that is being mercenaries out of hunger and need, by not giving their people what everyone has stolen from them. They brought the corpse of soldier Camilo Ochoa to bury him in Cuba. They are mercenaries for giving food to their family but the real mercenaries are those who sell themselves for a few perks.

The national origin would have to be discussed, since many Cubans had to claim the foreign citizenship of their grandparents, greatgrandparents and parents in order to leave the country, because as Cubans they were all imprisoned on the Island, except for the Castro curia who had citizenship from different complicit countries that protect and help them. In Cuba, the only millionaires who exist are those who have stolen even the bricks, members of the political party, those who became rich with the illegal games of bolita, those who have known how to negotiate with the foreign money that is sent to the country from the USA and other countries, those who have businesses from the city of Miami with the approval of the Cuban and American authorities, involved in these businesses, such as the business of house number 32 of Victor Mesa, in Havana.

The intelligent ones of the poor class, who have known how to steal, as well as the leaders. Remember that in Cuba they closed the institutions that did not suit them, they intervened by passing them to the government, without compensation to the owners, and they left those that they considered to keep. From then on, no Cuban could build any institution of any kind again. They are not free and yet Cuba was elected to the Human Rights Council of the UN.

Cuba was elected, for the sixth time, to join and lead the Human Rights Council, as a sign of the prestige achieved by the country in the work of this body. How far does social shamelessness go? What prestige is the UN talking about? Does it mean that there are 146 corrupt members in the UN by naming Cuba for its great development in destroying its people? By selecting Cuba, the corrupt voters have shown that they do not know what they are doing, or that they support dictators who marginalize their people. Only the United States has opposed it and if any member abstained from voting when its representative at that time Nikki Haley was in charge of representing the USA before the UN in the Donald Trump Administration, then in addition to being corrupt, they are also great IGNORANTS. It is necessary to be cunning, hypocritical, shameless, and ignorant to affirm that Cuba was the country with the highest number of votes in the region, ratifying the recognition of the international community for the very significant advances in the enjoyment of Human Rights for all people. That does not exist in Cuba.

What drug did those members of the United Nations General Assembly who voted in favor of Cuba use? Cocaine, marijuana, ecstasy, or the leftovers sent from the White House? Or the pleasure of using the power they have to maintain dictators abusing the citizenry? Can you tell me what extensive history Cuba has of international cooperation that is not based on lies and corruption?

What the UN says. As a founding member of the Human Rights Council, Cuba shows an extensive history of international cooperation in this area, based on a respectful, frank, and open dialogue. We wonder as spectators: Are the members going to this UN Assembly to talk nonsense, or are they going to expose the realities? Can there be a fair and equitable order in an extremely corrupt organization like the UN? Good God! So they say that Israel committed genocide in Gaza, and not that Hamas terrorists kill them daily and Biden is helping them to continue with terrorism, that is, for the laws of the Americans "without intentions."

Many of us are not religious, but we are sure that a new order at a global level must come and end all those exploitative and lying Organizations, accomplices of terrorism. (I am happy not to practice any philosophy that marginalizes me to express myself rudely) but it is what they deserve, when these insensitive and irresponsible members rudely before the world, vote in favor of selecting Cuba as a defender of Human Rights without respecting those who suffer it, the people, not the leaders, and accuse Israel of genocide without mentioning Hamas as terrorists.

Visit the website of the United States Embassy in Cuba where you can read what the United States thinks and offered under Donald Trump to the Cuban people in his wonderful speech at the UN presented by Nikki Haley.

Every Cuban, out of morality and gratitude, must adore the United States. Except those who came to do business between Cuba and the United States. We came with twisted behavior due to the moral and social human deterioration we had under a communist dictatorial regime, but more than communist, corrupt. Millions of immigrants from all latitudes came to this land, twisted by corrupt rulers, but individually each one can straighten up and millions have done so. Today we have the opportunity to change those fraudulent attitudes with which we had to live and begin the new era of admiration and gratitude for the country that welcomed us, and this goes for any Cuban in any country that extended a helping hand to them or for any immigrant who leaves their country and others protect them, except for the accomplices of the Cuban communists from this territory. These will always be the snakes of society that the authorities must investigate and DEPORT. Respecting their laws is the fundamental basis for healthy social integration.

Thank God I do not practice the philosophies of Confucius, Buddhists or Zen (wonderful and idealistic), in addition to the philosophies of the greats like Marcus Aurelius and Seneca, passing through all the great philosophers that none of these organizations, their members, read, analyze or practice, and they are the ones that govern us worldwide, destroying with their actions what their corrupt documents say. In order for the corrupt to understand, we must speak to them in their own language. In order for the Democrats to understand the same, and so on.

The philosophy of the people is to pay the bill to the corrupt with the electoral vote, for that reason the concepts of choosing candidates for any presidency or for any organization that is formed with communist ideas or not have been created. While intellectuals and academics use the learned language of ethics and correctness, the people have the right to return the same medicine, but with absolute truths, not for our thoughts or ideas, not for hatred but for facts, but for what we see and suffer, the shamelessness of all the organizations that are there to make a better world turned into cover-ups for things done wrong.

Let it be clear to you. Since the disastrous triumph of the Cuban Revolution in Cuba, all rights were lost, including human rights. Mrs. Haley was in the cabinet of former President Donald Trump in front of the US diplomacy of the UN. She served in this position for one year and 10 months. Mrs. Haley denied the rumors that linked her with a race for the presidency in 2020. There is not a single politician who does not dream of the presidency of his country at a global level, just as writers dream of the Nobel Prize, athletes with their medals and trophies. Nikki Haley ran for the US presidency in 2024 and we are thankful she did not run because if she says she was inspired by Hillary Clinton and not Martin Luther King, she has already told us everything.

Member states voted to condemn the blockade that the United States imposed on the Island since the 1960s.

The United States sells Cuba food, medicine and other products but they have to pay in cash because they no longer have the correct credits (due to fraud and thieves) for negotiations and grants them a quota in dollars every year for humanity, which is not the payment for the Guantanamo base, and the people are starving. In the speech to the UN, the United States has asked the members of the assembly to vote not only on the famous US embargo. They are asked to vote on political prisoners, the lack of freedom of expression, on the oppression of workers in Cuba. It would be useful to know what some journalists say about this.

Cuba has commercial relations with several countries that can sell medicines, equipment, food, etc., such as England, Germany, Spain, Mexico and many more, and if they do not provide the people with what they are owed, it is because they STEAL it. It's that simple. There is no such blockade (another sustained lie) as such, there are shameless acts of robbery and persecution of Cuban citizens by corrupt Cuban leaders. In the Biden administration, due to damages caused by the cyclone in October 23, the United States provided, through the United States Agency for International Development

(USAID), two million dollars in funds for emergency aid to the affected communities on the island. The houses are on the ground. Diaz Canel is in trouble for having been a puppet of the Castros. (That money is only seen by the thieving leaders of the Cuban government) the people do not participate in that aid, nor have they participated in the clothes that are sent through the churches, to alleviate social misery. Instead of thanking the churches and good-hearted people for what they do, they open second-hand shops, but first the authorities choose what is of good quality and the people have to pay to get what is left. Cuba receives MONETARY AID from the United States for different reasons, in addition to the remittances sent by Cubans living in different countries, which has developed in this century the current discrimination that exists on the Island in relation to those who receive money from abroad and Cubans who receive nothing. "Monetary Apartheid"

Those who receive money live better and those who do not have to eat even the cats and dogs they find. These are part of the family diet, which has never happened before in Cuban culinary art. Making "ropa vieja" meat or "carne ripiada" from banana peels is already the latest in Cuban culinary recipes under the corrupt communists. We are already tired of hearing in these conversations that in the name of Human Rights they want to resolve what cannot be resolved due to political corruption. What can the oppressed Cubans and citizens of the world think when they elected Cuba to join the UN Human Rights Council for six consecutive times?

Look at what the US State Department says, not only Cubans denounce these sad miseries that the Cuban people live through because of the members who defend Human Rights in the UN. Diaz Canel, who has a video on YouTube where this puppet of Cuban corruption gives orders for revolutionaries (the gang members of every communist society as well) with baseball bats and sticks, to go out into the streets to beat up citizens who ask for radical changes in the country and want to live with dignity and freedom without weapons. Cubans did not want to emigrate, they want a country like Cuba was. "The Pearl of the Antilles" and that name was not for nothing. Communism destroyed the pearls. Let the Americans look at the fact that they admire the rulers of Cuba and spend their dollars disguised as humanitarian, literary, scientific trips, etc. Double standards affect all countries globally. https://www.state.gov/reports/2022-country-reports-on-humanrights-practices/cuba. Anyone who tells the truth will be pounced on by predators, regardless of whether they are housewives, workers, intellectuals, students, presidents or scientists, regardless of whether they are friends, family, or strangers, as happened in Donald Trump's presidential election in 2016.

Many of us who supported him in California were unable to put the turrets on our cars because of threats from the mobs of blacks, Hispanics and whites, lackeys of the Democrats and those paid by Soros. Do they have brains? Do they need to be guided? We are totally stunned and disappointed.

That had never happened before. When the elections to elect Obama took place, every citizen decorated their car, their house, their establishment with flags and banners allegorical to the political party of their preference, even though they were voting for a black candidate, but not one of the correct ones, but rather the friends of the immoral. Because a person who is going to represent the American people should never hide his personal information, that is cowardice, he should be moral and transparent, and for those reasons I never voted for him. My vote is sacred, and it is not for cowards. If he had presented to the American people what he had done "belonging to the Black Panthers" or whether he was homosexual or not, it did not matter, because honesty speaks for itself. I would have given him my vote because I wanted to show that the white American people are not racist. I would have liked to be part of those transcendental elections, when the American people elected their black president, demonstrating that the racism that black criminals talk about is false. Of course, he marked American history by being a black president elected by the American people twice (there are more whites than blacks statistically speaking and more than Hispanics) showing the world that the current myth of discrimination is a weapon of convenience for groups that ask for donations to defend blacks, without remembering the act that says that one cannot discriminate by race, color, religion, etc. But groups are not created to help the country and rescue children from the Foster Care Program regardless of their race. There was so much hatred towards Donald Trump by a dirty press, incredibly sold out to monetary interests, that no one wanted to read what the correct journalists (very few) wrote, because the wave of hatred fomented by the press and the corrupt politicians in Washington D.C., Soros buying them and those outside, set out on the path to destroy AMERICAN DEMOCRACY.

This is how communists act, the destabilizers in countries to make money as Soros has done, a very good friend of Biden since Soros' son has visited him several times in the White House and it is certainly not to take an interest in his "mental health", but rather preparing the new coup that may happen, because they have the power and the money to do it. It remains to be seen if the American democratic people begin to take account of their leaders who are destroying their political party to which they all joined with respect and patriotism.

The facts are what say who we all are. Unfortunately, those of us who have lived through the agony of a communist country cannot believe Senator Bernard Sanders, an activist politician (socialist or communist) from the state of Vermont, who always wants to do something and can't. On his Web page he says: "There is only one way to transform this country: and that is together." That is what communists or corrupt people always want, to transform everything because it is not convenient for them to follow the established status of society.

What we must do together is to remove all those who have been in office in Washington D.C., for more than three decades, destroying the country, regardless of their party. Another of his aspirations: "End greed for profit in our criminal justice system, from top to bottom: banning for-profit prisons and detention centers, ending cash bail, and making communications, reentry, diversion, and treatment programs in prison and jail free. The ideal of communists in any country is that all the rich stay poor, giving them their capital and they steal it."

In short, continue feeding social parasites. What they should do in the USA is follow the example of the smallest Latin American country on the map in Central America. El Salvador, which received thousands of deported gang members from the Mara Salva Truchas by Donald Trump, defending the American people from organized crime, death and injustice, from those gang members, in El Salvador they have built good prisons for them, but they do not have the right to cell phones in the cells, they have to work and paint all the graffiti that they painted in their towns and cities dirtying them, so that they know the effort it takes to keep a country clean, both physically and mentally. Not like in California that considers graffiti urban art.

If Nayib Bukele could put his country in order, giving free rein to his soldiers and police to achieve it. We can do it too, because in the USA they jail the police and leave black criminals out for fear of riots. An unjust, unconstitutional and immoral practice, for the police, and for the people, who have to live in fear of criminals free on our streets, whether they are black or not. Bring to the television cameras the group that defends them from the judges who have done their job by violating their rights.

If American Democrats do not take the time to analyze that making changes is painful but necessary, they do not have to be Republicans, nor vote for Trump (no one asks them to, but it would be ideal), but if they deeply analyze voting for politicians who have been in Washington D.C., for several decades, destroying patriotic concepts and civil liberties, it is extremely dangerous, they will have to seriously think about how to vote. Nothing free is good coming from the government. Unless it is a contest, a gift from any company, etc., benefiting its users or clients. All those who want to give free services end up millionaires themselves, and the people in misery, or involved in scandals of theft and embezzlement.

To the organizations in defense of some and marginalization of others, as has happened so much in the past with the Black Panthers, in the present with the Antifa organization, and the Black Lives Matter, and by the way with the independent White and Black Supremacists. It is time to walk straight and stop having a psychosomatic limp. Use your minds, not the minds of others, to make good decisions. None of these organizations affiliated with Marxists, Leninists, Communists, left or right will give you anything, they take away starting with the money they collect, they steal it from you, etc.

They are not exactly idols to follow, for all their bad actions of vandalism, threats, racial hatred, and death with which they have structured their philosophies. All these organizations betrayed the concepts of the most gallant, intelligent professional, and intellectual, Martin Luther King and the whites, in their effort to be whiter every day, have darkened their conscience, betraying the concepts of Abraham Lincoln. All these groups under the Constitution have the right to demonstrate publicly and chant their slogans as they wish but peacefully.

None of these organizations of black or white members, have fulfilled their social goals in these times, because those who are based on violence, do not receive respect and support from the correct citizens. The concern of the American people is serious, seeing so many examples of corruption outside and inside their own country, the alarms are ringing. If there is something that all communists, socialists, social democrats, etc., agree on, it is the lies and abuses of their people for the sake of free benefits. Others hear theories about it from those who brainwash them in schools and universities, who paint a beautiful picture of taking from the rich, to give to the poor, and the poor sitting while the rich work.

The first thing that communists or terrorists do, because they are the same, is take away the weapons from the people, destroy religion, divide families and suppress freedom of expression or peaceful protest in the streets and in the process they have to think how they think. Total control.

It is better to be surrounded by many millionaires, opening businesses and giving jobs to the population, than to be next to those who live sitting in the chairs of mental idleness using discrimination as a weapon, when in reality the election and reelection of Barack Hussein Obama II ended that myth.

Let us all join together correctly to move forward without manipulation or lies. This is no longer the time for that, it is for preparing for a better future using digital technology, in the good, not that sadly every time they go out to demand rights about discrimination, that is not what people see precisely in street riots. Let us do what Psalm 119-37 says. "Turn my gaze from what is useless" keep me alive on your path. It is not necessary to be religious, but to love God by loving one another. Little by little everything is changing around us. Recognizing mistakes is wise. Repenting is also intelligent. Accepting our ignorance is daily learning. It is not cowardice, it is reasoning.

The Tower of Babel represents the spread of the various languages spoken in the world, also the beginning of something as important for humans as communication. It represents the sin of pride, the desire to reach heaven and therefore God, to be like him. The story of the Tower of Babel explains the origins of the multiplicity of languages. God was concerned that humans had blasphemed when building the tower to prevent a second flood, so God created multiple languages. Thus, humans were divided into linguistic groups, unable to understand each other. King Nimrod wanted to be famous, so he convinced the people of Babylon to build a great tower that would reach heaven. God could see that people were becoming arrogant and decided that he should come down and mix their languages so that they would not understand each other. We are not going to challenge God, but even if we have a Tower of Babel, we can communicate with the universal language that is love.

The United States does not have an official language because the founding fathers must have been inspired by this biblical story?

PETER PAN – COMMUNISM

The power to want o destroy Donald Trump and the envy of never being able to be like Donald Trump, no matter how rich they are, has led us down the path of hatred and moral destruction of our current politics among American citizens.

Two factors that have sickened the American people are those who are carried away by what others say, and those who resist lies and injustices, regardless of the political party they are from, but have annulled their democratic way of thinking, by following the guidelines of mentally ill politicians for power and money that are totally toxic to the Nation.

In so many decades of our politicians in power, we have not seen anything substantial. Let us remember Ronald Reagan when he gave amnesty to almost all illegals or undocumented or whatever you call them, favoring them with an upright life in the country under the Republican mandate, those who could have met the requirements for change and how many promises made in the Democratic mandates have favored illegal immigration? Only DACA, but without these young people being able to help their relatives to legalize. Everything is half-baked.

All those years of false promises led the Democrats and Republicans to deport entire families, except for Donald Trump who tried hard to clean our streets of criminal gangs, who threatened us all, and was crucified by those who like false promises, they could have fallen into family deportations like Obama did, who was the president who deported the most families with a smile from ear to ear. He was applauded by the democratic people. Wake up please!

The Mara Salva Trucha were not low-profile gang members, they were terrorists just like the Mexican gangs, or any other group. Those who criticized do not say that their own gang members killed and threatened even their own families. The metaphor of Stalin's plucked chicken has worked for the Democrats. Here I repeat the last lines so that you do not forget them, and you can analyze what is good for the country. This metaphor of Stalin, "The Plucked Hen" can represent any of us, white or black as a people and we must get out of that henhouse. "That is how easy it is to govern the stupid. Did you see how the hen chased me despite the pain I caused it? Most people persecute their rulers despite the pain they cause them for the simple fact of receiving a cheap gift, a stupid promise, or some food for one or two days."

As you can analyze, this is happening to us daily. Political disputes between politicians and excuse the redundancy affecting us all. These disputes that we see daily on TV or read in the corrupt news, or in the few that remain sacredly fulfilling their journalism, are what we have as a guiding panorama, that our country is being attacked as Abraham Lincoln said, from within, and the only ones who can save it are the voters.

2024 will be crucial in the financial stability of our country when deciding whether to vote or abstain. Luckily, in California there are many Republicans who will vote for Donald Trump. Many Democratic citizens will not want to make changes thinking that they are traitors to the party, but we do not live or act for parties, but for the leaders we select through votes and they betray us and enrich themselves like Nancy Pelosi in the end, using her knowledge to earn millions in the stock market by buying shares, Wall Street? Enriching herself due to the information she handled or still handles is not moral, not because she wins or loses or participates, but because she uses information that others do not have from her political position.

When we all have dirty homes, we clean them, we give cleaning tasks to our children, if we are poor, and those who pay employees, it is to keep the house clean, trying to ensure that harmony, a clean environment, provides peace, lasting this among all families and friends. When our houses are dirty, we mobilize the whole family to clean them, paint them, fix what is broken, etc., and we do it because we like our houses to look nice and clean, and many times even our neighbors or friends help. Those who have money do the same, paying companies to do the repairs. The United States is the Big House of all its citizens, it deserves to be painted, cleaned, and disinfected by all of us at the time of voting.

Our country is the main house where we all take refuge, where we have hopes of living in peace, without wars, and much less internal wars like the ones we are seeing, based on big lies and deceit. Our fundamental duty is to clean it and we are going to do it with our political responsibility, analyzing what have the democratic politicians given them? Unless it is taking away the civic rights of parents in front of their children, trying to remove a candidate from the ballot, and it does not matter if it is Donald Trump or another, for them to benefit from the votes in those states where the candidate does not appear democratically for the people to vote is immoral and unconstitutional.

Trials without following what the Constitution says. Interpretation and we have already seen on CNN in Spanish the comments of Sonia Soto Mayor, a member of the Supreme Court about Donald Trump's immunity, which if she had dignity she would sign her resignation. Lies from the FBI. Excessive fines constitutionally violating what is written in those documents. Increased racism by violent blacks, who consider that their rights are violated and they end up violating the rights of other citizens.

Crowds entering by the millions with Open Borders, immigration laws being violated by the current president Joe Biden, the balance of destruction is excessively high. That must stop, put a brake on the runaway Democratic horse, which is the one that has driven these races.

Let's hope that institutions such as the FBI, the CIA, the Pentagon, the Department of Justice and the Supreme Court of the country, have the reins ready to stop the political disaster that we are experiencing. Or from the point of view of the housewives, decide to put on the APRON and start cleaning together with all American citizens, our Big House, which is very dirty!

We are saddened by those who have seen the Supreme Court fail the Constitution in the form of interpretations, without first fixing it with two thirds of the chambers by restricting the use of weapons by violent people, which the Constitution clearly states. Amendment II. "A well regulated Militia being necessary to the security of a free State, the right of the people to keep and bear Arms shall not be abridged."

Who can we place our hopes on if all institutions are infiltrated with the destruction of the country and its laws? On the voters. We have the power to cleanse them all with our united electoral votes.

Nancy Pelosi could have ended her years in Washington D.C., full of glory and a millionaire, unnoticed, if she had not allied herself with the mastermind of the Witch Hunt, Mrs. Hillary Clinton and Obama.

She has said explicitly in her emails in this 2024 campaign for power "We will remove Donald Trump from the ballot at any cost" and he is a BULLY. (It turns out that the one they ordered killed was Donald Trump. Who are the thugs? The sad thing is that they will continue trying.

It seems unbelievable that so many decades in power and he did not dedicate a day to read the Constitution, and that is why Donald Trump was tried while he was serving the country, in a BIASED way when the Constitution says that trials must be done IMPARTIALLY. No Republican member has ever done that. Why do we have to allow a handful of ambitious people to power, to destroy our country? Whose responsibility is it? Ours as voters, who must defend the country, not its corrupt politicians. Do we have to repeat it until we assimilate it? Of all American citizens with the right to vote in different languages, since the Americans did not make arrangements for there to be only one language in the country, something that I would have liked to see. English Only! But when the founding fathers decided not to put an official language, they never imagined what would happen. Taxpayers' money is used to pay translators in all government organizations, creating chaos and discrimination, because they are not assigned to all languages, but to the most used ones, English, Mandarin, and Spanish, while the American people have to fulfill their political duties and the rest do not.

Those who vote in our presidential elections are those who do not even read carefully in their own languages who vote for them. Today we are a tower of Babel and everyone votes for their monetary or patriotic interests. Or to receive the wheat from the plucked hen. This is shameful in the international image. What can we criticize Putin for? If our politicians are up to his level. Putin wanting to take land from Ukraine, sending young people to a senseless war, for ambition and power. Turning himself and his people into a chicken coop.

Let's hope that the Russians one day remove him from power too. That's how all communists are, they stop at nothing and neither do the Democrats. We are in the same situation without being "officially communists", with the difference that we refuse to enter the henhouse. Who is really destroying our democracy? The Democrats, and this directly affects the voting Democrats. Many will feel offended, but it is reality, and in the face of the truth, lies die.

If they do not analyze how serious we are facing in 2024, we will have worse times, the wheat from the plucked hen will not be enough for everyone, whether we are Republicans or Democrats. Who in Washington D.C., can throw the first stone on morality or politics?

No one and from no party, because since the time of Abraham Lincoln these dangerous tricks have already been happening in our government, the difference was that cybernetic information did not exist and the people today know it the instant the events occur. Because if there had not been internal destruction, this serious thought would not have been left for us to have in our hands and to know how to defend a country without weapons or scandals, and now in the world we know that we can take off the yokes as happened in Poland without firing a shot.

Many will ask: Why did this author or housewife not solve the problems in Cuba and end communism or corruption and now she wants to come here to denounce?

Simply put, communism, socialism, or whatever you want to call it, bases its indestructible government on the destruction of the family, on demoralizing the people with divisions within the family and among friends, lowering their self-esteem, moral values, religious and financial values. One group accepting communism, and the other fleeing the country to save their children. Here the elderly flee to other countries because their money is not enough to live within, and many young people do too.

Their weapons were to spread terror so that the people would be silent. Are we here when they look to the side and do not see what the violent communists are doing? Political destruction came and only one group governed, there could not be political parties to choose from. Do they want to get the Republicans out of the way, similar to what happened in Cuba? In religion, they closed the churches and halls of other denominations in the country, preventing the people from even praying.

Socially, if you did not applaud at a meeting or showed dissatisfaction or did not do so-called "voluntary" work and it was forced, they called you aside and threatened you, not only towards the dissatisfied adult, but towards the family. Can we tell the truth in the USA without offending those who oppose the opinions? In Cuba it was worse.

Children and parents with different political ideas arguing aggressively and without being able to change things, or protesting because they were imprisoning you and even so, many always raised their voices. If there is no unity, the objectives cannot be achieved.

That is why I denounce what is happening to us here, because I left my third world country, which before Castro was the Pearl of the Antilles, and not by choice. I do not want communism to dictate the rules to follow here in the USA or for it to happen anywhere in the world. From the Pearl of the Antilles to the Great Misery, the cost has been excessively high and I do not want that for my new country, the United States of America.

In Cuba, they collected the gold, with the story of buying tractors and those who had it and believed them, gave it away, and it went to the coffers of the shameless leaders or ringleaders of the famous Cuban Revolution. Have you ever wondered why the politicians in Washington D.C., have enriched themselves for decades by serving the people? Because the people have always received the same promises and very few results. The government is slow to act and quick to pursue its objectives.

In Cuba, they collected the weapons of the citizens, fearful that they would rise up to defend their democratic ideas, which the people had. It was mandatory to hand them over. Another of their great deceptions. Have you ever wondered why the Democrats want to limit the use of weapons or restrict them? The Constitution does not specify what type of weapons citizens in the USA can or cannot have. Amendment II Being necessary for the security of a free State a well-organized Militia, the right of the people to possess and bear arms should not be restricted. The Supreme Court violated this Amendment in the month of June 2024 by 8 to one. Do you see similarities in what happened to Cuba with the communists?

Everything that the people accept as good, without analyzing what has happened to other countries through different decades under Marxist, Leninist, communist, socialist, social democratic philosophies is what leads us to social ignorance and that is what the famous communism is based on. That is why I wrote this book, so that if someone reads it one day, they can analyze it deeply and recognize for themselves which political party has done the most harm to the American people and which party has engendered hatred. The people want good results from any party, but unfortunately, the Democrats in these four years of Biden-Kamala, exceeded the limits of taking away citizens' rights for the sake of the incoming ones by illegally violating the laws. The least they deserve is for the democratic voting people to open their eyes and punish them by denying them the electoral vote until they regain their lost sanity. They took away a president's immunity, even if only for a time (while the Supreme Court interprets the laws) so that he could be prosecuted civilly. The plucked chicken is prophetic, Nostradamus was small compared to Stalin.

Many people believe that illegal immigrants who have recently entered through Biden's open borders against Donald Trump should not be rejected or deported. But those same people do not take responsibility and bring a group of them to their homes to help them, even if they are paid for it. Do you know why? Because it is very easy to talk and judge about that aspect of uncontrolled immigration, those who oppose it. Those people do not want to lose their privacy, they do not want to deal with emotional problems, they do not want to fight with different cultures and lack of education in the majority and expose their children without knowing who enters their homes.

They demand that they be helped, but the country is the Big House and if in the small ones they do not want them, why does the Big House have to bear the misery of all the countries that for the most part call themselves democratic? Think about it, it is unfair to ask the government to protect them all when their citizens are full of needs, but the latter Biden told them to come. It is his responsibility now and yet he blames his counterpart Donald Trump who wanted closed and controlled borders.

Where communism enters, we all become the forced plucked chicken, because without weapons, without purchasing power, without believing in God, with broken families, without honor, without the desire to fight for the pain caused by those who must defend us, they become chicken coops. Venezuela, Cuba, Nicaragua, have been for decades. Now the intention is the USA. That is the communism that the ignorant want and I have already gone through that serious mistake of living in fear. I decided to adopt the USA as my homeland, not my second homeland, and I must defend it. We learn from mistakes, and I learned and we will all learn. I hope that the democratic voting people also learn by knowing about others. In this decade there are no democratic politicians who can come out clean from the debates. Obama is fighting to remove Kamala, although they do not say it clearly. Obama is not stupid, and he knows the risk they run but the establishment spoke. He and Michelle had to accept it and approve it. Today, based on what is happening to this country and based on my experience as any person who has already lived it, I share it with the American people (my brothers without colors or races). It does not matter that those I have criticized do not like me, not out of malice, but so that they change individually. Remember that changes are not collective, but individual and by conscience, not by laws.

This is my answer to those who have thought why did I not fight communism in Cuba? But those who know me know that I made several attempts to fight it, with my voice, and I never gave in to saying that I liked communism and obeying as they wanted. One of the first popular trials in the Manuel Ascunce Domenech Hospital in the city of Camagüey, Cuba, was mine.

Perhaps as it was the beginning of the destruction of the country, they have erased the files as the communists are accustomed to do so as not to leave traces. I won incredibly when I opened my mouth, gushing out truths that killed the lies of my accusers. I never went to "forced" volunteer work and there was no mortal who knew I was not anti-communist.

In this way, communism marks you indelibly, harassing and persecuting citizens. They persecute them at work, in schools, in parks, streets, and above all in their own homes. So that you do not tell the truth, but what they practice and should be applauded.

THUS, THE WITCH HUNT AGAINST DONALD TRUMP INSPIRED ME TO DENOUNCE THEM. I do not defend Donald Trump as President, but as a compatriot. He has his good lawyers for whom many of us have prayed that God would enlighten them when defending earthly laws. I defend truth and justice, which is being lost in our country. That belongs to all of us. I defend democracy, the right to think differently, mutual respect in society, the respect for accepting different religions, genders, white and black supremacists, adult prostitution, respecting the right that the Constitution grants us, equality before the law. Because we are not defending a group or a man, we are defending Democracy by which we should all be governed. I respect the right to defend children who are so harshly attacked in elementary schools, and although the American people made the Communist Party official, I respect it, but I will never follow it, nor will I remain silent about how cruel, underhanded, liars and murderers they are, and it is my duty to tell them who they are and how they act, so that young people do not follow them. Academics know it, but the people in general doubt it. Rectifying is wise and those who have taken the path towards communism should rectify their errors by helping others not to follow crowds.

That is why I take the reins of exposing what is happening in our country, the United States of America, so that you can compare, if it resembles or not, what the Democrats and the Communists do. You do not have to believe me, just think how you can get away from the henhouse that they prepare for us. Even without knowing about politics, without knowing about American history, without knowing about religions, I risk presenting you this compendium of the situations that are happening daily, and it is a trigger towards the abyss that the Democrats have dug in these modern times. Many will say, "Is this lady crazy?" And I accept it. All of us who are crazy, whether we are workers, housewives, intellectuals or scientists, the majority is not because of what they do, but because of what they know and have learned from their lived experiences, in any branch, considering them crazy. Accepted epithet in advance! You can freely express your opinions, because that is what it is about, starting to raise our voices telling the politicians that we are not willing to fall off the cliff, that we will be on the edge, but no one will push us with their lies and violations of the laws, not even the Supreme Court.

You can say that I am ignorant, and I am not offended, because it is the truth, and that word "truth" is the one I want all of you to wield as the best weapon.

When you hear in the States of the country the Governors and their collaborators, the members of the Supreme Court who want to remove or restrict weapons alleging that crimes in schools, streets, domestic violence, churches, etc., are the product of weapons, do not believe them. Weapons are not the problem, it is the mental deficiencies of a people abandoned to their fate, by all of them to enrich themselves. I confirm: Donald Trump did not make his millions in Washington D.C. Therefore, he deserves to be in that place helping us to recover our country. Donald Trump, having it all, risks his life for us and we already proved it when "someone" ordered him to kill, but we all suspect who is behind the murders and attempts. The day I posted the protest asking for the Secret Service lady Kimberley Cheatle to resign, the entrance to President Biden's White House website was not open, nor was the intelligence website, I had to pass it on to Kamala Harris. They hide when the water reaches their necks.

Bloggers know more than the Secret Service. The orchestrated attempt to assassinate Donald Trump has to do (due to so many irregularities) with the famous separation of Trump from politics at all costs. Our country is deteriorating more and more every day and there is very little time left for the resurrection of American politics on November 5, 2024. I think that the American people collapsed the Web or they, cowards, closed it so as not to receive comments and be recorded in history. Let us be grateful.

We do not need to remove or reduce weapons. We need honest parents who see their children suffering from these mental illnesses and keep quiet so as not to be criticized (it is a taboo) instead of seeking therapeutic, psychological or psychiatric help.

Do not criticize or make dramas when a person needs to stabilize their emotions. The lack of monetary income to build hospitals to treat these mental illnesses is precisely what they do not do in any state. Politicians currently prefer to make Sanctuary Cities and the people are fine thanks.

These democratic-communist political stratagems are organized by the left wing. The coup de grace of the communists is the currency to which they make changes by devaluing them so that those who had saved some capital would lose it with their limiting laws and disarming the people by taking away their weapons and purchasing power. It is a country CONTROLLED by the power of all of them, not by any current political party.

If all this does not seem to you to be happening here, it is because everyone is blind, deaf and dumb. All that has been experienced in Cuba, in addition to hunger and corruption, where in order to survive we had to lie, accept as good what the leaders did and approved, without the consent of the people, steal, smuggle, because if we did not do it we would not live, is what corrupts the people and suits the aggressors.

All the people became corrupted by the bad habits of all of us who have set foot in the USA, but those of us who understood that in this country, it is not necessary to live as we did under communism, overcame those situations created by corrupt communists. The new man created by the communist revolution affected the new and the old, demoralizing Cuban society. Is that what they want for the United States?

Creating a corrupt government society and taking away the rights of parents over their children is what I do not want for my new homeland, the USA. Remember the PETER PAN program between the United States and Cuba. Naturally, the American people were opposed to bringing so many children and supporting them with their contributions (taxes), but the Cold War made them favor that plan. In a letter to Congress, Kennedy proclaimed the United States as "a refuge for the oppressed" with a "long humanitarian tradition of helping those who are forced to flee to maintain their lives as individual human beings, self-sufficient, free, with self-respect, dignity and health." The Catholic Church took the lead in helping them among other religious denominations that helped.

Bryan O Walsh, an Irish priest, described his role in Operation Peter Pan as "an opportunity given to me by Divine Providence to fight communism." He had broad support from the Church, which also opened its doors to Catholic leaders isolated and exiled by the Cuban government.

Those who have not lived under communism will never be able to sympathize with the abuses that are experienced and arise daily as a cursed condemnation. Envy and misunderstandings about why Cubans are helped and not other groups in Latin America. There is only one answer. In Cuba, communism operated and still operates, taking away the rights of parents over them. We already have it in our Casa Grande. In the rest of Latin America, there was no communism, but social misery due to theft and embezzlement by politicians and presidents in those times that still persist. The political and social conditions were totally different.

This has always caused envy, resentment, criticism and hatred from groups that did not have or do not have these privileges, but what they never say is why millions of people have to emigrate to other countries to survive their misery without having a devastating communist system, and it is that their rulers push them because they do not spend their budgets on the right thing. Government misappropriation, corruption. Are we experiencing this in our country because we want to help, or because we want to sustain ourselves in the corrupt government and turn North America into a third world country?

Journalists do not want to report properly and subjectively make their own analyses. This is how the red color began in Cuba. This journalist takes for granted that young Cubans lived comfortably in Cuba. It is a product of the fact that none of the journalists have lived under communism, and if they are, it is from a capitalist country, they have never moved to a communist one to experience all the situations. The first thing that communism would do to these journalists is censor them. When communism arrived and took hold, no one lived comfortably in Cuba again. The Los Angeles Times journalist continues saying: These young people come from places devastated by violence and economic scarcity. Referring to the children who come to the United States seeking support because they do not have it in their countries, among them Mexico in the first place. Never do journalists, and much less from the Los Angeles Times, report in reports like these, that the devastated places and the economic scarcity come from the negligence and theft of capital by all the irresponsible Latin American presidents who did not take care to clean up their miseries and the USA has to bear the results, without any of them having had communism in their territories. If this is not the truth, then they should go out with television cameras in all the small towns far from civilization and see the great miseries that tourists do not see.

It was very painful for parents and children to separate, but the Cuban parents thought it was better for their children to be saved from hell, even if they died in it. There are many cases of young people who used that program and came to this land, they did not feel happy, and it is that no child wants to be away from the warmth of their parents. Communism destroys families, and the democrats with their actions in these years, are showing us that they are more on the side of the communists, than on the side of democracy.

In Cuba, the morale of the Cuban was destroyed, and in turn the solid infrastructure. All the houses and buildings damaged along with the economic decline left the balance of large immigrations to different countries by Cubans. At that time, as always happens with communists, they blame others and they are unscathed (It reminds me of Obama blaming Bush for all his labor deficiencies). Fidel Castro with his usual verbosity, publicly blamed the United States for its campaign of hostility against Cuba for the development of the Peter Pan protection plan.

At that time, 14,000 Cuban children entered and were distributed in several states in the care of families who participated in those sad moments. Today, helping 14,000 children is not the same as helping 400,000 unaccompanied children reported as arriving from 2021 to 2023, according to a report from the U.S. Customs and Border Protection office.

Another of the most corrupt and significant situations of the left wing is that wherever they land, Justice dies. Corrupt judges, lawyers unable to practice their profession, because if they defended a dissident, they both went to jail. Corrupt Courts, Corrupt G2 Surveillance Department, Corrupt Army. Corrupt Police Force. A hell, and for that reason many parents sent their children abroad to save them through the Peter Pan program. The sacrifice was great, and many, upon arriving and meeting their children, suffered the ravages of separations and claims between children and parents. The indoctrination was such that teachers resigned daily in different schools, refusing to introduce communist books into the classrooms. Something that has not happened in the USA when they wanted to introduce books dealing with homosexuality, which is an adult issue. Today, books on homosexuality are almost obligatory.

I feel that it is the duty of all of us who have experienced these misfortunes, from whatever country we come from, living in the USA, to have the consideration to look back and remember our past, so as not to relive it in the present. We go to the past to see what we should not do in the present, not to cry misery for what we lived, because every moment lived, were excellent life lessons. To leave our children and grandchildren a prosperous and democratic country! Absolute development.

When you said that you were leaving the country, those of us who were lucky enough to have our relatives in the USA rent or buy with options that if the ship sank there the Contract ended. Many boats to rescue us left the USA, when the Mariel Exodus happened. From the moment the telegram arrived at our homes and we decided to leave Cuba, the "Communist Repudiation Acts" immediately began in front of our houses. In one day they gave me three safe-conduct passes, after a 98-kilometer journey, throwing stones, eggs, bottles and whatever else they could get their hands on at us, in addition to dirty and offensive phrases, for not wanting to be communists and leave the country.

Each safe-conduct pass was intended to offend us. One was for being a prostitute, another for belonging to the Jehovah's Witness religion. One of the groups that confronted the regime suffered prisons for not following its mandates to take up arms, other denominations also suffered it by persecuting priests, but there was not much information about it. The last was for being a lesbian. In Cuba, that word "lesbian" was offensive, because they were telling you that you were a lesbian without being one.

That was how it was socially. I saved them to bring them back, because they all had the stamp of the police of Camagüey Cuba, but my mother asked me to keep them for her and burned them. She was more offended than I was. I have to repeat everything so that they understand and do not forget that the Casa Grande is our country, to which we owe respect and love and we will always defend it.

Slander is also the potential weapon of the communists, because they are constantly repeated on the radio and television, and we, the people of the plucked chicken, believe it without analyzing it because of the constant repetition. Slander went very far in Cuban society.

Many men pretended to be homosexuals in order to come and many women too. What do we American citizens expect in the USA? When socialist ideas take shape in corrupt politicians and in corrupt organizations of black or white racists, we are facing a serious problem. The fear of unmasking the lie. The Democrats have acted along that line of covert socialism silencing the people. Supporting the communists is like playing Russian roulette.

By taking away the rights of citizens to vote for a candidate, by taking away the rights of parents to sexually instruct their children based on tolerance. By taking away or restricting citizens' rights to use weapons, we are in the presence of the famous Woke. Biblically, God says that parents are the ones who must instruct their children. They impose it in schools. By defending groups, marginalizing others, who were classified before the 60s as immoral in dictionaries and in medical literature, as abnormal. They say they defend everyone and it is not true.

In the communist-socialist system nothing is certain, nor with the democrats, and that has happened with their influence in these times. Nothing is certain, everything is based on fabricated trials followed by corrupt judges who serve them, not for us, the people, but to earn money and keep their jobs and in the face of this patriotic negligence we are all exposed. Not in all countries there are men like Lech Walesa, an electrician from the shipyards. It is necessary to love your country and unite, something that unfortunately is not achieved by thinking that we owe favors, when in reality we are the ones who do the favors to the politicians and unfortunately for the worse, most of the time.

A successful pro-democratic advance and effort that in 1989 put an end to the communist government in Poland marking the beginning of a cold war. Unfortunately in the Latin American and Caribbean countries that have suffered these corrupt socialist-communist dictatorships, they have not united to end them. Mexico has a new president appointed by López Obrador and the people play along by voting for them without seeing who they really are, showing that in all third world countries, "plucked chickens exist."

When you see a socialist on the ballot, whatever party they are from, do not vote for them. They are a social plague, worse than those the world has had due to diseases. Today we have the internal Cold War between the love of power and money of the Democratic representatives and the betrayals of their party by some Republicans who, instead of asking for their salaries to be lowered, because they have not done anything substantial, want a salary increase, when in reality they are our servants. The political career is extraordinary, everyone ends up being millionaires at the end of their time and the people in basic needs. The elderly do not receive an increase in the retirement they earned honestly by working (Democrats or Republicans) not living off public aid. Here, the politicians who promise us and do not fulfill have not worked either. Everyone in Washington D.C. has a secure future, but the people do not. If we wait for them, who have grown older and become richer in their jobs, and have not remedied illegal immigration by having laws, have not increased the insurance for the elderly, have not ended the drain of pharmacopoeias to our medicines, when they have not opened their factories in the USA or have moved them to any foreign country with the desire to earn more without caring about the exploitation that those workers suffer, what can we expect in the future? More false promises?

When a people sleeps peacefully in its territory, the enemy foments new plans for a new awakening. Every day more immigrants were arriving from all over the world and the sleeping Americans remembered the old times. They did not prepare themselves as happened in England, for example. Anchor children were born (children of undocumented or illegal parents or visitors who tried to give birth to their children in this territory) and the country baptized them and accepted them by the Constitution. That is the law and it is respected even if many people do not like it. The English worked differently. Children of undocumented people or of business transits are born, and these children obtain an English birth certificate, but not English citizenship.

Immigrant parents in England have to register their children in their respective embassies. There are no anchor children in that territory. When their parents apply for a green card or English citizenship, then those children born there can receive the status of English citizens, but there is a health program for everyone. Something is something. It is not as good as it seems, but it solves the problem for the poor, undocumented or not. Something that should be implemented here but in an orderly manner. The American dream was to have a good job, a car, and to own your house, and by the way give the neighbor a cup of sugar or borrow it. When you get sick they bring you an apple pie or other flavors in terms of help and solidarity. Each citizen was worthy of representing his country anywhere in the world, but he was also defended and everything has changed. To say "Made in the USA" was to say "Quality." Everything was changing while together we dug the grave of our own country. The common slogan was "The Constitution." In all the destroyed countries, the first thing politicians do is undermine it in order to implement their laws, whether they are communist, liberal, or corrupt, and that happens all over the world. We are not the only ones. We have seen all of this in corrupt countries like Cuba, Venezuela, Russia, etc., and now we are seeing it in leaps and bounds within the United States of America. American voters, open your eyes!

We are all guilty of that gigantic grave where we will bury the best economy in the world, "The United States of America."

If we do not participate with our protests, there will be no change. When we talk about the economy, the people do not make an exhaustive examination of the nation's assets, nor of the private profits of entrepreneurs with new or old companies; the poor people have their own barometer to measure the amount of well-being that is obtained or not. It is when there are many companies hiring citizens, giving work to the people, not having to visit the Department of Unemployment, the Department of Social Assistance, is when the poor measure the economy. In the Lord's vineyard there is everyone, from the least intelligent to the geniuses. For any provider, having a job is vital to support the family. It is what we commonly call "working with the sweat of your brow" and having the family budget enough to enjoy a Sunday with a barbecue and your friends.

Something that is not happening in the Biden-Kamala economy. This is how the poor measure the country's economy, filling up the gas tank and going for a walk, without thinking that the next day they have to make the same expense and they cannot. When you go to buy groceries and you see that a hundred dollars are spent on four or five products. When you cannot buy foods with less sugar or sodium because they are more expensive than those that are loaded with them. When you cannot pay for expensive medicines and you have to use generics that will be the same but you do not have the free option to do so. Politicians forget their duties and then do not want there to be demonstrations of dissatisfied people. Let them work, that is why they collect their salaries and receive bonuses from the Treasury Department.

That is the economy that every citizen wants to obtain, and not public services. Jehovah warns that each person must strive to earn his livelihood. "He who does not work, shall not eat." Epistle of the

Thessalonians 3:10, and the Democrats criticized Donald Trump for wanting to bring companies home and give jobs to his compatriots, reduce unemployment, and lower it to figures that had not been achieved in the country for many years, especially among Hispanics and blacks when he governed.

They criticized him for reducing unemployment and trying to give jobs and not Welfare. They hindered him so that we would not supply ourselves with oil or coal. Today Biden with his plans asks Maduro for begging favors and possibly compromising the country's reserves by giving oil to the Chinese.

Little by little the governors of the states, the Senators, the Representatives took over the country and the people by constantly reelecting them, and none of them has wanted to change the laws that divide us. The people have begun to have another social and political perspective. You give me benefits and I give you my vote. This has always happened in third world countries due to political corruption.

All of this is a product of politicians who in different times have continued to enrich themselves, just like Latin American presidents, and all because of dirty lobbying that gave millions to achieve their objectives. "The shark bathes but splashes." Allegorical to when the corrupt in the government steals, but gives something to the people to keep them happy and quiet.

What have we seen in recent times? A pack of politicians defending their income and positions, and not the interests of the people. We have seen corrupt politicians from all parties, but the Democrats must be on the pages of the Guinness book at the top because we have seen them testify under oath and their lies and falsehoods have been silenced, and not prosecuted.

Many believed that communism had fallen asleep, and that the ravages of previous decades would no longer occur worldwide, but we were wrong. When a country tolerates or admits that communists have the same rights to have their party registered, it is inviting them to exercise their rights and ideas and that is what is happening now, and with these wonderful ideas and corruption, the people continue to vote for those who do not solve their real problems.

If there are no laws to limit politicians by time limits serving the people, and others come with new ideas, the people must change their same behavior of repeatedly voting for all those who have always failed them. It is logical! 314   For decades, Americans forgot to vote. They were safe in their country, regardless of whether the president was a Democrat or a Republican. Everything seemed to be going well, but it wasn't. What is happening today was brewing. Little by little, civil rights were defending their thesis and gaining ground daily, whether they were right or not. Along with all this, they began to place liberal professors who would be in charge of changing the course of things, and they changed them. The Constitution was not taught. At the end of the courses, young Americans did not even know how many amendments the Constitution had. Today, journalists, like we saw with Jesse Watters, go to universities and ask future professionals questions, and out of ten students interviewed, only one answers correctly, the rest scratch their heads. Who was the current president? And so on, a series of basic questions, and they didn't know them. This means that the

The educational system in different states of the country has changed extraordinarily, they have forced the parents of the children to carry out the curriculum that they estimate, whether the parents agree or not. But they do not teach them that there is a God. But no parent should protest because it is homophobic, no parent should ask that if they teach sexual tolerance, they should tolerate religious tolerance. We have to tolerate homosexuality and not adult prostitution. Everyone has the same rights to choose what they do with their lives. It is unfair to favor one group and leave another in social misery. Although you do not like their arguments or their philosophies, that is where the

It means that single men cannot have sex with women, without politicians understanding that adult prostitutes should also have rights and be responsible if they sell their body or not, and repressing the right of men who request these services. They should open brothels for them, because if they opened spaces for the porn industry, why don't they integrate them in the same way they did with homosexuals?

All the governors in each state should be tolerant with this group as well. There are homosexual governors. And can't there also be prostitutes serving the government? Don't they ask for tolerance in primary schools? Let them start by putting these topics in the elementary school curriculum. We see that the governors are intolerant with this group, and if I continue further, they are not only intolerant, but they are frauds so that the word hypocrite does not sound rude.

The trafficking of children and young people would decrease extraordinarily if prostitutes were given the same level achieved by homosexuals. Both know that they have suffered from persecution. Venereal diseases would be reduced because of misinformation on these issues as well. Both homosexuality and prostitution are adult issues, and should be treated as such.

Prostitutes are outside the law. Homosexuals have every right to express themselves, to publicly declare themselves homosexual, prostitutes do not. Why do they get paid? Well, they should pay taxes.

Nowadays, if a neighbor has sex with anyone, she is treated contemptuously, because she is a prostitute, an adulteress, etc. But the prostitutes who make porn films are not prostitutes, they are "respected artists." "Sex workers." That is how society is, changing terminology and making idiots out of others. We are totally tired.

Conservative teachers have no place in schools. Nowadays, you cannot correct a child who misbehaves, you have to tolerate him and give him all kinds of privileges, including putting his feet up on the desk, using his cell phone in class, not obeying his teacher, and giving him homework outside the classroom, so that his selfesteem works. Here in California it is like that. Consequences: no teacher can exercise his authority, because he is offending the child. Here is Nancy Pelosi in San Francisco with social misery making waves, corrupt Gavin Newsom with a city subjected to misery. This is the California that voted for the corrupt Adam Schiff seeking the senator and not for Katie Porter who wants to clean up the party and Washington D.C. This is how we are full of social misery. California is disgusting, more rights for some and less for others. Rampant corruption and the people voting irresponsibly. "Telling all these truths causes discomfort, but it is in the interest of a better economy by undermining the power of the shameless and not letting themselves be carried away by the hatred of corrupt people that have served them very little in four decades."

The same thing happens in universities. In universities and colleges, if the professors refuse to follow the directives of the uncontrolled students demanding rights, they fire the professor, leaving the students unruly and undisciplined, trampling on the rights of others, for their absurd requests that they defend. This is the society that many politicians want to maintain, because being "liberal" which they have confused with "libertinism", brings them more votes than being conservative. They no longer know what to invent to secure the position they have and the lobbying that provides them with many thousands of dollars selling themselves worse than the prostitutes they pursue.

Liberalism (Dictionary). Political doctrine that postulates individual and social freedom in politics and private initiative in economic and cultural matters, limiting the intervention of the State and public powers in these areas.

Attitude that advocates freedom and tolerance in the life of a society.

These young people who consider themselves "liberal" and seem not to understand that freedoms and tolerances belong to everyone in society, do not study or prepare themselves properly to know what philosophy to maintain, falling into Libertinism. Libertinism (Dictionary) Unrestraint in works or words. Its similarities are: debauchery, immorality, vice, dishonesty, sensuality, impudence, lust, indecency, and frivolity. The Bible does not say it. The damned Dictionary that has almost disappeared from Universities and colleges says it.

Every day the voter is more irresponsible than in previous decades. The voter carefully analyzed who he gave his vote to, the political platform of the candidate, etc. Today everything has taken a turn towards immorality (libertinism). They spend their time listening to sensationalist news that makes money for the big news companies. They don't analyze, they let themselves be carried away by hatred towards the candidates, instead of seeing if the country benefits or not. The majority of voters from other third world countries vote according to how they did in their respective countries. Fraud was essential, the candidates gave food packages, promised villas and castles, and then never fulfilled their promises, but they voted for them again in the next elections, and that is happening with the candidates we have in Washington D.C. The people elect them out of habit, because none of them solve anything.

There is talk of justice and equality and all that is a lie, it is only written in a Constitution that should be better interpreted. There are laws that discriminate and they are made in the states. We are not equal before the law, as the Constitution says, because they make state laws according to the erroneous concepts of those who propose them, and accept them.

Can someone tell me that the Spanish language was made official in California, if the founding fathers considered not doing so when they wrote the Constitution. And why was the language in which documents are written not made official from the beginning? The swamp has been going on since Abraham Lincoln left us his beautiful thoughts.

Another great state fraud is the laws to obtain public aid "Welfare." They are designed for fraud and lies throughout the country. If you take money from the bank, give away or transfer your property to your family, and appear as a person who has no assets (cars, jewelry, etc.), you can obtain public benefits. You can have a person who drives you around, helps you at home, and takes you to the doctor and to buy groceries. If you ask for that help without first getting rid of your assets, even if they are a pittance, they deny it to you. Those who have never worked (officially) enjoy good laws, where they are given help to pay for the houses or apartments where they live, food stamps and for rent, help at home, etc. But they have had the intelligence to hide the money. (Lie, manipulate them and not own property). In short, lose dignity for a handful of wheat like the one offered in the metaphor "Stalin's Chicken."

This is how society is corrupted. In Riverside California, on its website it says that it has money for illegals. The citizens do not have it. Are we equal before the laws that the Constitution says? No, because our laws are manipulated with the word Intention. Single mothers and fathers, the elderly, physically or mentally helpless, should have them. Most who can work, consider it a duty of the government to support them. God says that he who does not work should not eat. Searched in the Catholic Bible. 2 Thessalonians 3:10-15.

"For even when we were with you, we gave you this command: If anyone will not work, he shall not eat. For we hear that some among you are living disorderly, not working at all, but meddling in other people's business." Very clear, and that was what Donald Trump wanted for us, work and not disorderly living, and even the Democratic people destroyed it. That is social injustice.

Honesty does not work with those good laws that no politician wants to change. Equality does not exist in this matter, nor does justice, but the violated Constitution says that we are all equal before the laws. We would be equal if the citizens who have worked, and have not asked for public assistance, in our old age, had the same benefits as those who have never worked. Now, with many insurance companies, the situation has changed a little for the better, but they deduct from your Social Security check as a retirement of approximately $165.00 dollars a month. If you receive a Social Security check of $735.00 dollars, because you made the mistake of retiring at 62 years of age, you already have a monetary deficit. Many laws have now changed. There is monetary aid for undocumented citizens (illegals), they obtain all kinds of public aid through their children, and citizens do not have those rights. American politicians do not worry about those laws, or about amending them, because they earn good salaries, they lobby companies and earn money, they have good retirement benefits, good medical insurance, and blind citizens continue to keep their jobs through voting. They do not need to change anything, because the less they do, the better they live, and the sooner they become corrupt. If many of us had the power of a "magic wand," the first thing we would do at UEA is schedule the time of the Senators, Congressmen, Representatives, Judges, and Supreme Court Justices. It is ridiculous that a president has two terms, and the justices have their seats for life. They go straight to corruption and violate the same laws they are representing. Any government position that is held for life, in the end, ends up as corrupt as common politicians.

That position must have limits. And voters can limit Senators, Representatives and Congressmen to short terms by voting. But the people vote for the faces of individuals, and that has been demonstrated with Dianne Feistein in California, with an estimated net worth of $87,938, 540 in 2018. And Nancy Pelosi in California with another estimated worth of 290 million or so according to some articles read. And the same thing happens throughout the country. If these two ladies had been eliminated by vote, they would not have been corrupted.

They made the money from the halls of Washington D.C., but for the Democrats, the word audit does not appear in any dictionary. The vote is very important so that corruption does not occur and who has the most to do is the Democratic voters who have to accept that they have been wrong for many years. But it is wise to ratify. God gives them wisdom to take up the weapon of personal determination and not vote for Democrats again until they restructure.

Many millionaires in California are rectifying their political direction. They have more to lose than we the people, even if you don't believe it. When the communists, helped by the democrats, come to power, the first to fall are the rich. That is a very well-prepared plan by the communist system that cannot be deprived of that disastrous merit, but merit.

When we talk about justice and help, everyone thinks of the police of their towns, states or nations, of their politicians, etc. Crime has grown enormously because along with that crime, politicians, in order to earn more money than the drug cartels, have decriminalized marijuana. Today that is the best option. Having a zombie brain, driving and running over anyone, because drugs affect them even if the politicians say they don't. What good does it do for a police officer to arrest a drugged individual and for the town's liberal judge to get him out of the problem with a single stroke of the pen?

The police become demoralized, and the day comes when they have to turn their backs on the other side, and that is how we are currently living. There is a fierce struggle to see who will destroy the country first: the politicians or the urban criminals.

The majority of blacks and Hispanics. Do you know why that happens? Because they fear the riots of undisciplined blacks and criminals, defending the indefensible, accusing the police of being murderers, and the corrupt press, prepared for these riots, which are attacks on the citizens, reporting police abuses but not reporting the murders committed by criminals. In 1992, the riots in California left it destroyed and the politicians have promoted these policies precisely so that the people will submit. Deficits of millions of dollars due to attacks on buildings and businesses. In Los Angeles, during the riots, the Koreans took up arms to defend their property because the blacks, enraged by the beatings given to a black man, came to his defense but to the social deterioration of the others. This is how California works, with very high taxes and reducing services dedicated to beautifying cities, obtaining funds for illegals.

Morality is on the ground, taking away rights from parents and giving them to children. That is communism, the disgrace we have and there is no order and we are fed up. Donald Trump had to come to clean our streets and deport all the criminals he could, among them many Mexicans as well.

JOURNALISM

Journalism and its definition 1- masculine noun. Professional activity that consists of obtaining, processing, interpreting and disseminating information through any written, oral, visual or graphic medium. This is what the dictionary of the Royal Spanish Academy says.

We continue to delve into the subject and we ask ourselves: What is the ethics of a journalist? And all the rules that most do not comply with appear. Ethical journalism strives to ensure the free exchange of accurate, impartial and exhaustive information.

Impartiality is what citizens expect from the press, from the judgments towards Donald Trump, but all the corrupt people who hate the country have decided to offer us fake news and biased judgments. They have become biased with immoralities of all kinds. An ethical journalist acts with integrity.

The Society declares the following principles as the foundation of ethical journalism, and encourages its use, in its practice by all people in all media. The press is direct communication with the people and if it fails, so do the people.

These principles are: Respect and truth. Being open to the investigation of the facts. Pursuing objectivity, even if it is known to be inaccessible. Contrasting the data with as many journalistic sources as necessary. Sadly, in these decades the principle of "respect for the truth" has been lost in current journalism in almost all media. Objectivity is what journalists and owners of newspapers, magazines, etc., and television channels in the news do not practice, considering the public incapable of understanding when it is true and when it is a lie, (lack of respect for the public regardless of which political party they belong to, what religions or philosophies they practice)". Making subjective reports according to their preferences and resentments in their minds, towards the country and its citizens.

Contrast the data with as many journalistic sources as necessary" None of these principles have been fulfilled in our dirty press, on the contrary, there are very few journalists and news channels that are still spreading the truth as the sacred duty of journalism implies. Never before had anything like this been seen in the country. It is a rampant madness that must stop.

Many immigrants of all colors and races stopped watching Univision and Telemundo because the cheap news they offered us daily crossed the line between truth and lies. They were taken from the filth that they themselves fostered and we were tired of. This is what happened to the American people, many of whom abandoned television networks and newspapers because they were covered in the same material that the Hispanic networks had when giving the news.

The muddying in the swamp full of manure began in Washington D.C., extending to a corrupt press. We have to flourish with baths of wisdom and begin to be selective if we want to save our nation. Let us remember that wisdom is something common to our lives and we must take care of it by returning to the steps of God, to have the strength to survive these political declines that surround us. You don't have to be religious or congregate, although religions love that because that's what God wants. You have to follow the healthy impulses of common sense or the good feelings of each person. Corrupt journalism has destroyed American society and it's time to rescue it. If there's one thing that television channels and newspapers don't want, it's losing users because that means losing money. The counterbalance to destroying our society with lies, plots, hatred and dirt is to move to channels that are more conservative.

As a society we must understand that if we do not educate ourselves, corrupt politicians and journalists corrupt us with their lies, blasphemies, deceit and brainwashing, which exists daily even if many do not believe it, and it will happen to us like the metaphor of the chicken that communists historically use. This metaphor represents very well those who vote negligently, those who are still deceived, those who vote out of apathy and give their vote to any politician without reading the political platform, those who by chance are living off past glories and do not care about the present, and many more reasons that we all know. Do we see ourselves reflected in this metaphor or not, these days?

Searching for information about what they call "Big Tech", I came across this article and it had been a long time since I read so much nonsense in several paragraphs coming from a communication professional. The least a journalist should do is get informed. As a housewife who likes to write, I can make mistakes and have a margin of error in the face of the social problems we face, but a journalist cannot be excused for his lack of common sense. If human misery is kept in Pandora's Box, in this article Envy, Disinformation, Hate, Resentment and Lies have come out hastily, among many others. They have played an extraordinary role in these paragraphs of this article, as has the immense amount of hatred and resentment read in all these years.

For your pain and to mitigate your envy, we are going to make a better place, and many of us are already doing so from different trenches, and the first step is to refute all of you for your malicious information, following in the footsteps of the communists who are envious of the rich, but end up stealing and becoming great magnates. Who are you trying to fool? I am not part of the plucked chicken that you want to turn us into.

The Democrats for 2024 want the best for the people with unfulfilled promises for several decades, without caring about the needs of the people, only their personal monetary enrichment. (It must be emphasized). Now they want the best for all of us. Can we give them the benefit of the doubt? Of course not! Let everyone remember that the philosophies of the communists are brutal, and the "intelligent members" divide families with any argument at hand. That must end, because if not, we are being complicit in all these social miseries. Journalism must inform, educate and entertain society, but also denounce, question and transform reality in a dignified way and that is what the people appreciate. Today the information is disastrous. You do not know who to believe because almost all of it seems true and is dressed in lies. Precisely journalism is the one that can begin to have moral responsibility when informing in order to believe them again. That is why these thoughts only go to the corrupt and congratulations to honest journalism which is what exalts us and provides us with the correct information from which we learn.

Two thoughts very much in line with the situation regarding the press that we have and totally dedicated to them because they are corrupt.

"A cynical, mercenary and demagogic press will produce a cynical, mercenary and demagogic people." Joseph Pulitzer. Do we have it or not?

This thought is dedicated to those who follow the concepts of journalism.

"Only those who know about journalism, and the cost of disinterest, can truly appreciate the energy, the tenacity, the sacrifices, the prudence, the strength of character that reveals the appearance of an honest and free newspaper." José Martí.

SABBATICAL YEARS

A sabbatical year is designed for a period of 12 months duration, but it is adjustable and can vary, depending on the time the person needs, so it can have a suitable term of between two months and a year. Generally, six months is the standard time period for a sabbatical year. According to the RAE. Royal Spanish Academy. A Sabbatical Year is a year of paid leave that some teaching and research institutions grant to their staff from time to time. All the Democrats, judges, mayors, and others involved in their great plot against Donald Trump should take not one year, but four to six sabbatical years to restructure themselves and become DECENT AND FAIR again.

Lawyer and commentator John Bolton attacked former President Trump by warning that the Russian government would celebrate Trump's reelection because they see him as an "easy mark." Unfortunately for the envious, Donald Trump's mark has gone down in history. A strong mark, showing that the cowardice of the Democrats did not erase it. Putin will be a murderer, another one who got rich in power, but he knows that Donald Trump has the intelligence that the Democrats lack, and that he is a man of solutions (already demonstrated while he served us), and not of theft in power. One day the Russian people will throw off the yoke of the shameless communists, more than common communist thieves. That happens when they want the distribution of wealth to the proletariat.

If Donald Trump has done dirty business, he is at the level of those who have gotten rich, and nobody cares about that, what the millionaires do and how they get their millions, but far from the power of Washington D.C., that with that show that it is not necessary to be in the government to get them. Those who have used the halls of Washington D.C., are not persecuted like the Democrats Nancy Pelosi, Schumer, Hillary Clinton, Obama, Biden and family, the Republicans and Democrats all millionaires in power like Mitch McConnell, the minority leader.

The serious problem for the Democrats is the tenacity and integrity of Donald Trump in having denounced them, and many did not believe him. Who are the Democrats talking about from their workplaces? Donald Trump! They have no other topic. They do not think how do the international leaders see them who also expect consequences from the USA? Donald Trump is a pacifist, he proved it during the four years he served us. Remember that Bush left his wars to Obama, he continued them and the web of shameless Democrats began to be woven by awarding him the Nobel Peace Prize, something that Obama himself did not want to even mention again because he knew he did not deserve it.

Many Democratic leaders have not agreed with the Witch Hunt against Donald Trump, but they do not go to the press to say so. Many want to make drastic changes in their party to separate themselves from the filth caused by so many decades full of lies and deceit, hypocrisy, and illicit enrichment through dirty lobbying and betting on the Stock Market. They will have to work hard and systematically until they manage to work with decorum and impartiality, since the American people deserve it the least.

Democratic voters will have to vote WISELY or grant their party sabbaticals, so that they return to the decorum and political decency with which their party was founded.

The persecution of Donald Trump with the chain of unconstitutional trials that have been done to them, has done so much damage to the country's democratic morale that the international community is living the results as a dark movie series, and they do not want to miss a single chapter.

The end of that dark movie will be when Donald Trump returns to work with dignity. While the Democrats of Washington D.C., will leave for history, the collapse of the dirty politicians who created the movie the "WITCH HUNT."

*They hate him, discredit him, and defame him completely and hating him in this way is to demonstrate the moral weakness that many suffer and all driven by his political rivals and the communists in addition to the individuals who fight to destroy him. Many were even glad during the pandemic that he had been infected, and that lowered the morale of the people who are not grateful without seeing that Trump served the country, and although the press, the Democrats and his hidden detractors hate him, he served us all equally without charging his fees. Which were donated to many institutions. But this gesture, which is commendable for many, is not the first time that it has happened in the United States. Two other presidents, John F. Kennedy and Herbert Hoover, also decided to give their presidential salaries to charitable organizations. Only three presidents in the USA have donated their salaries. (According to the information). We are not saying that Donald J. Trump is perfect. We are saying that he is the Right One to Govern the United States of America after the 2020 presidential elections were stolen from him by not using the laws to prove it, serving us for free, and having worked efficiently during the four years that he served us. Enough of changing the history that belongs to all of us! Persecutions of a former President without irrefutable evidence, but rather rigged. If they made up the case by editing the Prosecutor's report when he sentenced him as a "forgetful old man," can we believe that the trials of Donald Trump are not made up and edited to destroy him? Thanks to technology, we can be aware of what is happening, and be able to make the right decisions when voting in 2024.

TECHNOLOGY

Technology has changed our mentality. We have all the windows open with Google. In all countries, users are entertained on Facebook X, Instagram, You Tube, and many others, looking for information from the present and the past. Several decades ago we had to go to libraries, bookstores, etc., looking for information. Today, through all of them, it comes to us for free and many do not use it properly. Nothing is more important than enjoying them in our homes and we must thank all those millionaires who have left us a cyber inheritance. Without computers, phones, tablets, etc., and all those programs, we can no longer live. These platforms have transformed our lives and ideas, of course. They have even given humanity a door of love by communicating globally, being able to do so in different languages thanks to their language translation programs. That is wonderful and we have to appreciate it.

Before, politicians stole and nobody knew it, but the people imagined it, especially in third world countries. Today, Forbes magazine tells us the details, newspapers, blogs, news pages, etc., keep us informed to inform us of what each one wants to search for. The Wikipedia and others at the service of humanity, (with many dubious articles that experts must correct). Amazon with its thousands of books that each one can learn in their own way and possibilities, even publishing them and becoming writers totally free is a divine gift. (Among them me). All the dictionaries at our disposal, including the best-selling books that are in almost all homes worldwide and the least read or interpreted ones at our disposal in a single click. The Bible! The Constitution! Dictionaries! and countless topics and writers at our disposal.

The Witch Hunt for Donald Trump has its meaning for the Democrats that represent us. Let communism be perpetuated, let our moral values be destroyed, let laws not be enforced under legal destruction, let capital be controlled by the shameless, let education expire and let us have foul-mouthed young people wherever we are. This is how society is being destroyed etc. Democrats deserve the absolute help of those who preserve moral values and want to recover them together. Witches were the new scapegoat of Christianity in those times. Donald Trump from 2016 to 2024 is the scapegoat of the dirty white and black Democrats united in the shameful policy of revenge, racism, and destruction in our country USA. Are we moving forward or backward?

Democratic politicians remain silent, but acting, erasing the beautiful era of the party when Kennedy gave this beautiful speech. "Therefore, I am going to ask the Congress to enact legislation giving Americans the right to be served in all places open to the public—hotels, restaurants, theaters, department stores, and any similar establishments. I am going to ask the Congress to allow the federal government to participate fully in the design of laws that will end racial segregation and to include in those future laws the right of the Negro community to vote." (Televised speech of June 11, 1963, after the race riots in Alabama led by Governor George Wallace.) If you can recognize that both Kennedy and Martin Luther King were referring to Americans, not to "Afro" Americans, it is a sign that both meant it constitutionally. Kennedy ended by saying "the Negro community," and those words were the correct ones, without divisive prefixes that only serve to separate.

I always held a certain resentment towards Kennedy for what we Cubans considered a betrayal of the battle in the Bay of Pigs, Cuba, at that time. But I was able to eliminate the resentment from my heart, both towards him and Fidel Castro, and to come to see that every coin has two sides, the good and the bad. And that both were the driving force that drove us Cubans to adopt this wonderful land called "The United States of America" without even knowing its language and its history. Kennedy has always been considered to have betrayed the plan that he promised to help. If he had fulfilled it, Cuba would have recovered and been free many years ago.

The former President would have gone down in history in a positive way. For those who suffered prison and died defending it in the Bay of Pigs, Cuba, Kennedy was seen as a traitor. The United States of America betrayed them. Although we all learn from bad experiences and the Kennedy name was never erased from the minds of the Cubans who were betrayed by him. Nor should we penalize those who carry it, and want to serve the country. A president should not promise what he cannot deliver, for whatever reasons.

The first documentary evidence of the phrase "United States of America" dates from a January 2, 1776, letter written by Stephen Moylan, an aide in General George Washington's Continental Army, to Joseph Reed, Washington's aide-de-camp. Moylan expressed his desire to go "with full and ample powers from the United States of America to Spain" to seek aid in the Revolutionary War effort.

The first known publication of the phrase "United States of America" was in an anonymous essay in The Virginia Gazette newspaper in Williamsburg on April 6, 1776. In June 1776, the name "United States of America" appeared in drafts of the Articles of Confederation and Perpetual Union, written by John Dickinson, a founding father of the province of Pennsylvania, and in the Declaration of Independence, written primarily by Thomas Jefferson and adopted by the Second Continental Congress in Philadelphia on July 4, 1776.

The Kennedy surname has a bad reputation for Cubans and because of their internal or political miseries like any family has, and thanks to a Kennedy, the Peter Pan children were able to escape communism at an extremely high price, family separation, and reside in the United States of America.

It is our decision to choose the good in order to live in harmony. Those who choose the path of resentment will always live as prisoners or slaves of their bad thoughts and attitudes. The Democratic Party, the Republican Party, and others, must work to help the people, or at least that is the objective, but never to persecute them, as they have done with Donald Trump and tomorrow they will do with our children and grandchildren, whatever race they have. We are waiting for Justice to return or for it to wake up from the eternal sleep that currently subdues it.

These are times of rejoicing and working hard so that the country once again takes the leadership it needs, and not the weaknesses and anguish that we are witnessing in these times, where we are all divided, resentful and weak in character, which all these destructive philosophies are based on. The more they divide us, the more they win. It is not necessary to live like this, it is only necessary that politicians recover the lost values and the Department of Justice return to work for its people and we, who more than once, have been The Plucked Chickens, analyze deeply that we have to unite to protect our Homeland. Now the problem is not Republicans against Democrats or vice versa. Now is the time to join hands and show the world that if we unite, on November 5, 2024, we will recover the country from the clutches of the famous Woke and its internal miseries, who are the ones who are pulling the strings together with the destabilizing George Soros trying to destroy us all. They will not succeed! We Americans say NO!

The American people have always been prosperous, because their white or black men have been the engine of their progress. Making changes hurts and bothers, that is true, but when it is necessary and prudent to recover the moral and patriotic values of future generations, we have the unavoidable duty to do it, and all together so that the dream of Martin Luther King, Abraham Lincoln, Mahama Gandhi and all of us who dream as a people for peace and spiritual harmony, turn the bad into good, and together we will turn them into beautiful realities in a society that belongs to all of us equally. The words of M. Luther King "I have a dream" or "an American" are still alive when he marched to Washington D.C., in pursuit of alleviating poverty and segregation. "This Country is Sick" he said when Kennedy was assassinated. Today history repeats itself, and we all say using his words "This country is crazy" but he meant "these people are crazy". Almost the same as what Eric Trump said "this country is shit" he was referring to the people who affected his father, not the country itself. What Michelle Obama said hurt as well and former First Lady Laura Bush minimized the comments. We must interpret better than judge, something that the Supreme Court is already failing us. My wish is to see Artificial Intelligence in the first instance, in the Supreme Court of the country, since all the judges form a group of vested interests according to the President who elected or appointed them, plus the effect of the different individual neurons in operation interpreting according to their information, not what is in the documents. One test was the restriction of the individual's rights to bear arms as the Constitution says that no one wants to touch, not to read, interpret or edit it.

And our distrust and insecurities have reached the Supreme Court upon hearing the words of Justice Sonia Soto Mayor to CNN in Spanish.

Witnessing the persecution of Donald J Trump, the 45th President of this beautiful nation, we all unanimously say "the Democrats are crazy." All of us who have been attacked for our skin color, hatred, envy, patriotism, different ideas, whether we are white, black or of other mistreated races, sitting in the history books of any country on any continent, understand the great concept of persecution being innocent as abuses towards citizens.

We do not want food for two days. We want a healthy economy, the American people tell the Democrats. "Biden is not a forgetful old man" as the Prosecutor described him, forgiving him for taking unauthorized documents to his house. Whether they are classified or not. He committed a crime because he was vice-president and had them since he was a Senator. He is an old man with cognitive problems governing the World Power and corrupt. Can you believe it? Violating and signing executive laws at the same time and without sense. But he is not the only one with those problems, but those who draft executive laws are almost the same. A cabinet worthy of an inept President. All brought to our homes thanks to the technological world we are enjoying.

A disaster of destructive magnitude in the Biden-Kamala government, which will always be remembered for encouraging racism, divisionism, non-compliance with laws, illicit financial scandals and hypocrisies, etc.

They wanted to remove Donald Trump from the government with the 25th Amendment as Nancy Pelosi wanted to remove Donald

Trump for hatred towards him and now no one thinks of asking for the same thing and with obvious reasons that Biden has been prosecuted for not being able to govern and having hidden it for so long that in Washington D.C., they did not find out and on YouTube there were videos going around the world. Do we deserve that? Of course not!

OPINIONS OF OTHERS

Many will say: this lady is crazy, but I am crazy to see my country free of politicians from all parties getting rich by serving the people, creating Sanctuary Cities instead of complying with the laws. Money disappears due to rampant corruption. All countries comply with them. Mexico deports those who do not suit them. Crazy to see that the existing laws are complied with, crazy to put a stop to the entry of immigrants in a reasoned and gentle way, with serious immigration reforms, or that the laws regarding immigration are respected. It's crazy that there are no privileged groups like Haitians, Cubans, Nicaraguans, Venezuelans who have to enter with an affidavit and are not supposed to be burdens on social assistance, and that is not true. They should consider immigration in a different and reasonable way like the one Democrat James Earl Carter Jr. did in 1980. A well-organized entry into the country and following the laws and the Biden Kamala administration violating them all. They do not deserve the Democratic vote. With Kamala's ideas of opening the doors to Cuba without having been tried for the abuses and crimes, only to impress the Cuban electorate in Florida, that tactic is known to Cubans and they do not fall into the traps, it will not be of much use. Cubans want Cuba to be free and for capitalism to come through democracy, not communism along with all of you.

In California, they make state laws according to the concepts of those who are hypocrites. Politicians, including the Governor and the Attorney General. They are already making futuristic plans for the distribution of powers and money, as the Attorney General wants to become the Governor and the latter the President of the nation, leaving a trail of political corruption stored in the national archives and all of us fleeced in the future. We do not want that either.

Those who come with the affidavit do not have their expenses paid by their relatives, they are paid by the California government from food to medicine. Do Mexicans in California deserve the same or not? Mexicans who have the vote should pass the bill to the Democrats and I do not invite them to vote for the Republicans if they do not want to, but this 2024 is the opportunity for those who have the vote to analyze all the years of darkness in which their communities have lived without positive results and if they do not want the Republican party, make changes. Biden has humiliated them by letting in 10 million illegals and distributing the benefits that are taken away from other groups or reduced. Open your eyes. They have left Mexicans in immigration limbo, and they are the ones who have been in the shadows for many years. Many call those of us who protest crazy. Those who are detractors will say a hundred thousand times that illegal immigration does not take away jobs and we all know that it happens. Due to needs or other causes, but it happens.

It is possible that we are crazy, because they leave children in primary schools free of homosexual or political concepts. Teachers are not the parents of their students, they are their guides in the subjects they need to get ahead. Corruption does not come from black or white supremacists, from criminals, from decent people, it comes from Washington D.C., and our politicians are responsible for these bad practices and for many decades allowing the unacceptable where many Governors have become confused and take the role of dictators.

Power is a drug and money is another, when it is not earned in private business, but rather by stealing donations that the people generously give them for their disastrous purposes and sadly we are the voters who have caused this great evil, by electing them year after year without analyzing what these true criminals of politics do.

Political apathy is maintained for this very reason "Due to the lack of patriotism, not the patriotism that immigrants bring to the country falsely, but the moral values that should be taught in schools and are not done. Our children and grandchildren grow up blind from the country that they should defend like those who defend us in the army. They leave the universities blind with underhanded programs changing their ideologies without letting them act and choose for themselves.

Soldiers are made to be strong in their training to defend us by planting ideology in them, something that we should all have without going to the army, coming from Kindergarten. The ministers of education have failed in our country, as have the corrupt governors who want to make their own state laws, violating the most sacred thing in the country, which is the Constitution, which, along with the Bible, should be corrected many things while Jehovah or his son does not arrive.

Socially speaking, those of us who think that everyone has the same rights and duties, have the free will not to follow the unhinged crowds that, in the name of their rights, trample on the rights of others. If we spoke biblically, we could interpret "following the crowds" as blindly going after the unbridled majority in our society and that is not good. Every human being is endowed with a brain that belongs to him, so he does not need to think like others. He has the right to think for himself but practicing positivism.

Those who hate are those who then walk around with a Rosary in their hand or a Bible, praising God and hating their neighbor, who is Donald Trump. We are already tired of so much street tale. Nancy's time has passed. I stopped adding her emails because she is obsessed with Donald Trump. I have never seen a male figure who has become the MASSIVE OBSESSION of both male and female Democrats in Washington D.C., of a dirty, jealous press, of Democratic voters who really don't even know why they hate him. What is rude? Well, if we don't want to bring him into our homes, we want him in Washington D.C. Remember what Paulo Coelho said. "Life always waits for a moment of crisis to reveal its magical side." And that moment will be when Donald J. Trump returns to Washington D.C., as president again.

He deserves it for the abuses his government has subjected him to, and for the respect of those of us who believe that working always leads to success and Donald Trump proved it. Nancy was furious when he returned to Washington D.C., saying that he had to be removed and even involved Trump's children so that they wouldn't let him leave. That video revealed a totally insane person.

She is unhinged. Mrs. Pelosi needs an exorcism. All her emails, like Schumer and Schiff Adams, are a fraud because they do not work properly for their people.

PROSTITUTION AND HOMOSEXUALITY

Through the previous pages I have been informing you how sad it is to see a Democratic Government asking for tolerance for homosexuality and not for adult prostitution. They chase prostitutes in the streets, (I repeat this as many times as necessary), but they do not have the courage to go and imprison those who generate billions of dollars with prostitution films called "porn" and this is what makes the police force of California and perhaps many other states of the nation act hypocritically. This is a very important industry that generates a lot of money and those who produce them cannot be persecuted or imprisoned. A mafia. A woman on the street offering the services of her body is just as much a prostitute as a call now in this dirty liberalism where they want us all to be blind, deaf, and mute. "PORN ACTRESSES: They are pornographic prostitutes who sleep for money, Judges who are homosexuals and act outside the law wanting to impose rules and laws outside the Constitution."

Former US President Donald Trump has been charged in three criminal proceedings on charges related to his attempt to interfere in the 2020 electoral process (Insurrection invented by the Democrats because it was actually a demonstration calling for redress of grievances by not counting them). The improper handling of classified documents (Biden Obama and many more who have kept them in their homes, libraries or the garage of their houses, they do not even analyze it and when they do, do we know the results? Trump must be destroyed and Biden must be saved by saying that he is "a forgetful old man." What kind of prosecutors are in office?)

They accuse him of diverting funds from his presidential campaign to try to hush up an extramarital relationship with a prostitute from the porn industry who also changes her name to Porn Artist.

Now the prostitutes of the porn industry are also called "ADULT FILM ACTRESS" Double standards of our government! Double standards of the laws! They accept the Mafia of the Porn Industry and crucify the prostitutes on the streets who have chosen for themselves that work preference. The preference for homosexuals is accepted and the so-called cheap prostitutes are punished in comparison to what they pay those in the Porn Industry, which is totally justified in the nation. Is this logical?

Homosexuality has always existed and prostitutes too. We are not gods to tell the two groups who to sleep with. That preference is personal, and children should not be involved in schools for the sake of the famous tolerance by introducing books with inappropriate themes. Children should be respected for their right to be children and not be involved in the social or political affairs of adults. Parents are responsible for all this debauchery with their children, not schools and much less governors. Parents why don't they protest.

Sure, it was easy to remove religious books from schools, but it is not difficult to introduce almost pornographic books without the consent of the parents. Do you know why they don't put the Bible in schools? Because God offends homosexuals just like He offends prostitutes, extortionists, drunks, etc. If they repent of their practices, God loves them; if they don't repent of their practices, He detests them. There are groups of activists, homosexuals, Governors and lawyers discriminating against children who are religious by not giving them the opportunity to be tolerated in schools. This has happened in Florida and now the Governor of California wants to impose these tolerance books in primary schools, defending the "vulnerable" who are used by them for electoral votes, leaving out the Christians who are on the list of the "vulnerable" because their religions are not accepted in schools (Separation of powers) but they widely discriminate against children who profess the Christian faith, by not providing them with religious books, to go against Governor De Santis. The hatred of the Democrats towards the Republicans has involved children and the fights between all of them, should not affect citizens.

Human beings should not judge homosexuals or adult prostitutes, we are not God. Let God be the ones who judge themselves or repent, and if they do not want to, that is their free will, to do with their body what they wish. But if they removed homosexuals from the dictionaries with their classifications of immoral, before the 60s, let them also remove prostitutes.

According to the Dictionary. Prostitute: "Person who has sexual relations in exchange for money." Those who make porn films are exactly that. PROSTITUTES, NOT ACTRESSES, and they are not persecuted.

HOMOSEXUALITY: It is the sexual orientation for which an individual feels physical, affective, sentimental, sexual and emotional affection towards individuals of the same sex.

So the democratic politicians and activists, like everyone else, think that only homosexuals can have physical sexual affection and they defend them and prostitutes outside the law. Many homosexuals also prostitute themselves and are not persecuted.

The law is for everyone, and not for different groups. We are not a society of groups, but of citizens protected by the same Constitution. They separate us as groups to count the sheep and provide them with money for different purposes, marginalizing some and defending others. Homosexuals have already turned it into a political group, it is a sexual preference towards their own sex, blacks, Hispanics, Indians, etc., we form the group of sheep. So, only homosexuals can have physical sexual attraction and prostitutes cannot, because money is involved and it is not indicated in the laws. They have their monetary preferences to sell their body just like the prostitutes who work for the PORN INDUSTRY, who are not persecuted and both should be respected just as homosexuals are respected. If we have to say things, we should say them as they are and happen, not as the liberals want us to say them.

The web designer from Colorado who has the right to offer in her business what she offers as a religious person had to go to the Supreme Court. If the homosexual did not like her decision, he should have gone somewhere else where religion was not involved. The problem is that many in the state of Colorado, homosexuals and their organizations that defend them, want laws by force, that benefit them as a homosexual community, and not others, and they end up with cases in the Supreme Court because they have not even had the time to read the laws before acting. The fact that the Governor is homosexual does not give them the right to change society by force, but by the existing laws.

We must be fair and follow the canons of the Constitution. In many doctor's offices and gas stations there are signs that say: "We have the right to not give you services if you do not agree with our policies." They are private businesses, which have the right to not give us service if they feel affected. I fully support the Supreme Court's interpretation that gave religious people the right to express themselves and not do what those who do not know the law want and that is to reform society. Because if activists and politicians have forgotten what the Constitution says, they should go back to it to review it. Violating the Constitution would be totalitarianism on the part of the state or federal government, and it should not exist in our democracy. These are the citizens who destroy the country from within, like the 8 Supreme Court judges who voted in favor of restricting weapons to those who are involved in domestic violence. God says about this in the Bible: 1 Corinthians 6:9-11

Do you not know that the unjust will not inherit the Kingdom of God? Do not be deceived. People who are sexually immoral, idolaters, adulterers, men who engage in homosexual acts, men who practice homosexuality, thieves, the greedy, drunkards, revilers, and extortioners will not inherit the Kingdom of God. And yet, some of you were like that. "But you have been washed, you have been sanctified, you have been declared righteous in the name of our Lord Jesus Christ and with the spirit of our God."

It is not the people who say it, it is the Bible, the same God who praises homosexuals who have these practices and gets married by the church. That is why Jehovah should have included politicians. I would have liked to see them biblically represented as political thieves, unjust politicians, those who are sexually immoral according to the Bible (there are quite a few). Governors, greedy ones like Nancy Pelosi, Chuck Schumer, Adam Schiff, the senator-elect from

California (demonstrating how overwhelmingly INCOMPETENT he was by failing to find him guilty), corrupt judges who want to destroy Donald Trump by holding almost a hundred trials before the 2024 elections, drunks who laugh at what is happening, slanderers like the governor of Colorado and his Secretary of State, inciting the people to division and resentment by wanting to accuse Donald Trump of what they call INSURRECTION, wanting to remove him from the ballot in the primaries and going against the principles of others.

The Democrats and some Republican traitors who staged a chain of sham trials against Donald Trump in Washington D.C. And finally, the extortionists who want to brainwash the population will not inherit the kingdom of God if they do not repent. I thought the arrangement was fantastic, but it is a shame that the Bible does not accept propositions or amendments!

We might even think that Jehovah was a Republican back then! Because he wanted things to be fair, correct, loyal, and conservative. (Remember that only Jehovah can judge me for calling him a Republican or using the Bible verses in this book since we are "imperfect."

We are living in a totally HYPOCRITICAL society, but that is what has been generated, and we have the right to point out and express our concepts freely as well. That is called tolerance between all groups and free expression without offending or defaming, because the topics discussed are those we are experiencing in American society day by day, and they belong to all of us, from millionaires to the homeless. How are we going to structure the topics, if every day the same topic takes on extraordinary proportions? It is total madness that of the politicians in Washington D.C. They have lost their minds and that is how they govern us. I confirm: There are even strong rumors among the population that the attempted assassination of Donald Trump was planned in Washington D.C. Since we no longer believe in our institutions, it occurred to me to send a note to the President and his page asking for the resignation of the inept head of the Secret Service Kimberley and the page of Intelligence closed, I had to pass the email to Kamala Harris.

We MAGAs have the right to participate by expressing our points of view with the truths in front and without fear and so should the 343 Democratic voters, denouncing all of you for being liars. We will not tear down statues, nor the architectural infrastructure of cities, we will not steal from private property, or from any, because we are not thieves, we are citizens who want the common good. But we can wield the weapon of free expression and send letters to those who are not working correctly, to make them reconsider or at least to let them know that we participate in defending our country from any trench, and sadly defend it from our politicians and from those who want to destroy it from within or from outside.

California Governor Newsom's rant against De Santis regarding children's tolerance of homosexuals due to political rivalries discriminates against religious children and families who have to endure being humiliated and discriminated against in the name of defending homosexuality, which is a personal matter, not a political one, as they want to make it seem in California.

For this reason, I sent this letter to the Attorney General of California, Mr. Bonta, and the first message through social networks Facebook, the second by letter to his office. They never respond to those who point out their faults. That's how Democratic politicians are.

Dear Mr. Rob Bonta. When you won the election, I sent you a message and told you that you would do what our government wants, to defend your position. I wished you luck. Now I read the email I received from your office "AGAINST LGBTQ+ DISCRIMINATION" and I agree that everyone should have the same rights as our Constitution says, but you are forgetting about adult prostitution. In many states like California there are laws and despite them they are still persecuted by our undercover police, and they do not have the courage to pursue prostitutes in pornographic films that society calls "porn actresses" when in reality it is an accepted prostitution that generates billions of dollars and they only persecute street prostitutes who earn a pittance selling their bodies. There is a double face in our system and it smells of corruption. YOU WHO MAKE OR APPLY LAWS, DO IT WITH THOSE WHO

INTEREST YOU FOR THE ELECTORAL VOTE, not to look for good solutions. If you are going to fight to introduce books for the homosexual community in schools for the sake of "tolerance," you must be impartial and introduce Bibles for the different students who believe in God and if there is a separation of law between the state and the schools, then let all those philosophies of life be separated. No child goes to school for that and because of so much nonsense, everyone ends up not learning the subjects and they are passed to the next grade and that's enough! That is called equal conditions. The hypocrisy in the Democratic government is bordering on madness. Be "fair" with all groups and then I will personally believe you. For now I continue to think that we must follow the path that the party points out to you, because with these actions defending one group and leaving several groups marginalized is a betrayal.

With all due respect, analyze this situation well and ask for tolerance for religious students and that they have the same opportunities for books that homosexuals will have, who must also learn to tolerate religious people and adult prostitutes and their children. What California should not allow is for homosexuality, prostitution and lack of tolerance to affect any minor. No one is fooling me with many nice words and disastrous actions of intolerance towards other groups. Everyone should enjoy the same rights and then we will talk about "equality and justice."

Respectfully

Alila Barreras

Did you answer me? Neither did they! The separation of powers is good for some, for others it is a blatant discrimination in these democratic times. This is how we are living at the mercy of political disputes between the parties.

Each Governor feels like a Roman emperor, and wants to cut off the head of the one they choose. They feel omnipotent, and these are the governors who lie to us daily and tell us in a recital the beautiful things they have done, wanting to be the Presidents of this great nation to use power and continue destroying the country from a bolder platform, the presidency of the Country.

Nancy's last email in this book because there will be more in the coming months but after the Republican Convention we do not want to deal with so many toxicities. The end of the book will be on November 5, 2024 signed by all American citizens in a giant red, blue, and white wave voting for Donald J. Trump. We get the feeling that she is exhausted, sad and disillusioned with her Democratic Party, seeing a Biden who can no longer continue in the Presidency and she understands that she is because she vociferated so much about applying the 25th Amendment to Donald Trump and she could not do it with Biden who is sick and not being able to apply the 14th Amendment to her enemy but also to her friend who violated it by providing aid to the Palestinians. After all, they should feel ashamed because they are corrupt in the eyes of the citizens and that is shameful. Nancy is depressed because even the assassination attempt on Donald Trump has left her without the strength to continue her crazy race of destruction, perhaps understanding that God has returned to our country after the communists and all the evil philosophies along with terrorism expelled him from schools to homes. Fortunately, the failed assassination was because God returned to protect the right man in the presidency and for many reasons Donald J. Trump, and we are placing him on his throne, the United States of America.

And when we say together God Bless America, that strength reaches all citizens of different political parties knowing that November 5, 2024 is the new birth and return of the values requested by giving us their hands in the crucial moments that the country requires. Nancy Pelosi, Chuck Schumer, Adams Schiff, the Clinton Family, the Obama family, and the Biden family have already done their part, including Alexandia Ocasio Cortez, whether we like it or not. They are toxic and we cannot live with hate behind us, we need the power of love, which is the best theory. Now it is our turn to clean up Washington D.C., and every department that previously refused to work by not wanting to count the electoral votes of 2020, an event that has gone down in American history so that it will never happen again.

WORDS OF BERNIE SANDERS DEMOCRAT SOCIALIST

What are radical communists disguised under the name of socialist democrats? Yes they are. Do you remember the presidential campaign of this candidate and his denunciations of corruption? We see that Donald Trump is not the only one in these denunciations. But Donald Trump is the bad boy of the Democrats. The American people know about government corruption and we are responsible in 2024 to put a stop to it, because the end is a very specific word and it will not be achieved easily, so we must work together.

Sanders attacked the speech of his main rival in the party, Hillary Clinton, and attacked the **"fraud and corruption" that "reign" on Wall Street** and the large financial institutions of the United States.

Democrats fighting for power. A Democratic senator says so. The senator continues to attack Hillary since he wanted to be the President and thanks to the voters, neither he nor she won.

Sanders. "Greed, arrogance, fraud and dishonour are the words that describe the business of Wall Street, which only cares about pleasing the banking corporations and destroys the American middle class," Sanders said at a rally held at the Town Hall auditorium in New York.

They all have the same pattern of behaviour.

Sanders: repeatedly accused Hillary Clinton, the first in the polls to be the Democratic candidate for the White House, of being "wrong" in her proposals to regulate the main financial institutions of the country.

Answer: It is good that Sanders, a Democrat, said it, but he only wanted to be the president and when the political campaign begins, everyone falls apart. But then peace must reign.

Sanders continues: "We are going to end this reality and the illegal behaviour of the corporations on Wall Street." Sanders called for the restoration of the Glass-Steagall law, approved in 1933 after the Crash of 29 and repealed in 1999 by then-president Bill Clinton. This law separated financial institutions for decades between deposit banking, or commercial banks, and investment banking (stock exchange).

Answer. Is it in the stock exchange where everyone has gotten rich while serving the American people from Washington D.C.?

Another little message. "In this sense, the Democrat recalled that if the 2008 financial crisis was about to end the economy of both the country and the rest of the world, it was because of the Clinton administration, which he pointed out as a friend of the financial titans."

We are going to agree with Bernie, because it is true that with the corrupt financial titans, the Clintons got rich, but not only them, almost everyone.

Bernie. "No president can do this alone," Sanders admitted, so the Democrat called for a political and citizen movement in which no one is left out because of their color, gender or origin and thus "govern for all and not for a few."

That is what I am asking, that the people open their eyes, but not to serve a so-called socialist, who in the end are communists. We must identify who the fraudulent ones are in American democracy, and our civic responsibility is to give our vote to a representative who puts Americans first and has not enriched himself in Washington D.C., receiving money from corrupt governments. Donald Trump is the only one who did not steal peace, money, or lobby to increase his millions, simply because he is not a politician, he is a citizen who has sought so many problems for us, that we must repay him in gratitude for what he has done for our country, even stoically enduring the attacks of the Democrats to the point of imprisoning him. Have they imprisoned any president before? No, and much less if he is a Democrat. We all know how corrupt the situation is, but it must be made clear to Sanders that the Democratic politicians, already at the extreme of government corruption, for the most part, advocated approving the drug "Marijuana" so that they could have money and compete with drug trafficking, allowing our young people to get addicted so that they do not see their disastrous administrations and they have money from the drug cartel that they formed in our states to continue promoting the swamp in all the states that have approved it.

You said that day: "When a young person goes to prison for selling marijuana but Wall Street executives, who cause pain to millions of people with their illegal businesses, are not even prosecuted, it is because we have a corrupt financial system," you said.

It is true, and I share that opinion. So corrupt, that you are swimming with all of them in the swamp, for not having made decisions to dredge it even if it would have been very little in this nefarious era of the Witch Hunt. No Democrat has condemned what they are doing from Washington D.C., publicly. Not only financial, Mr. Sanders, but also governmental, and we have never seen you, before the television cameras, condemn what you are doing to Donald Trump, all of you obsessed with obtaining power. None of you has spoken out to protest so that the WITCH HUNT ends and everyone can participate decently in the presidential elections of 2024.

The same thing happens to you Democrats as to Hispanics who when they tell you that you have criminals in your groups, you get offended and want an apology for the word, but they do not ask for it for the crimes of their groups. The same thing happens to blacks who do not use that word because it offends them without thinking that they are not defending their race. The same thing happens to all of you political Democrats, from Washington D.C., who when we call you corrupt, you get offended, it is disrespectful, etc., but you do not think about the disrespect that we have suffered for generations forming the famous swamp.

You say this to each other to climb up to the poor presidency that is already asking for help. All these Senators sooner or later end up millionaires and that is good, I am not against that, but not profiting from the dirty politics that they have always maintained, and negotiating from their positions that is to serve the people, and not their monetary interests, and the sad and frustrating thing is that: they cannot be differentiated from each other because they are all the same.

DONALD TRUMP'S LAWYERS

All those who in one way or another have had the opportunity to defend former President Donald J. Trump in any of the trials will go down in history as the defenders of a man who in the United States has had so many trials and complaints in different districts that he has never been living or committed them and if he did commit them, the same was done by the previous ones and they were not prosecuted. Excessive accusations, excessive trials, excessive fines, excessive sexual defamation, spilled the cup of Democracy. All the accusers are the intellectual aggressors of the Witch Hunt. Unfortunately, the country has gone crazy, as Martin Luther King said when Kennedy was assassinated. Donald Trump's detractors all settled in Washington D.C., are not crazy, they are immoral before the society they must serve.

What they serve the people by corrupting themselves, and do to a man unjustly and publicly, they will do to our children and family members. It is already happening to the police who protect us. (Facts accomplished). They are not after Donald Trump but us, the people. It is the objective that comes from secret and powerful sources. Destroying the empire, something that has been quietly discussed in our homes at a national level, and the people are already afraid to mention it, erupting like a volcano since 2016.

Citizen responsibility is placed on the shoulders of voters, through legal truth. This is what will put the "manly toga" on all citizens and work bipartisanly offering us justice, respect, unity so as not to be Stalin's plucked chickens in the hands of politicians. Human criteria are changed for any reason. Being impartial is a gift of the human being, based on honesty, conscience, and respect.

What we call the Golden Rule refers to **Matthew 7:12 "So in everything, do to others just as you would have them do to** you. **For this is the law and the prophets."** Few can be partial or impartial and in the case of Donald Trump, who has had his immunity removed to demolish him and remove the Republican Party from the presidential political contest as the opposing party.

Donald Trump has pleaded not guilty to 34 serious crimes for falsifying business records according to his accusers but they insist that he is guilty. Do you consider that having 91 trials against him is not a factory of moral and political demolition by the Democratic hatred? Not counting the lawsuits in each state that his detractors with anti-democratic ideas have wanted to file.

This trial was that of the prostitute Daniel Look at the shamelessness of our government. They call prostitutes those who work on the streets with minimal payments and they persecute them. Prostitutes who work making pornographic films and get paid for it, are called Porn Actresses. Liberalism has changed the name of reality. Street prostitutes are the same as prostitutes in the Porn Industry. With the difference in rank and payment. But both groups do the same thing and get paid for the same reasons.

To whom do they sell the medicine that they are called Porn Actresses? In New York, a Harlem resident, who Blanche asked if he understood what was at stake in the trial of Donald Trump for the case of the prostitute (porn actress Stormy Daniels). He summed it up in this wise way and with deep insight into what was coming to the country when he answered: **"THE LIFE OF THE MAN IS AT STAKE. THE COUNTRY IS AT STAKE. THIS IS SERIOUS."** Taken from the published article "How the strong opinions of the people of New York about Trump make it difficult to select the jury in the trial against the former president." The hatred directed at Donald Trump by the Democratic Party and its allies in Washington, D.C., has damaged civil peace. It has damaged judicial impartiality. All of this is too serious not to protest and ask those who serve us to end this hatred. Hate begets hate and love begets love. Let us always choose love.

That vision of: **"THE LIFE OF MAN IS AT STAKE. THE COUNTRY IS AT STAKE. THIS IS SERIOUS."** This gentleman, whose name is not mentioned in the article, his words are and will be prophetic if he knows it. Naturally, at that time he was referring to the danger of being partial in the judgment, but when he extended his words he covered everything in perfect harmony.

They were so prophetic that the attempt to assassinate former President Donald J. Trump happened. I have always been against the people's juries, because there are few who think like that before belonging to a group that can harm or save an individual.

We wonder, did this gentleman only visualize it? No, the 335 million American citizens are seeing it and thanks to the irresponsibility of President Joe Biden, he has placed us in the third most populated country in the world. India, China and the United States. The world is watching us without filters, just as the Democrats have behaved in their government, weak, irresponsible, and miserable with their people. Is Donald Trump's life at stake? Yes, unfortunately yes.

How serious is this Witch Hunt for the country? Extremely serious. The fall of the Berlin Wall had an international impact because of the search for political reconciliation on both sides. The fall of the prestige of our government institutions since 2016, demolished as the wall was, has left us with a bitter balance. The fall of the Berlin Wall called for freedom and love among all. Mrs. Pelosi's hammer destroyed American democracy calling for power and hate. Along with her, the accomplices of the democratic demolition, Mr. Chuck Schumer and Mr. Adam Schiff, their irresponsible and hypocritical allies enriched by power.

What can trigger the seriousness of this matter? The seriousness of the matter can trigger unimaginable acts when the 2024 presidential elections arrive if the laws are not properly applied. This gentleman summarized what is at stake, the country, the life of a man who tomorrow could be all citizens, and that everything that happens is extremely serious if the vote counts are not applied through the laws if crimes were to occur as in 2020.

Words that summarized what has developed into the unconstitutional witch hunt. You will analyze what you should do in 2024 if you want to take a step forward, or many steps back. You can criticize me and tell me what you want, but it is my duty to react by seeking harmony in the country that I will leave to my grandchildren and all the grandchildren of the nation, who will be the future of tomorrow, and fulfilling my oath when I took American citizenship very seriously, which was and is to defend my country from internal and external enemies. Let us hope that our government institutions react positively in harmony, and comply with the laws, whether they are interpretive or not.

May God save America and, summing up with the thought of Abraham Lincoln, I invite you to reflect. As Abraham Lincoln said, "You can fool all of the people some of the time and some of the people all of the time, but you cannot fool all of the people all of the time."

The truth is a powerful weapon in our possession, to solve problems and to get ourselves into trouble. If we lie, we are congratulated and applauded; if we tell the truth, we are harshly criticized and offended. Each person chooses his or her comfort zone according to his or her interpretations, feelings, and patriotic duties.

ANONYMOUS MORAL

✱ A teacher asked her students to share a story with a moral. Little John raised his hand and said: My parents told me a story. The teacher encouraged him to share it, and John began:

"There was a little bird flying south for the winter. It was so cold that the bird landed in a big field and lay there. A cow came by and threw manure on it. Curiously, the frozen bird began to feel warm and well. It stayed there warm and happy, and even began to sing. At that moment, a cat that was passing by heard the singing and went to investigate. The cat discovered the bird under the manure and quickly took it out and ate it.

1. The teacher was stunned, and asked: My God, what was the moral of that story? Little John calmly replied: Well, it teaches us some valuable lessons.
2. Not everyone who throws manure on you is your enemy.
3. Sometimes, being up to your neck in manure makes you see life differently.
4. Not everyone who gets you out of the manure is your friend.
5. When you are up to your neck in manure, it is better not to say a word.

THOUGHTS OF MARTIN LUTHER KING

I have one dream, one dream only, to keep dreaming. To dream of freedom, to dream of justice, to dream of equality, and I hope I no longer have the need to dream them.

Peace is more precious than diamonds or silver or gold. This is how he ended his speech when receiving the Nobel Peace Prize. Another of the admirable aspects of Martin Luther King was his pride in his black race, distinguishing him before the world. He never had color, he had gallantry. Many years have passed, and someone thought of saying that the word Negro was offensive, when in reality it is a source of pride for those who have that race and no one is more accurate than a cultured man with a giant heart, to say it several times with pride in his speech when receiving the Nobel Peace Prize so well deserved. Martin Luther King led us along the patriotic, peaceful and glorious paths of blessed racial, patriotic and civil changes.

Sadly, we never follow the right leader, but history is in charge of saving them so that the current generations follow their example and make their changes to pacifism, to the truth, to the pride of knowing who we are, where we come from, but serving the country united, with pride, and dignity. Accepting our mistakes and changing them for the sake of others. Let us live together their beautiful thoughts that will always inspire us.

"The greatest tragedy is not the oppression and cruelty of bad people, but the silence of good people."

"Nonviolence is a powerful and just weapon that cuts without wounding and ennobles the man who handles it. It is a sword that heals."

"Freedom is never voluntarily granted by the oppressor; it must be demanded by the one who is being oppressed."

"Sooner or later, all the peoples of the world will have to discover a way to live together in peace."

"I want to be the white man's brother, not his stepbrother."

"The end of our lives begins the day we become silent about the things that matter."

"It is always the right time to do what is right."

"If I knew the world would end tomorrow, I would still plant a tree today."

"If you can't fly, run."

"I'm not black, I'm a man."

CHRISTIANS IN DEFENSE OF ISRAEL

Dear Alila. For anyone who loves Israel like you and I, this is heartbreaking, outrageous, and infuriating. All at the same time. And I'm not even talking about the unspeakably cruel Hamas attack that killed over 1,200 Jews in southern Israel on October 7. On that day, Hamas monsters raped, mutilated, burned, beheaded, and slaughtered innocent Israelis in a heinous attack. No one was spared from the demonic frenzy Hamas unleashed against Israel. Elderly Jews were killed, a pregnant mother had her womb cut open, and there were murderers, along with her unborn child. Babies were thrown into red-hot events and burned alive. It was unimaginably vile. And I condemn Hamas for its barbaric atrocities. But that is not what I want to discuss in this letter. Instead, I am outraged by Israelhating Hamas defenders who celebrated the horror of Hamas… Who marched and demonstrated all over the United States to denounce Israel! And they did so just hours after the worst attack on Jews since the Holocaust.

The true horror and extent of what Hamas perpetrated inside Israel was still unknown when Israel's enemies took to the streets across the United States. In New York City, the Democratic Socialists of America (DSA) held their "All Out for Palestine" rally the day after Hamas marauders killed, raped, and pillaged southern Israel. Throughout the rally, these friends of Hamas displayed a Nazi symbol, burned Israeli flags, and cheered on Palestinians.

It was disgusting and a perfect reason for DSA members in Congress, like Alexandria Ocasio-Cortez and Rashida Tlaib, to quit the far-left party in outrage. But of course they haven't. That ugly hate-fest in New York, however, is just one example. The Anti-Defamation League reported that there were about 150 anti-Israel rallies across the United States the first week after Hamas massacred more than 1,200 Israelis, injured 5,000, and took 240 hostages. These demonstrations were characterized by hostility toward Israel and cruelty toward suffering Israelis. In Philadelphia, Pennsylvania, one speaker criticized Israel and defended Hamas, declaring:

What happened was that freedom fighters were fighting for freedom... Not all the people who died yesterday were innocent. All Israeli settlers are, by default, terrorists.

In Washington, D.C., rabid Hamas fanatics demonstrated on October 8 to express their hatred of Israel. One speaker told attendees to "take the fight to the Zionist institutions in the West" and said, "Duty calls us to fulfill this war."

In Denver, Colorado, a speaker at a pro-Hamas event urged attendees to search the Internet for photographs of kidnapped Israelis taken from the "house they robbed" to put a smile on their face.

In New York City, a speaker at the October 15 rally shouted that Israel is a Zionist extermination campaign that began in 1948.

In Anaheim, California, a speaker at the rally celebrated Hamas's slaughter: "Our fighters have started fighting again... the people in Gaza right now are fighting so hard... and we are here in the United States fighting this battle with them, aren't we?"

And in Dearborn, Michigan, a place dominated by Muslims, one speaker declared that the only hope Palestine has is its armed resistance... If you are pro-Palestine, then you are pro-armed resistance."

And this brief report only begins to describe the seething antiSemitic hatred that has erupted across America since October 7. The Palestinian war on Israel has reached America, and a black cloud of anti-Semitism darkens our land.

Will you help Christians in Defense of Israel speak out now in defense of the Jewish people and the State of Israel? I ask for your generous year-end donation today to make our pro-Israel voice heard even louder across our nation, in Washington D.C., and in Israel.

CIDI informs, equips, and activates friends of Israel like you to speak out and act in defense of God's people.

We are on Capitol Hill, where we monitor legislation, engage lawmakers, and send pro-Israel petitions that you and others sign to push for pro-Israel policies in Congress.

With your help, CIDI is training college-aged Christians to be champions of Israel through a covenant trip, offering promising young people an unforgettable and life-changing 10-day visit to the incredible Holy Land.

You make all of this possible, but we live in a very dangerous time for Israel. Much more needs to be done to defend Israel and expose the truth of outright hatred about the Israeli people.

You will be equipped to respond to the top 10 slanders, libels, and slanders against Israel. Big Lies Answer the questions. A place where slander against Israel spreads and grows on American college campuses. It is appalling and endangers Jewish students. Here is a taste of the hostile atmosphere Jews face in American higher education. In the wake of the Hamas massacre of Jews on October 7, 30 Harvard student groups signed a letter oozing with hatred toward Israel.

In it, the student groups said they "hold the Israeli regime fully responsible for all the violence that is taking place. The apartheid regime is the only one to blame."

When students at Columbia University blamed Israel for the brutal and savage Hamas attack on Oct. 7, a group of Columbia professors came to their defense. And the faculty union at City University of New York sent an email to its 23,000 members sharply criticizing the Zionist genocidal campaign.

Hostility toward Jews is now so pronounced that more than a third of Jewish college students hide their identity on campus, according to a survey conducted Nov. 14 and 15. More than half, 54 percent, said they felt scared.

That, my friend, makes me angry. I'm sure you feel the same way. It is an absolute scandal that Jewish students do not feel free to come and go as they please, to openly own their Jewish identity on campus.

By the way, Joe Biden and Kamala Harris are not helping to defeat anti-Semitism. Biden included the Hamas-linked Council on American-Islamic Relations (CAIR) as an outside advisor to the White House strategy to counter anti-Jewish hatred, but CAIR is one of the most anti-Semitic organizations in the country. It blamed Israel for the October attacks and refused to condemn Hamas for its savage massacre.

Signed this letter by Mat Staver, President and Director of Christians in Defense of Israel

This letter was received by all of us who in one way or another support Israel. It is easy to analyze continuing to insist on rescuing our country from the clutches of communism. Anti-Semites are those who do not have the courage to show their faces, covering up at demonstrations so as not to be recognized as perfect cowards, they are those who in one way or another serve the Woke. Do young university students who vote for Democrats not understand that what is sought is not only to be on the side of Israel, but to clean up the Washington D.C., Swamp?

Those rebellious black citizens affiliated with communists like the White Supremacists, Black Lives Matter and all the others, what are they saying now? All of you were not, are not and will not be the last to be discriminated against as your leaders claim in a society run by communists, not by correct ideologies.

If Democratic voters do not make the giant red, blue and white wave with the Republicans by voting for Donald J. Trump and do not accept our invitation to save the United States of America from savage communist-terrorism, you will not go down in history as citizens giving everything for their country. Since 2016, 2024 has been a long time coming. They have tried to destroy Donald Trump using the same discrediting resources that communists use. Not in vain, whether the press likes it or not, it has Joe Biden's words on file saying that the only one who could stop Donald Trump from becoming president was him and Nancy Pelosi in her emails saying the same thing that Donald Trump would be removed at any cost. No more words are needed. The assassination attempt that all investigations point to Washington D.C., is enough for the people to know that the laws in the USA do not work.

In these elections, Democratic politicians have joined the large corporations, those who have used their money to destabilize the country, those who have paid a lot of money to the press, antiTrump organizations and the assassins recruited to eliminate him, among many, the Black Rock company, which is under scrutiny by independent investigators looking for links to national destabilization and the attempted assassination of Donald Trump. Not only paying the social scum to destabilize everything, but also those who sell themselves for money by becoming vile citizens. Each person will make the right decision seeking the well-being of all.

"Let us not try to fix the guilt of the past. Let us accept our own responsibility for the future." John F. Kennedy.

THE PEOPLE'S REFLECTIONS

Let us hope that government institutions react to the current destruction of our laws and that the world sees us with dignity and respect as when Donald J. Trump served us for four years, not as packs of wolves tearing each other apart. Citizen responsibility will be what determines in the next presidential elections in 2024 whether we fall into the abyss that Washington D.C., has created and they deny it, or if we all save ourselves without distinctions of philosophies, political parties, religions, etc.

We, the voters, are directly responsible by granting our electoral votes to politicians who do not deserve it, we must make favorable changes to the country and if we continue doing the same, that is what we will have. We all have different points of view, and each one will interpret it in their own way, and all concepts will become true or false, regardless of the political parties we profess, and of the historians and their concepts, whether these are fair or not. We have lost ethical values in these years from 2016 to 2024 with so many lawsuits accumulated against former President Donald J. Trump. These are not our values, they are the values of the communists allied to the Democrats who, due to their thirst for power, have usurped them from us. These values, and excuse the redundancy, are the behavioral guidelines regulating the conduct of individuals.

The fundamental ethical values are: justice, freedom, respect, responsibility, integrity, loyalty, honesty and equity. These are the values with which we have grown up regardless of whether we have been poor or rich. And these values are not passed from parents to children, as a rich family, social, human, political inheritance, and even through the media when these are moral.

Today nothing is structured by the politicians of Washington D.C., involving our institutions that are there to establish order and enforce the laws and they have crossed the line of non-compliance with the laws and decency. Enough is enough! We must defend those who bring us back justice, respect for the political party that voters joined decades ago, transparency in presidential elections, and these are the Republicans, who are conservatives who want the laws to be followed. The Democrats have lost their way. Give Caesar what is Caesar's and God what is God's. The sacrifice for the Democrats as a people would be to give the vote to Donald Trump, remembering that they are not going to make him richer or poorer, that what he has said is true, simply that the country needs a firm person to stop this wave of political shamelessness involving the most sacred thing in a country, which is its CONSTITUTION, and moving away from communism even though it is official in our country and fulfilling its disastrous function of contaminating ideals in all our organizations, especially in the Universities.

I extend a cordial invitation to you to reflect and meet with friends, family and strangers, Republicans and Democrats, for a beautiful democratic dawn in the USA, discussing the issues in our homes. Enough of Democrats like Nancy Pelosi, Chuck Schumer, Adams Schiff, Obama buying mansions, the Clintons and the Biden family swimming in the swamp, enriching themselves from Washington D.C., all and the other allies obsessively continuing to destroy their own country, which is ours too. Remember that Donald Trump worked for his millions and they did not.

Inspirational thoughts from John F. Kennedy (Democrat).

"Let us not look for the Republican answer or the Democratic answer, but the right answer."

"Tolerance does not imply a lack of commitment to one's beliefs. Rather, it condemns the oppression or persecution of others."

What they have done to Donald Trump and the police officers who stand up to crime to defend our civil liberties and end up in jail unjustly responding to the myth that police officers ARE KILLERS coming out of the mouths of Nancy Pelosi and her clique and that Donald J. Trump is a criminal. We are all tired of so many political injustices. See you together on November 5, 2024. My great dream is that the Democratic Party regains its prestige and dedicates itself to working, not to persecuting us all. We must unite to send a red warning light to politicians, to reflect that if they have been or want to be in Washington D.C., they must serve the people and work bipartisanly. We must unite to clean up the Swamp! "The ignorance of a voter in a democracy harms the security of all." John F. Kennedy.

God Bless America!

AUTHOR BIOGRAPHY

Alila Barrera was born in Central Macareño, Camagüey province, Cuba in 1945. She studied Pathology Laboratory in Cuba in 1969. She arrived in the United States of America in the famous Mariel boatlift with her husband and two young daughters in 1980. She lived for two years in the state of New Jersey where she studied Cosmetology in 1982. Later she moved with her family to California, receiving her American citizenship on December 4, 1988. She graduated in computer science in 1995. She attended a program at MT. San Antonio College called H.A.G.A.S.E. which stands for 'Hispania's Achieving High Ambitions, Satisfaction and Success' in 1996. Her passion is writing and she has already published several books. The first titled "WHAT AN AMERICAN CANNOT SAY IN HIS OWN LAND" (2001) and the version of the same in the English language titled "What an American Can't Say in His Own Land" (2007). The poetry titled "Dreams and Melancholies" version in the English language (2008). Her first romantic novel titled: "The Mansion" (2012). "The Stories of Alila" in 2014 in digital form for Kindle. The consumerist novel titled "Doña María" in 2018. DEMOCRATS PLEASE, DO NOT HURT ME. WE ARE THE PEOPLE 2024. Alila lives happily with her family in the state of California and is the grandmother of four beautiful granddaughters and a great-grandson. She is a cancer survivor.

Dear American Readers,

I wrote this book thinking about the great political situations we are living in and that we do not accept regardless of which political party we belong to. The theme of this book is the proposal to analyze the truth without following anyone. We are adults and we know what we must do to defend our country from the lies and communism that has infiltrated our current government and that we must not underestimate. In these social times called Woke which is nothing more than International Communism, moral values are lost. I am not an academic writer, historian, or politician. I am a Housewife like millions of people in our country with the status of poor. I was not born in this country, but it has been mine now since the day I obtained the citizenship certificate that tells me that I am a citizen of the United States of America. I did not get involved in American culture and of course, I didn't learn the language. I do not blame any Republican or Democratic government, it was my big mistake and I assume it. I am assuming that publishing should be done in the best possible grammatical way, but as a poor person, I could not afford to pay any editor to help me with the grammatical concepts (punctuation, question marks, among other punctuation rules). Please, make focus on topics. My sincerest apologies for that, but at this time when our country needs help, I run the risk of being criticized for it. Offering these issues that have been going on for eight years gives us the constitutional right to expose them publicly for critical thinking us reflection, not suggesting that you abandon your political party. We need to be united and love is our best philosophy to have a good bipartisanship. If we unite as Martin Luther King wanted, we will achieve a Sutnami cleaning up Washington D.C. Swamp.

www.ingramcontent.com/pod-product-compliance
Lightning Source LLC
Chambersburg PA
CBHW020453030426
42337CB00011B/93